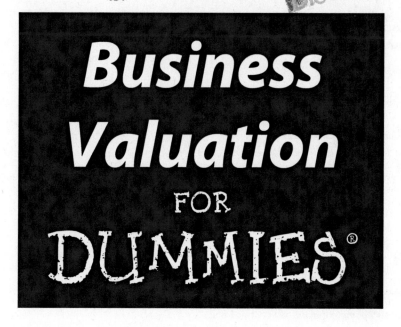

Business Valuation

FOR

DUMMIES®

by Lisa Holton and Jim Bates, MBA

WILEY

Wiley Publishing, Inc.

Business Valuation For Dummies®

Published by
Wiley Publishing, Inc.
111 River St.
Hoboken, NJ 07030-5774
www.wiley.com

Copyright © 2009 by Wiley Publishing, Inc., Indianapolis, Indiana

Published by Wiley Publishing, Inc., Indianapolis, Indiana

Published simultaneously in Canada

For general information on our other products and services, please contact our Customer Care Department within the U.S. at 877-762-2974, outside the U.S. at 317-572-3993, or fax 317-572-4002.

For technical support, please visit www.wiley.com/techsupport.

Wiley also publishes its books in a variety of electronic formats. Some content that appears in print may not be available in electronic books.

Library of Congress Control Number: 2009925028

ISBN: 978-0-470-34401-9

10 9 8 7 6 5 4 3 2

WILEY

About the Authors

Lisa Holton: Lisa Holton heads The Lisa Co., an Evanston, Illinois–based writing, editing, and video consulting firm founded in 1998. She is a former business editor and reporter for the *Chicago Sun-Times* and a former editor for Thomson Corp. She is a busy writer for corporations, associations, and universities nationwide.

Holton has 26 years of experience writing about business, workplace, education, and investment topics and has written or co-written 14 books. Her titles include *For Members Only: A History and Guide to Chicago's Oldest Private Clubs* (Lake Claremont Press), *The Everything Guide to Mortgages* (Adams Media), *How to Be a Value Investor* (McGraw-Hill), *The Essential Dictionary of Real Estate* (Barnes & Noble Books), and *The Encyclopedia of Financial Planning* (FPA Press). She also ghostwrites books for corporate professionals.

In 2005, she became a contributing writer for the Financial Planning Association on consumer finance and retirement planning issues. She also writes on corporate governance and business planning issues for a variety of publications, including *Corporate Board Member* magazine.

Since starting her company, Holton has written for national magazines and newspapers including the American Bar Association's *ABA Journal, Parents, American Demographics, Latina, Working Mother, The Boston Globe,* and the *Chicago Tribune.*

She is a graduate of Northwestern University's Medill School of Journalism and a former national board member of the Society of American Business Editors and Writers (SABEW). She is a current member of the Authors Guild, the International Association of Business Communicators, and the Society of Midland Authors.

Jim Bates, MBA: Jim Bates is vice president, Transaction Support, for the Christman Group, a middle-market investment banking firm based in Palatine, Illinois. He ran his own business valuation company after managing the business valuation division of a national consulting firm.

Bates's responsibilities include providing the managing directors of Christman's regional offices with complete transaction support, including but not limited to preparing business valuations, writing offering memoranda, doing industry research, identifying and contacting buyers, and helping with virtually every other aspect of serving clients. He has been involved in more than 30 sell-side engagements and has prepared more than 500 business valuations.

In his spare time, Bates is a competitive tennis player at the national level and serves the Professional Tennis Registry as its representative for Illinois. Currently, he is five-time defending champion of the Midwest Hardcourt, 35 and over, doubles championship. He has been playing and/or coaching tennis competitively for more than 25 years and is certified by the Professional Tennis Registry at the highest of its three levels.

He holds a bachelor of business/economics degree and an MBA with concentrations in finance and marketing from Western Illinois University.

Acknowledgments

Many of the people who contribute to the process of writing a book are unsung, so we'll do the singing here.

We'd like to start by thanking Tom West of the Wilmington, North Carolina–based Business Brokerage Press for graciously allowing us to reprint excerpts from his rule-of-thumb industry bible, the *Business Reference Guide*.

Darrell Dorrell of Lake Oswego, Oregon–based Financial Forensics was a font of information on the forensic accounting field and a great storyteller regarding the criminal side of valuation and finance. Justin Cherfoli, managing director of the Dispute Advisory and Forensic Services Group of the Chicago-based financial advisory firm, Stout Risius Ross, provided great guidance and harrowing commentary on what some families go through in the valuation process.

Above all, Mike Adhikari of Business ValueXpress and the Kellogg School of Management at Northwestern University was a great conduit to basic valuation knowledge and many of the sources within this book.

We couldn't have done this book without substantial help and support on the *For Dummies* side of the street. Natalie Harris, Chrissy Guthrie, and Stacy Kennedy worked tireless hours to make this book a reality.

Lisa would also like to thank her agent, Marilyn Allen of the Allen O'Shea Literary Agency in Stamford, Connecticut.

Jim would like to thank his family: Brad Bates, Mary Ann Bates, Mary Agnes Bates, and Meredith Spiering. Without their love and support, his career would not have been possible. In addition, he would like to thank his colleagues at the Christman Group: Pete Christman, Rich Jackim, Jack Emmons, and Anneke Chamy. Their feedback, experience, and friendship are invaluable.

Publisher's Acknowledgments

We're proud of this book; please send us your comments through our Dummies online registration form located at `http://dummies.custhelp.com`. For other comments, please contact our Customer Care Department within the U.S. at 877-762-2974, outside the U.S. at 317-572-3993, or fax 317-572-4002.

Some of the people who helped bring this book to market include the following:

Acquisitions, Editorial, and Media Development

Project Editor: Natalie Faye Harris

Acquisitions Editor: Stacy Kennedy

Copy Editors: Sarah Faulkner, Krista Hansing, Kathy Simpson

Assistant Editor: Erin Calligan Mooney

Editorial Program Coordinator: Joe Niesen

Technical Editor: Anneke Chamy

Editorial Manager: Christine Meloy Beck

Editorial Assistants: Jennette ElNaggar, David Lutton

Cover Photos: © David Muir

Cartoons: Rich Tennant (`www.the5thwave.com`)

Composition Services

Project Coordinator: Katherine Key

Layout and Graphics: Reuben W. Davis, Christin Swinford, Christine Williams

Proofreaders: Amanda Graham, Bonnie Mikkelson

Indexer: Infodex Indexing Services

Special Help: Christina Guthrie, Danielle Voirol, Amanda M. Gillum

---

Publishing and Editorial for Consumer Dummies

Diane Graves Steele, Vice President and Publisher, Consumer Dummies

Kristin Ferguson-Wagstaffe, Product Development Director, Consumer Dummies

Ensley Eikenburg, Associate Publisher, Travel

Kelly Regan, Editorial Director, Travel

Publishing for Technology Dummies

Andy Cummings, Vice President and Publisher, Dummies Technology/General User

Composition Services

Gerry Fahey, Vice President of Production Services

Debbie Stailey, Director of Composition Services

Contents at a Glance

Table of Contents

Part II: Getting Familiar with Valuation Tools, Principles, and Resources 73

Introduction

No two businesses are exactly alike — even those that are part of a national chain with exactly the same sign on every door. Each business or outlet of a business has its own complexities that determine whether it's worth a little . . . or a lot.

That's why business valuation is actually a pretty complex affair for someone who's never taken a finance class. If you go online or into a bookstore looking for books on business valuation, you're likely to find volumes that are written more for people who've already been exposed to business finance, accounting, or management training. If you're considering buying a business or have operated one for years without a lot of that training, we're pretty sure that a complicated textbook isn't what you need.

We think that valuation should be the first thing you think about before you make a move into or out of any business. Consider this book to be a starting point for a bright, well-informed future in buying or selling a business, because the dream of owning or selling a business should always begin with dedication to understanding the true value of what you're buying. If we can give you an understanding of the basics of business valuation and of the tools and expertise you require to get the right valuation for the job, we'll have accomplished our purpose.

About This Book

This book is very cautious because we think it should be.

We'll state this upfront: This book will not make you qualified to handle most business valuation tasks by yourself. Nor will you have a complete background in business accounting or business law when you get to the last page. The purpose of *Business Valuation For Dummies* is to give you an overview of all the critical skills, issues, and methods involved in small-business valuation without taking you through all the detailed theories and number crunching necessary to the process. Other, more-advanced resources are out there to show you those processes when you're ready. But by the time you're done with this book, you'll know which basic processes, resources, experts, and tools you need so you can put together the fairest and most affordable valuation solution for the business in question.

We tell you what various professionals do in the valuation process, but we don't tell you that you can do their job. We also tell you the many steps you can follow to educate yourself about valuation in general and your target business in particular, as well as how to make the right decisions to get an accurate valuation of a business. For instance, you can consult resources, free or nearly free of charge, to build a baseline of the business you're considering and then move on to the basics of valuing that kind of company. We tell you about those resources in this book, discussing rule-of-thumb valuation and other resources you can consult early in the process to start building knowledge. We encourage you to do this basic research before you even think about buying or selling a company. (And yes, even if you've owned a business for decades, you need to do this research before you sell!)

If we've done our job, this book will give you a thorough summary of all the steps in effective valuation and show you how to plan and execute that process. We give only two detailed examples of valuation in this book: one for the sale of a business and the other for a purchase. This way, you get a close-up look at how an isolated example works, which we think makes a lot more sense than attempting to generalize for every possible situation, which might mislead you.

This book adopts a holistic approach that involves expertise not only for business valuation but also for your personal and family finances. Why? The decision to buy or sell a business is a major life step; it's not just about the business. Ownership is tied to one's personal finances and family goals, and business valuation needs to tie into all those things. Even if you have a small business and a small family, getting advice tailored specifically to your circumstances is usually smart.

Last thing: Because one of the authors of this book is a valuation professional, you may say, "Oh, that's why they keep saying to use an expert." Keep in mind that we don't say which experts you need to use; you have a choice. But anyone who wants to be in business needs to know that tax, valuation, legal, and finance issues are interconnected, and you need people with excellent skills helping you manage these subjects if you don't have the expertise yourself.

Conventions Used in This Book

When this book was printed, some Web addresses — which appear in monofont — may have needed to break across two lines of text. If that happened, rest assured that we haven't put in any extra characters (such as hyphens) to indicate the break. When you use one of these Web addresses, just type exactly what you see in this book, pretending that the line break doesn't exist.

We use *italics* to highlight new terms, and we follow them up with easy-to-understand definitions.

What You're Not to Read

If you want to lighten your reading load or just simplify your understanding of the concepts, take a pass on any text preceded by the Technical Stuff icon. Also, although we encourage you to check the chapters that have a significant amount of formulas and math in them (which we haven't overdone, by the way), you may want to take a break on those or just save them for last. Finally, you can skip the sidebars — gray boxes containing related but nonessential text — if you want to get straight to the good stuff.

Foolish Assumptions

This book is designed for two kinds of people: those who are thinking about buying a business and those who are considering selling one. We consider this book to be optimal for people who want to go into business for themselves for the first time, because it addresses the critical knowledge that all good businesspeople have: the ability to maximize value at all times. Yet if you're planning to sell a business, we provide a planning outline to allow you to maximize the value of your business before the for-sale sign goes out front.

Here are a few assumptions we make about you, the reader, whether you want to buy or sell:

✔ You're probably looking at a company of less (sometimes significantly less) than $5 million in annual revenues. This book focuses mainly on the purchase and sale of private companies — that is, companies that don't trade daily on a major exchange.

✔ You have some experience with the business world. However, we don't assume that you have a background in finance or valuation, which are frankly two different and very complex disciplines.

✔ More than anything, we assume that you don't want to be taken to the cleaners on your first foray into business or your last decision with the business you own. Perhaps you've watched other people go into business, and you just know that they don't have any idea what their business is truly worth; they've negotiated up or down with a seller, but they haven't fully kicked the tires. That move isn't the kind you want to make. You realize you need industry, financial, and operational knowledge to make the best decision.

How This Book Is Organized

Like all other *For Dummies* books, this book is divided into parts, and each part is divided into chapters. What follows is a summary of what you can see in each part of the book.

Part 1: What Business Valuation Means

We start by telling you what business valuation is and why we think it's the first thing you should understand about being in business. We talk about why valuation is such a challenge, and we give you the basic accounting approaches that experts take to uncover value — or the lack of it — in an organization. Last, we talk about the greatest valuation challenge today: how experts evaluate what intellectual property means to an organization.

Part II: Getting Familiar with Valuation Tools, Principles, and Resources

This part is where we spend the most time talking about paperwork, process, and expertise. We talk about what a valuation report looks like and what various professionals do in the valuation process; we offer a primer on financial statements and how they're used in the valuation process. We also offer an important chapter that talks about rule-of-thumb valuation information — where it can help and where it can mislead.

Part III: If You're Selling a Business . . .

People sell businesses for lots of reasons. They're sick of running the business, for example; or they've made the business a rousing success that's ripe for a nice price from a new owner; or they're ready to retire or to pass on what they've built to the next generation. The reasons can vary, but one thing is clear: Planning for the sale of a business is something that you don't do just a few months in advance. The planning takes years and is best thought of as part of a founder's overall estate strategy. If you build a business, you want to get the best value for it in a way that allows you to enjoy the full rewards of what you created.

So if you're trying to figure out what to do with a family-owned company, this part is for you. Family businesses supply an incredible amount of drama in the valuation process. This part also introduces a detailed case study on the sale of a fictional business.

Part IV: If You're Buying a Business . . .

Knowing about basic valuation issues is the key to making a deal. Buyers have to do their own planning for a transaction because they may be going into business for the first time or buying another company in a series of companies to complement existing business interests. And of course, buyers have their own succession and estate-planning issues to deal with. In this part, we discuss valuation issues for the buyer and feature another major detailed case study, this one on the purchase of a particular fictional business.

Part V: Don't Try This at Home! Turning Things Over to the Valuation Experts

The purpose of this part is not to win business for valuation experts, even though we clearly believe that these chapters cover situations in which you need help. The idea is to communicate why the complexity of certain valuation situations should encourage you to seek help.

This part includes three chapters that discuss situations in which business owners definitely shouldn't go it alone. Which situations did we choose? Divorce certainly qualifies because it endangers many family companies. Estate planning and gifting are tied in with the value of the family business; therefore, they need joint coordination. Finally, people need valuation advice when they're preparing to attract outside investors to a business.

Part VI: The Part of Tens

These three chapters offer ten points of interest each on the following topics: reasons to consider a prenuptial agreement, elements to build into a partnership agreement, and things to consider before transforming a conventional business to an employee stock ownership plan (ESOP).

Icons Used in This Book

This book uses the following icons to highlight key information.

This icon calls your attention to particularly important points and offers useful advice on practical financial topics. This icon saves you the cost of a yellow highlighter pen.

This icon serves as a friendly reminder that the topic at hand is important enough for you to put a note about it in the front of your wallet. The icon marks material that a college professor would put on the board before class starts, noting the important points that students should retain at the end.

This icon warns you about speed bumps and potholes on the valuation highway. Taking special note of this material can help you steer around a financial road hazard and keep you from blowing a fiscal tire. In short — watch out!

This icon marks nonessential information, such as statistics and history lessons. The ideas here are interesting, but you can skip this text if you want to get back to the basics.

Where to Go from Here

We really enjoyed writing this book. We particularly like the idea that we can get small-business people thinking about the importance of valuation early in the life of a business.

If you know nothing about the business valuation process, we suggest you start with Part I. But this is a reference book, so feel free to jump around a bit. For example, you can see how specific situations are handled in Part V, and if you want to see detailed case studies on valuations, by all means, head to Chapters 13 and 18.

Part I

What Business Valuation Means

In this part . . .

Many people think that business valuation is all about getting to a price for a business, and that's certainly a big part of it. But we think that valuation is the central concept of what makes a business a business — and that very few people really understand it. In this part, we discuss the reasons valuation happens in a business, and we introduce the accounting concepts in the process. Most importantly, we discuss valuing business ideas.

Chapter 1

The Value of Understanding Business Valuation

In This Chapter

▶ Why the price of a business is only half the story

▶ The importance of planning in valuation

▶ Basic due diligence

▶ Why families are so important in the process

*Y*ou're here for one of two big reasons: You have a business that you want to sell, or you want to buy a business. Very likely, the business in question is a small business (with less than $3 million in annual sales), and it may be the first and only business you ever own.

Before we go further, we want to pay you a compliment. Right now, you're doing something that painfully few entrepreneurs do: thinking about what a company is actually worth before you make a major decision or take a major action. You're already ahead of the game. And because you're reading this book, you obviously know that business valuation is an important part of that game.

Business Valuation For Dummies is for people who want to understand value. This book can help you get your arms around the many tasks and variables involved in effective valuation of a company and help you decide what kind of help you should enlist to complete a deal. In this chapter, we discuss the importance of valuation, talk about doing research and calculating value, and include some notes on valuation experts and intellectual property. We wrap up with a discussion of passing a family business from one generation to the next.

Basic Tenets and the Importance of Valuation for Businesspeople

Everything has a value. Putting value in dollar terms is the cornerstone not only of running a business but also of investing in almost any form. Knowing how to arrive at a value for the physical and intrinsic characteristics of a business is essential to building wealth of all kinds.

To that end, people who invest in companies need to look beyond the current state of the business they own (or want to own) and consider what decisions they need to make to boost value. People who have experience in those industries are often best equipped to make those decisions, but it often helps to engage a business valuation expert for guidance. In this section, we discuss the concept of value and note some of the main principles of business valuation.

Value differs from price

As the celebrated investor Warren Buffett once said, "Price is what you pay. Value is what you get." We would add one more line: "If you do your homework."

In business deals, most buyers and sellers have a singular focus on price — and price is hard to avoid. Negotiations ideally produce numbers that both sides can be happy with. But getting to the right price in any deal involves understanding what business assets are truly worth and then structuring a deal around financing and tax realities, which can be quite surprising to those who fail to plan.

Planning drives value

Creating value is a transformative topic in business planning and execution. If you're creating a product, granted, that product is the focus of the business for customers and your employees. Creating *value* — long-term growth in asset value in a company you've built — is something you need to focus on, because a company is the sum of real and tangible assets, investments, ideas, and management talent.

If you can look at all those working parts of a business through the prism of value, the desire to determine and create value in a company can become a much more important driving force in its growth than simple profits and losses.

Proper valuation takes time. People buy and sell businesses for a variety of reasons that aren't all about business. For instance, they may make moves in and out of companies based on career goals. Others devote a lifetime to a business so they can finance their retirement or simply pass the business on to their kids as a legacy. All these motivations drive valuation and should require three to five years to account for owners' estate, succession, and exit planning. We talk about the importance of planning throughout this book.

One of the best places to start finding out about the planning process for starting a business is the U.S. Small Business Administration's Web site (www. sba.gov).

No two valuations are exactly alike

No two businesses are exactly alike; neither are the goals and circumstances of business owners. You may be in any of a variety of situations, such as the following:

- ✔ You may be the child of a company founder, wondering whether you want to take over the company when she retires.

- ✔ You may be a corporate executive who's ready to start a new career with a new business purchased with a cash buyout.

- ✔ You may be a worried sibling trying to figure out what to do with the family company because the company's founder, your father, has died suddenly.

Valuation isn't an exact science for another reason as well: The risk inherent in any business situation is far from static. Depending on the economy and the state of the industry the business operates in, the company may be under tremendous pressure to stay afloat, or it may have great opportunities for growth. Any time the economy goes through a major convulsion, people take a fresh look at what value means and at the realities of any deal. As we write this book, the nation is in the grip of a worldwide credit crisis — an economic slowdown that is redefining the values of a host of assets, from companies to private homes.

All these variables are one reason you won't emerge from this book with the skills to do a top-to-bottom business valuation. Also, proper business valuation takes a lot of practice. People with finance degrees and long experience in accounting or other numbers-related fields aren't always naturals at valuation, either. Don't worry, though. This book does cover the ins and outs of business valuation and points out the areas in which you can handle valuation on your own — and those for which you should hire some help.

Valuation isn't a one-time deal

If you're already operating a business to its fullest potential, valuation isn't something you should put off until you're ready to sell or close your doors. Most tax, business, and personal finance experts say that even if you're years away from retirement — or years away from your next business idea — keeping your valuation numbers current is a good idea. This way, you can make changes and investments in the business so you can leave the business with the highest valuation possible.

A strategy of continual valuation tells you the following things:

- ✔ Whether selling your business or merging with another makes sense
- ✔ Whether you can make enough money from the sale of a business to support your retirement
- ✔ When you want to set a timetable for your kids or other family members to take over the business
- ✔ The optimal time to set up an employee stock ownership plan (ESOP) as a way to pull money out of the business in a tax-advantaged way

How often should you run valuation numbers? Frankly, it varies based on need. With computerization, it's easy for many businesses to program their numbers so they can keep a constant eye on their main value indicators that have been developed for any goal they have on their radar.

If you're working with a business or tax planner, discuss the creation of a valuation system for your business, whether it's something you access yourself or have an expert handle at regular intervals.

Seeing what the finished product looks like is a good starting point, so flip to Chapter 6 for a description of a typical valuation report.

The Basic Building Blocks for Calculating Value

The three top associations for valuation professionals are the American Society of Appraisers (ASA), the Institute of Business Appraisers (IBA), and the National Association of Certified Valuation Analysts (NACVA). These organizations agree on three major approaches to business valuation:

✔ **The asset approach:** Also known as the *cost approach,* this valuation approach is based on finding the fair market value of assets (the easiest ones to value are tangible assets) and deducting the liabilities to determine the net asset value or the net worth of the business.

✔ **The market approach:** This approach compares your company or a target company with similar companies. You can use comparisons to publicly traded companies or actual sales transactions for similar businesses. These valuations are frequently expressed in ratio form.

✔ **The income approach:** This approach focuses on the future economic benefits you're anticipating from a business — better known as income. This amount is expressed in today's dollars, and is also known as *present value.*

For more information on these three approaches, see Chapter 4. In this section, we discuss some of the basic ideas that go into calculating value.

Discount and capitalization rates: The numbers that really matter

Most of the number crunching that goes into valuation doesn't take on real meaning until appropriate discount and capitalization rates are assigned to the valuation itself. These computations allow valuation to become much more meaningful in light of the business the company is in and the various attributes to its industry. We discuss these concepts in Chapter 6.

Doing your homework: Due diligence

The term *due diligence* means investigating a company with the cold eye that you should bring to any investment. For anyone doing the job, due diligence involves reading everything, asking plenty of questions inside and outside an organization, and generally leaving no stone unturned in finding out what makes a company tick and how much it's truly worth.

Due diligence involves not only basic research and calculations, but also the ability to forecast how a company will do years from now.

Whether you're a buyer (see Chapter 16) or a seller (see Chapter 12) — whether or not you're enlisting help with a transaction — due diligence starts with your intentions toward any company. Both soft and hard skills are involved in valuing a business correctly, and in the chapters in Part I, we talk a great deal about the early stages of company research and what you can do to inform yourself about the worth of the business, even if you've never been in business before.

How rule of thumb enters into business valuation

Rule of thumb is a starting point for civilians in valuation — a way to get a general idea of what companies in certain industries are worth. The rest, you have to investigate thoroughly on your own and with the right help. But here are some key points concerning what you're about to see.

Tom West is a founder, past president, and former executive director of the International Business Brokers Association (IBBA). For the past 18 years, he's been the author of *The Business Reference Guide*, an annual bible on pricing for hundreds of categories of independent businesses and name-brand franchises. In Chapter 9, we feature rule-of-thumb guidance for ten kinds of businesses from data West has compiled for the *BRG* and listings on his subscription Web site, Business Brokerage Press (www.bbpinc.com).

In West's guide, rule-of-thumb guidance comes in two formats that most valuation experts recognize:

✔ **Percentage of annual sales:** If a business had total sales of $100,000 last year and the multiple for that business was 40 percent of annual sales, the price based on that particular rule of thumb would be $40,000.

✔ **Multiple of earnings:** An earnings multiplier makes the most sense to prospective buyers. It directly addresses the buyer's motive to make money: to achieve a return on investment.

In many small companies, this multiple is commonly used against what is known as *seller's discretionary earnings* (SDE), which are earnings before accounting for the following items:

• Income taxes

• Nonrecurring income and expenses

• Nonoperating income and expenses

• Depreciating an amortization

• Interest expense or income

• Owner's total compensation for one owner/operator after adjusting the total compensation of all owners to market value

Chapter 9 gives you more details on how rule-of-thumb guidance applies in specific business situations.

Getting Expert Help

The authors of this book share a very precise bias: We believe that no one should attempt this process alone unless he or she has been trained and licensed to value companies, plain and simple. It's a very good idea to enlist help wherever you're in the valuation process. Valuation experts can help a business owner locate key benchmark data and other information that shows the worth of companies demonstrating the best practices and best performance in an industry.

Valuation experts (the best ones, anyway) aren't generalists. They do have general skills in finance that allow them to make mathematical calculations — known as *tests* — that are relevant to finding what particular assets are worth. But certain valuation professionals specialize in specific industries and deals. Some work with manufacturing assets, for example, whereas others work with intellectual property; others handle mergers and acquisitions for companies of a particular size.

The various experts in the valuation process include the following:

✔ Appraisers and valuation experts

✔ Accountants and forensic accountants

✔ Attorneys

✔ Business brokers

We provide a few case studies in this book (especially in Chapters 13 and 18) that illustrate what we believe to be true: Owners lie (intentionally or unintentionally) about their results, and not every business owner is equipped to see through such obfuscation. Even in fairly small deals, much opportunity exists for assets to be overvalued or hidden.

Plenty of business owners resist getting help with valuation because that help costs money. But unless you have significant experience in business or in valuation finance, getting someone who can help you confirm that the asset value of that business is real is a good idea. We encourage you to ask people who work in business valuation plenty of questions, because you need to know that these people understand what you need to value and for what purpose.

You can find detailed books on business negotiation, but unless you can match valuation knowledge with the process of negotiating for the business itself, you may not be fully prepared to make or receive an offer by yourself. In Chapters 13 and 18, we offer case studies that show how buyers and sellers go through the process of valuation. In Chapter 18, we also talk about how mistakes in valuation can damage a deal.

The Move toward Intangible Asset Valuation

Perhaps the greatest philosophical debate going on in the valuation industry is how to place a value on companies that derive most of their asset value from intellectual property. We talk about that debate in some depth in Chapter 5.

Some people argue that old formulas and approaches to valuation have been blown out of the water by the transition to a world that's overrun by Internet-driven companies that outsource much of the production of things you can touch. We don't. Our position is that whether a company's most valuable assets are sitting on the shop floor or inside the minds of some really smart people, those assets need to produce one thing to prove value: profit.

Today, as before, the central identity of an asset is its capability to generate a return. Yet businesses that deal in intellectual property — everything from old-line medical practices to cutting-edge software — need to keep their eye on the production of real earnings.

Family Businesses: Important Valuation Targets

We spend a lot of time throughout this book talking about families because they control the lion's share of business wealth in the U.S.

In 2004, *Insurance Journal* estimated that approximately $40.6 trillion will change hands by 2052, as Baby Boomers pass their accumulated assets on to their heirs. A portion of that wealth transfer will be due to the deaths or retirements of the owners of closely held or family businesses. Yet according to a 2006 report in *Business Week,* the oldest Boomers aren't so willing to die in the saddle. Many owners in their 50s and 60s are willing to move aside after they've made enough money to retire and possibly start new careers.

Many founders or previous-generation leaders are seeing retirement as a chance for new possibilities, so they're willing to get out of the way of the next generation. But are they willing to plan for the smooth transition to the next generation, with clear leadership roles defined and wealth-management issues settled before they go? Not so much. According to a 2003 Raymond

Institute/MassMutual survey, 19 percent of family-business participants hadn't completed any estate planning other than writing a will, and only 37 percent had written a strategic plan for their companies.

Working with family members from the time they're young to gauge their interest and involvement in the business will be crucial to valuation later on. Enthusiastic and talented employees who just happen to be relatives tend to be much more dedicated to growing the company than those who use the family business as a fallback employer. Family members who know where they stand as participants or nonparticipants in the family business are likelier to pull together and do what's best for the business as transitions occur.

Chapter 2

What Triggers a Business Valuation?

In This Chapter

▶ Looking at reasons for buying a business and what they may mean for you

▶ Getting a valuation to appeal to lenders and investors

▶ Knowing what your company is worth before it changes hands

▶ Setting up an exit plan

*B*usiness valuation is about as dry a term as you find in finance (admit it — didn't your eyelids flutter a little when you read this book's title?). But when you start looking at the *reasons* people want to value a business, things start to get sexy.

The motivations behind getting a valuation right go beyond finding out whether a mom-and-pop store is worth what Mom and Pop really say it is. Most business valuation efforts are tied to finding a number that describes wealth, no question. But dig a little deeper, and you find some very real emotion behind the process: One person wants to realize his dream of owning a business. Another realizes her dream is failing (or maybe her creditors are trying to convince her that it is). A longtime family company finally runs out of heirs willing to take over, and it's time for the business to be sold or split up. A husband and wife divorce, and both want their fair share.

Yet business valuation isn't an idea only for existing companies. It's also an important concept in buying a new company or developing a business idea. Why? Because if a business doesn't produce value for customers, suppliers, and owners on a day-to-day basis, it's just not a business. This chapter discusses the concept of value as a starting point for anyone who wants to buy an existing business or start a new one. It also covers valuation for when you seek a loan to support an existing business or for when you need to sell or pass the company on to someone else.

Exploring Reasons for Wanting a Business

Many people start or buy their business with money they have in their pockets (or more realistically, a sizable bank account) or money they get from others. The money from others may be in the form of loans, gifts, or cash exchanged for partial ownership in their new company. The money in their pockets may be from savings, an inheritance, or possibly a company buyout.

No matter where the funds come from, knowing the unbiased value of a business concept is critical. You may think that your business is worth a lot or that the business you want to buy or start is great. But if people with money to offer don't see what you do, how much is it really worth?

The first step in valuation is determining the motivation for the valuation. In the following sections, you can find some prime motivations for valuation that you'll likely find familiar.

It's time for a new career

Whether facing a bad economy, a bad boss, or an early buyout, plenty of people think about self-employment. According to 2005 figures from the Ewing Marion Kauffman Foundation, approximately 10 percent of the U.S. workforce is employed in businesses they own, and 0.29 percent of the total adult population starts new businesses *each month*.

Unquestionably, new businesses provide new jobs. But how *secure* are those jobs? Valuation is one way to determine the level of risk one undertakes in buying, selling, or starting up a company.

And how many new entrepreneurs do a professional, detailed valuation of a target before they take this chance? Well, no firm figures exist, but it's a safe bet that the answer is "not enough." According to the U.S. Small Business Administration in 2005, two-thirds of new employer establishments survive at least two years, and 44 percent survive at least four years — and the numbers fall from there.

The role of valuation in a career context isn't one-dimensional. You're not just talking about valuing a company so you'll have someplace to go every day. You want to know whether this company can provide a steadily increasing income stream that will not only keep your personal finances ahead of inflation but also give you and your family financial security in the short term and the possibility of a legacy in the long term.

Are you ready to be in business?

If you've never had the experience of owning a business, the first questions to ask have nothing to do with valuation. Consider this list of questions to ask yourself if you've never operated an independent business:

Question	Yes	No
Are you an organizer? A self-starter?		
Can you tolerate a variety of personalities?		
Can you make solid decisions quickly?		
Are you in good health?		
Do you understand business finance?		
Can you work 10- to 12-hour days with no weekends?		
Have you discussed all the challenges of owning a business with your family?		
Have you created a business plan?		
Will you have to borrow money?		
Will you have investors in the business?		
Do you really believe in your ideas?		
Have you ever hired anyone?		
Have you ever talked to anyone in this industry?		
Have you thought about where you'll locate the business?		

Answering *yes* to these questions is important because they're true indicators of how prepared you are to build a company. If you find that you're answering *no* to more than a few, that doesn't mean you shouldn't start a business, but maybe you need to wait or refine your idea.

If you're seeking a career change, it's not enough that a business works well enough to keep the lights on, support its employees, and stay competitive in the marketplace; it has to support you from a financial standpoint and engage you from a career standpoint. You're not just valuing a business; you're valuing a career and a financial future. Can you see yourself working many hours in this field and guiding the business through good times and bad? Can you see it building you a better life at home? A thorough valuation process answers those questions, too.

You're fulfilling a dream

When your business plans are tied up with fulfilling a dream, valuation gets emotional — and therefore a bit dangerous. Absolutely nothing is wrong with having a dream of owning a business, as long as it comes with a solid plan to determine the value of its assets. And to get to a solid plan, you must have respect for solid valuation techniques.

Plenty of entrepreneurs successfully incorporate raw emotion and their dreams into the purchases and startups of new businesses. For instance, the lore goes that Jeff Bezos, founder of Amazon.com, got the idea to start Amazon on a cross-country drive between New York and Seattle after he quit a Wall Street job as a computer geek. Within days, Amazon was taking baby steps in his garage. And Sir Richard Branson, founder of the Virgin brand of more than 360 companies, started a teen magazine at age 16 that eventually morphed into his first mail-order music business, and the Virgin name is now on everything from airplanes to alternative fuels.

Entrepreneurial stories — particularly the success stories you hear over and over — are inspirational. But they don't take the place of cold, hard valuation techniques in the process of starting up a new business idea or buying an existing company. Valuation techniques are used to evaluate and quantify the following three basic elements, which determine the value of a going business:

- ✔ **Cash flow:** The cash that a business is expected to generate, and continue to generate, into the future

- ✔ **Growth:** The growth expectation of the cash-flow stream we mention in the preceding bullet

- ✔ **Risk:** The risk inherent in maintaining or growing the cash generated by the business

You're taking advantage of a strategic opportunity

It's great when opportunity knocks, but how do you know it's really a strategic opportunity for you and your business? Whether you're talking about buying a small company or a large one, the valuation process is necessary to determine whether the current owner's sales pitch conforms to the actual value of the business or whether the prospective buyer is representing himself accurately.

That's why when companies merge, both parties request a valuation assessment of the other. And in many cases, they may already have conducted such a process on themselves. When both sides get to serious talks, they bring in valuation professionals and, in some cases, forensic accountants (see Chapter 17) to begin a detailed examination of all of a company's assets.

Skipping out on the strategy

Before you act on your dream of owning or starting a business, you need to dedicate yourself to a valuation strategy. After all, the financial future you save may be your own.

One particular gentleman accumulated a nice nest egg working in corporate America and decided to purchase a business. It was a rather small business (with roughly $500,000 in gross revenue) that had been around for years. Through the seller's intermediary, the man submitted a professionally written offering memo. An accountant was the primary reviewer of the financial statements. He didn't bring in a specific expert on valuation.

The gentleman made an offer, and the purchase and sale agreement and other documentation began. However, he performed no physical inventory audit. He didn't spot-check the customer list. He didn't scrutinize the owner's add-back adjustments.

The result: The buyer drastically overpaid for the business, and its cash flow couldn't keep up with what the buyer owed on the business. He declared bankruptcy two years later, and his nest egg was gone.

Some people believe that valuation is important only for larger companies. Not true. Small businesses, even lucrative ones, may not be totally clear in their financial reporting or other factors in operating their business. That's why expert help comes in handy.

However, valuation isn't a process reserved only for pending deals. Valuation is also a strategic activity. Throughout this book, we talk about how companies prepare themselves for various actions in their life cycle by looking very closely at the value of their assets. This process should be constant at all companies because it enables management and potential buyers to spot potential opportunities in the marketplace that their competitors can't.

For sellers and buyers, one fact always remains the same: Knowledge is power. And qualified valuation professionals provide the best and most up-to-date quality of information to steer their business through the years.

You're buying a business to pass on to your heirs

Family businesses are typically smaller businesses — companies with annual revenues well below $1 million. They feed and clothe a houseful of relatives, and they educate them and provide them with summer jobs and full-time careers.

Family friction and the need for valuation

When a founder dies, families can go to war for reasons far more emotional than economical. Relationships forged in childhood don't always translate into effective working relationships in a shared business concern. At the same time, family members who have been longtime employees in a business may feel that they have a deeper stake in the business than cousins and siblings who have worked elsewhere.

Likewise, divorce breaks up more than a few family businesses, (see Chapter 19 for more info). Both parties in a divorce frequently do valuation if a family business is involved as a prime asset.

Family matters are critical drivers for valuation. For more information on valuation and the family business, turn to Chapter 11.

Family businesses may last several generations. However, most end in closure, sale, or some other ownership structure, and that chosen endpoint is one of many things that affect their valuation.

Just 30 percent of family businesses are passed down to the next generation. These so-called closely held businesses rarely outlive the founder because keeping the next generation inside the business is often tough. Kids generally want to make their own way in the world. Add that to the threat of estate taxes and the job of finding competent managers and employees inside and outside the family to keep the business going, and you can see why business survival is a challenge.

Passing on the family business to the next generation can include many hurdles, from tax issues and owner reluctance to family conflicts and greed that can rival a Shakespearean tragedy. And that's when a need for business valuation frequently enters the picture.

Shaking the Money Tree: How Lenders Make Thorough Valuation a Necessity

Valuation standards aren't always the same. When the economy is good and everyone is making money, banks and other lenders can be surprisingly loose about demanding adequate valuation of the assets they're basing their loan amounts on. But when times get bad, it's just like Robert Frost once said: "A bank is a place where they lend you an umbrella in fair weather and ask for it back when it begins to rain."

As we write this book, it's raining hard, and plenty of people are getting soaked. The nation is in the midst of a historic credit crisis led by a downturn in the U.S. economy and an even more severe crunch in the nation's commercial and residential lending environment. By 2008, U.S. lenders of all stripes started tightening up their borrowing standards to the point that even their best customers were starting to find obstacles to loan approvals for everyday business needs and long-term expansion. These were obstacles they hadn't faced for quite some time.

What has that meant for the business valuation process? Everything.

Lenders have done a complete turnabout on their desire for evidence of value in both tangible and intangible assets. And although long-term relationships with lenders still matter, lenders have grown far more demanding for this data.

In this section, we discuss valuation as it relates to borrowing money.

Borrowing to buy a business: What lenders want to see

Arranging for financing to buy an ongoing operation has certain appeal, to both buyers and lenders. Yet as most first-time buyers find out, the process of *preparing* to apply for a loan is just as important as that first meeting with the lender. In today's uncertain economy, that preparation process is more critical than it has been in many years.

If you're paying attention, you can see how long a particular company has been in operation, you can investigate its activities through the news media (check the clips to see how good business has really been), and you can go online to see whether you can identify regulatory problems or court actions the business may have suffered. You can also gather a fair amount of word of mouth from customers, suppliers, and other key constituencies of that business.

Lenders want you to know that they want to understand your value equation for your business before they lend you money. Banks lend to reputable borrowers who have the following elements:

- ✔ A well-thought-out business plan
- ✔ A solid credit history on a personal and business basis
- ✔ A willingness to do business with them regarding other services, including checking, depository services, and so on

Both individuals and companies buy businesses. Smaller privately held companies and many individuals face considerable challenges in proving their value and qualifications to lenders who will enable the deal. Private companies don't have to disclose everything to the general public — although the IRS and industry regulators will want to know more than their fair share — but they have to put these details on display to prospective buyers. The same is true for individuals and small businesses making a purchase.

If you have the financial flexibility to buy the real estate your business needs to operate, do it. Lenders like to see a business with equity on its books, not just rent payments and depreciating equipment. However, it may make sense for you to hold and value real estate as an asset separate from the business for a variety of reasons that benefit both you and the business. By all means, talk to a qualified accountant about this issue.

Also, smaller companies generally don't mean as much to lenders as larger ones, and that goes for public and private companies alike. In a tough lending environment, the spoils don't go only to companies with valuable assets and spotless credit records, but size definitely matters. Bottom line: Bigger companies provide lenders with more business. So not only do smaller companies such as the ones we really focus on in this book need to have a quality valuation process in place for evaluating a future investment, but they also need to prepare for that degree of investigation by anyone helping them to finance a transaction.

We advise buyers or sellers of small companies to start preparations well in advance — sometimes two to three years in advance — to get their overall business health and reporting systems in place so lenders get all the answers they need when they need them. Many companies need to upgrade their financial reporting to be ready for an honest and thorough valuation. Some need to clean up their credit history.

Preparing for mergers and other big-money deals

If a company is planning a merger and is inclined to borrow a large amount of money to close the deal, a lender may demand significant valuation data from the potential borrower so that it can determine whether to lend. The lender often isn't the place where you have your checking account, although retail banks typically have commercial divisions where loans are made; investment banks and other types of lenders may demand valuation data on a business you plan to buy or sell.

Counting on Uncle Sam?

When private lenders cut back, don't expect the government to sweep in and pick up the slack. During the credit crunch that was happening while we were writing this book, government lenders were also tightening the screws. The U.S. Small Business Administration was taking considerable heat for tightening lending requirements. By spring 2008, the SBA reported that the National Association of Government Guaranteed Lenders had found "two-thirds of SBA lenders had tightened standards on 7(a) loans, SBA's primary business loan program, and more than 60 percent of SBA lenders said they are seeing a decline in demand from businesses for loans."

If you're planning a merger or big-money deal, get professional advice on this and do the valuation with enough time in reserve to make specific changes that may boost your business's valuation even further.

Seeking new or continued funding for an existing business

Business owners should never expect their relationship with existing lenders to stay the same, nor should they expect their reputation to mean all that much to new lenders they're approaching. So even though their business may be a known quantity in the community, they definitely need to view themselves through an outsider's eyes in evaluating their attractiveness as a borrower.

Depending on the amount of funding and the purpose for the valuation (funding a business may spring from many reasons), it may make sense for a company to prepare to borrow by bringing in a valuation professional to create a bigger portfolio of information for a lender to consider.

Attracting public or private investors

Many of the priorities of outside investors are the same as that of lenders: They want to see a great business idea, a solid business plan, and credit behavior above reproach for the various participants in the business.

Keep in mind that what your business is worth depends on three factors: the cash it generates today, how much cash it's likely to deliver in the foreseeable future, and the return any buyers would require on their investment in your business. Some businesses that have been operating for a while have such a track record, but many are too young for that.

Most new businesses tap friends and family for early seed money. This early money — and your handling of it — can make your business more attractive to angel investors if you have a hot idea and the talent to bring it forward. An *angel investor* is someone who provides capital to one or more startup companies and is usually a rich person who likes to dabble in young businesses with great potential. Angels tend to be the next rung of financing for companies hoping to take their business to the next stage — expanding the reach and scope of a product's distribution, bringing in advertising and promotions, or helping pay to expand staff. The next step is venture capital, firms that take companies at this still-young phase and prepare them for what will hopefully be a successful march into the public markets.

What If You Want — or Need — to Sell a Business?

Owners usually sell successful ongoing businesses for a number of reasons, and even in the best scenario, significant planning is required in advance to ensure a successful outcome. Valuation expertise can be an enormous help in planning not only the life of a business but your life as well, as we explain in the following sections.

Doing some smart estate planning

Valuation isn't something you do only when a deal is pending. Doing a proper business valuation is a necessary precursor to any number of business scenarios that can be incredibly personal — selling the business, buying a new business to expand your reach, or passing it on to the kids or qualified managers who have been with you all along.

Estate planning is the process of examining all your assets and determining your wishes for their disposal to family, friends, and employees at the time of your death or incapacitation. If you're a business owner, you have plenty of information to consider in this process. You need to take an unbiased look at what's there and what the real quality of those assets is. Sometimes it takes some time for those realities to sink in.

We suggest doing a valuation of a business as part of any estate-planning process anywhere from three to five years of a projected transition.

Business owners and their attitudes fall into two camps. The first include first- or second-generation business founders who welcome outside assessment of their activities and are willing to entertain opposing viewpoints about the value of what they've created. The second involves the same kind of people, only they have a lot less willingness to entertain such opposing viewpoints.

If you're in the second camp, you need to gravitate toward the first. Outside valuation advice, in tandem with qualified tax and estate advice, is absolutely necessary because of the following:

✔ Your family members will rely on the wealth you've created in that business to support themselves if you die suddenly or become incapacitated.

✔ Your kids already employed in the business see it as a legacy they can pass on to their children.

✔ Your most loyal employees also see their net worth as tied to the fortune of the company, and they should know your final plan for the business.

Reaching retirement

The notion of retirement in today's society is changing. Some business owners keep the traditional view: 65 and out. Other owners — particularly people who consider themselves serial entrepreneurs and who start one business after they sell the other — may retire two or three times before the end of their lives because they simply want to do new things at various stages in life. Still others view retirement as one step into the grave, so they *never* want to retire.

Business valuation is critically important for all three of these individuals. Obviously, death is the most unavoidable endpoint of all, but much like estate planning, retirement planning is something best done well in advance to see if you can retire the way you want.

Letting the kids take over

We spend much more time on this topic in Chapter 11, but a valuation strategy is necessary in the succession plan, both for children who are already working in the business and for the children who have a stake in the wealth created by the business.

Any number of family-owned businesses — some large, most small — have been torn asunder by owners who failed to plan and siblings and cousins who could not agree on anything from management decisions to the ultimate share of the business each actually owns.

Estate planning, retirement planning, and succession planning are inextricably linked. If the business is the central source of wealth in a family, you must have an independent valuation based on a set date that all parties are made aware of and hopefully accept.

Facing threats from market forces

Consider a small-town five-and-dime store that saw its business start to erode when the first Wal-Mart moved to town 40 years ago. Think of the 75-year-old family bookstore that started to see fewer customers when the first Barnes & Noble superstore opened at a nearby shopping center.

Even for multigenerational businesses, times change. Most importantly, the players change, too. All business owners must keep valuation in the back of their minds when they sense that a game-changing company has moved into their marketplace.

But competitors aren't the only market forces that change a company's fortunes. Look at what outsourcing and more modern technologies have done to established companies. If they haven't kept up, they have three choices: modernize (often tough for smaller companies to afford), put themselves up for sale (to a market that may not be ready to buy), or simply fade away.

Many business owners may not see the end coming, whereas the best valuation professionals do. Valuation is not all about that final dollar figure; it's about measuring a business's short- and long-term viability as well. A valuation expert with knowledge of your industry — or access to outsider experts who have that knowledge — is as much a central business advisor as your accountant or attorney.

Separating from a co-founder or partner

Partnerships are unincorporated businesses in which two or more individuals manage the business and are equally liable for its debts. You can find variations on that level of liability based on the legal definition of the partnership, but that's basically it. Partnerships are a particularly interesting valuation challenge because they typically don't have that many hard assets to value. In fact, a lot of partnership value is intrinsic — that is, it's tied up in the skills of the individuals who form the partnership.

Many law firms and medical practices start out as partnerships. If you're interested in buying into or selling out of an existing partnership, you're valuing not only the few hard assets the business has but also the many intangibles that lead to most of its value — literally, the brains behind the operation.

What buy/sell agreements do

In partnerships or closely held businesses, concern always arises over what may happen to the business if one of the owners elects to leave or dies or becomes incapacitated. Surviving owners want continuity of ownership and management — and no threat from a deceased owner's survivors — so smart businesses draft buy/sell agreements that spell out how transitions will occur. They typically cover the following:

✔ A definition of various "triggering events" to guarantee owners that their interest in the business will be purchased

✔ Who the owner's interest must be sold to, whether it's the company or the partnership or specific owners

✔ A mechanism for pricing that stake when a triggering event happens

✔ A funding source — either owners' funds or proceeds from insurance policies — that finances the purchase of the departing owner's stake

✔ The valuation process for a deceased owner's interest in the business or partnership, for estate tax purposes

For all business valuation, hard assets are only one part of the picture — an important part for many businesses but rarely the most critical. What any potential buyer wants is a company with cash flow or market comp values that are over and above the adjusted book values of the assets. That means you have a company that "has something," significant intangible value or goodwill. If the target company fails that test, the company may be "worth more dead than alive" and should be purchased only for the breakup value of its tangible assets.

Partnerships are unique in another way, too. Partnerships may be structured as an equal split in ownership: For instance, perhaps two doctors start a medical office as a partnership and are 50/50 owners. But as that partnership ages, they may take on associate partners in the practice who don't have the same ownership stake. Why? Because all the partners benefit from the patients and clients that the original partners brought in back when the firm or practice was founded.

Valuation professionals are handy at various stages of a partnership's life. Incoming and outgoing partners want to know the value of a partnership before they commit to working there or know their potential share of the partnership's wealth as they leave or retire.

Valuation may also be an important first step in drafting an equitable buy/sell agreement or updating an old one. Although not unique to partnerships, you'll hear about buy/sell agreements that determine various shares of ownership. *Buy/sell agreements* address how shares of a partnership may be bought or sold if a partners leaves or dies, and they're also an important consideration for the families of the practitioner who's transitioning out.

Dealing with divorce

Business valuation is often the central point of wealth separation when a marriage ends. And not only must spouses be considered, but so must children and possibly children the business founders had with previous spouses, as well as nonfamily employees whose futures are tied to the fortunes of the business.

As divorce and tax lawyers and accountants wrestle with the actual division of assets, the valuation professional has to establish a fair value on the business, even if opposing sides may not be volunteering much information.

Divorce is clearly a situation in which individuals can't take a complex valuation assignment upon themselves. Divorce is a complicated and emotional process, and it's best to have valuation experts with experience in such matters handle it. For more on divorce and business valuation, see Chapter 19.

Exit Plans: Writing the Ending

An exit plan in a business may be retirement. It may be the sale of a company. It may be a reduced role for a founder or a partner until she feels the next generation is in the best shape to take over full time. At any rate, having an exit plan is a good idea.

An exit plan is actually the precursor to any of the situations we mention earlier in the chapter. Before you decide to retire, you have to decide how you want to retire. And before you sell, you have to decide how you want to sell.

This book talks about exit plans in many valuation situations for a reason: Exits are a common fact of life, whether business owners want to admit it or not and certainly regardless of whether they want those exits to happen. Owners die in the prime of their lives. Business partners get sick of working together. Kids don't want the business. Economic or industrial realities change, and owners are suddenly forced to survive in ways they hadn't planned. In this section, we give you the basics.

Who benefits from an exit plan?

Many more people than the owner benefit from an exit plan. Co-owners need to coordinate their exit plans, and the families of each owner need to be aware of those plans so they can plan their financial future. Plus, family and nonfamily owners and employees in the business need to have a solid idea of the owner's exit plan so they can plan their own careers.

Spouses and siblings who work in the business need to have an exit plan in case they elect to leave the company and possibly purchase the stakes of others. Exit planning also gives a family an idea of which skills and talents they'd have to replace if key members were to leave.

When should an exit valuation be done?

A business valuation has many triggers, but the best reason to do one is to plan for best outcomes and unexpected events. With that in mind, exits can — and should — be planned well in advance. Valuation is key in the process, which should be done at least three to five years before an owner is thinking about making a move. If possible, exit planning should be an activity mutually undertaken by other owners and their families to make sure all personal and business issues are aired.

But back to valuation. Valuation is a key start of exit planning because it tells you the following:

- ✔ How much money you're likely to get for the business if you sell and, therefore, how much you'll have to use for your retirement or possibly the purchase of another company
- ✔ How big of a legacy you can pass on to your kids or employees as they continue the company's activities
- ✔ Whether any major or minor business problems need to be fixed before you put the company up for sale or pass it down to the next generation

Solo valuation and exit planning is tough to do. Most business owners are too tied up in the day-to-day activities of running their business to spend a lot of time thinking about how to pass on the business to children or employees.

Think about endings in terms of the startup and continuation of a business. At any time in a business's life, owners and other family members can be thinking about an ending in the most positive way possible.

Chapter 3

Understanding the Tangibles and Intangibles of Business Valuation

*I*n business, there's so much talk about the bottom line and the irrefutable truth of numbers. So why, then, isn't business valuation an exact science? Because the everyday competitive environment in which businesses operate is in a constant state of change. The economic tide that lifts all boats can sink them tomorrow. And overnight, unexpected world events can make a difference in the smallest business fortunes — just witness the economic downturn triggered by the September 11 attacks in 2001.

In good economic times as well as in bad, innovation and ideas are the toughest elements to measure because no one can foresee when an entire marketplace will respond to one great idea. Perhaps Steve Jobs had an inkling of how big the iPod was going to be, but at the turn of the 21st century, much less a generation before, few people understood how popular personal digital electronics would become.

Business valuation is as much an art as it is a science because numbers alone can't be trusted — successful valuation involves an understanding of business financial documentation as well as a nose for news and activities considerably more stinky. And a certain amount of gauging the risk in any business is subjective. In many ways, businesses are as unpredictable as people. This is why the best business valuation professionals mix solid mathematical and research skills with extreme curiosity and a sharp instinct for the good and bad in business. A good valuation toolbox combines hard data and soft skills. This chapter focuses on the information that a valuation professional looks for when valuing a business.

Examining Your Reasons for Valuing This Business

People buy and sell businesses every day, and sellers have just as many reasons for selling as buyers have reasons for buying. Determining why you want a valuation of the business is the first step in the process of buying or selling.

For a truly unbiased valuation, the valuation professional should strive to present only a fair market value, which (in the case of a willing buyer and seller with full knowledge) includes all the assessment and analysis required to make a solid estimate of earnings, growth prospects, and risk. This results in a valuation that can stand a test in court. Just remember that fair market value (FMV) and price are not the same.

The various personal, market, and operational situations facing a business can determine whether it will be worth more or less when it's time to buy or sell. Any current or prospective business owner may be in any of the following situations when valuing a company:

✔ **A desire or need to retire:** We see so many companies that are forced into transition when an owner becomes ill or is forced by family members or employees to end his or her career or pass on responsibilities to another generation. In the best of situations, retirement is an event that's planned well in advance. Valuation done in advance helps, too — it gives a sense of timing to a major business event.

✔ **A struggle to get money out of a dying business:** We often get word of valuation assignments when companies run into major — and sometimes irreversible — trouble. Valuation becomes necessary not only when creditors want to get a bead on the value of a company that owes them money but also when owners and families want to understand whether they'll be able to take any money away from the operation at all, even if it's only the liquidation value of the company.

✔ **A need to expand an existing operation:** A company can grow in several ways: It can grow through internal means by plowing its profits into new facilities and other methods to grow its operations; it can borrow by approaching banks for loans; it can approach investors for needed funds by issuing public or private shares in the business; or it can buy a separate company that complements its needs. Each option establishes the need for valuation to determine the value of the company so it can determine how it wants to grow.

✔ **A divorce between one of the owners and his or her spouse:** Marriage is a big factor in the future of a business, and so is divorce. Valuation may come into play when two spouses part company; the fair market valuation of the company often must be completed before the divorce can be finalized.

✔ **An exit from a business on one's own terms:** Several decades ago, a top executive wouldn't break her stride just to take a few years off or possibly start another business with money she earned from the last business she sold. But today, it happens all the time. Exit planning is now akin to estate planning in the number of issues that you need to consider, but the key word here is *planning;* the valuation of an existing business is a guidepost to the next step in many executives' lives.

✔ **A need to do some early estate planning:** Making sure the assets of the business stay in the family or with key employees isn't something you can do in a day. Estate planning is also not a singular process. An unbiased valuation of the company is necessary to put all constituencies on the same page before the division of assets is mapped out.

For more details on these reasons for business valuation, see Chapter 2.

Introducing Standards of Value

A *standard of value* is a choice for the way value is sought in any transaction or the type of value used in a specific transaction. It may be legally mandated based on the situation, or it may reflect the desire of both parties in a transaction. In this case, it's a measure of the motivation and knowledge of the parties — meaning buyer and seller — as well as other conditions that have a direct impact on the value/price of business.

The concept may sound a bit technical at first, but we go into more detail on standards of value in this section. Simply keep in mind that people buy and sell businesses for a variety of reasons and under a variety of conditions.

A business needs not only to make money but also to make progressively more money over the years to stay ahead of inflation. Valuation is a process that forces you to look at the viability of an existing business or a business idea and at whether an investment in a particular business will outweigh investment in other things like the stock market, currencies, or other securities. It's tough to avoid emotion when buying or selling a business, but valuation is a reality check.

The mother of all standards: Fair market value

The standard of value you hear about most often is fair market value. *Fair market value* — a term used colloquially with *market value* and *cash value* — describes a business valuation in which a buyer and seller, who are both willing participants in the transaction, can agree on a transaction based on a common knowledge of all relevant facts. The word *market* doesn't imply the stock market; it's basically the market of all buyers and sellers that would potentially be interested in making a particular deal.

Why do we emphasize that the buyer and seller are both "willing participants" in the transaction? Because someone having an urgent reason to buy or sell can definitely skew the valuation in one of two ways:

- Motivated buyers tend to pay higher prices to unmotivated sellers.
- Motivated sellers tend to accept lower prices from unmotivated buyers.

The valuation process would be so much easier to explain if there were only one or two motivations for a transaction. And of course, valuing businesses would be even easier if both people and businesses weren't so unique. But the value of any business may get personal, based on the individuals involved. One buyer may have a personal vision of what the business is worth, and of course, a valuation professional may disagree after he or she views conditions from specific data combined with training and perspective. All these viewpoints — and the desire to possess or give up a business — have a somewhat unpredictable up or down effect on price. Fair market value is an attempt to be objective.

Fair market value implies an equilibrium that, although it may not always be met, represents the theoretical fulcrum point in any deal. That's why fair market value is the most widely recognized and accepted standard of value, and it's used in all federal and state tax matters, including the valuations used in estate taxes, gift taxes, inheritance taxes, income taxes, and ad valorem taxes.

Perceptions of investment value

Whereas market value is objective, impersonal, and detached, investment value is subjective and personal. *Investment value* means that the value of a business is based on expected earnings or monetary return to a specific investor. Investment value, at least for most people, is in the eye of the beholder.

The investment value to one particular owner or prospective owner can be different from the fair market value. Valid reasons for this difference can include

- ✔ Perceptions in estimates of future earning power
- ✔ Perceptions in the degree of risk involved
- ✔ Differences in tax status
- ✔ Things in common with other operations you own or control

Keep in mind that we're talking about more than the stock of a company when we talk about investment value. For example, real estate is also a business, and investment value is also a standard used when determining whether a property should be bought or sold.

The fundamentals of intrinsic value

Intrinsic value — sometimes called *fundamental value* — differs from investment value in that it doesn't have as much to do with the investment as with the *investor*. Intrinsic value involves an investor who applies his or her own particular analysis and skills to the business as a whole or to individual assets to determine whether the business has value that isn't reflected in the current market or asking price. It is, as many say, the "true" or "real" worth of an item based on that analysis.

Going over going-concern value

Think about it: If you're considering buying a business that's still operating, you conceivably may pay more for it than you would for one that's going out of business. A *going concern* — also known as an *ongoing business* — is a viable operating entity with assets and inventory, staff and management; it's open for business with no expectation of closing for any reason in the immediate future.

If it's a well-run business, not only is it paying its expenses, but it's also making a profit. Profitability is one element of value.

Valuing assets is a different ballgame when valuing an ongoing business as opposed to one that's on the brink of closure. Here are a few reasons why:

- A business's brand identity is arguably more valuable as a going concern.

- Customers are still actively coming through the door.

- Products are still in an ongoing state of service and development.

- Marketing and advertising is ongoing.

- Management is still running the operation with intimate knowledge of how to make the business work.

Valuation on a going-concern basis doesn't necessarily mean that the business is being run at its optimum level. Frankly, you may have some better ideas about how to do that. But because you may apply more than one valuation standard to a specific transaction, looking for intrinsic value as well isn't uncommon.

Liquidation value

Liquidation value is the flip side of going-concern value. *Liquidation value* represents the net amount that can be gathered if the business is shut down and its assets are sold piecemeal. For example, liquidation is common in the restaurant business. If a restaurant closes, the assets such as the kitchen equipment, tables and chairs, and so on can be sold. (This is, of course, assuming the owners owned the assets in the first place and the equipment wasn't leased.)

Knowing the kind of liquidation that's taking place is important because it affects the costs connected with liquidation of the property, including commissions for those facilitating the liquidation (lawyers, accountants, auditors) and taxes at the end of the transaction. That entire outflow affects the final value of the business. Here are the gradations of liquidation value:

- **Orderly liquidation:** Assets are sold strategically over an orderly period of time to attract the most money for the assets

- **Forced liquidation:** Usually, creditors have sued or there's a bankruptcy filing that calls for liquidation, so everything gets dumped on the market in a hurry

In calculating the present value of a business or property on a liquidation basis, discount the estimated net proceeds at a rate that reflects the risk involved back to the date of the original valuation.

Adjusting or Normalizing a Financial Statement

"Adjusting" numbers sounds a little shady, doesn't it? Well, it's not. Not only is it legal, but it's also the essence of the science of valuation. To analyze and compare attributes of companies, it's appropriate to add or remove various financial data or apply various computations to get a true economic picture of the business versus the picture of the business for tax purposes. *Adjusting* is what accountants and business valuation professionals do to fully examine assets and companies as a whole.

Here are some common reasons for adjustments of figures in the valuation process:

✔ **Removing nonoperating assets:** In any sale transaction, you have some assets that aren't related to the production of earnings, such as excess cash. Those assets are generally not made part of the deal. For this reason, valuation professionals usually adjust the balance sheet to remove these items before making any comparisons.

✔ **Getting rid of nonrecurring income and expense items:** A target company's financial statements (see Chapter 8) may be affected by events that aren't expected to recur, such as asset sales, costs or proceeds from a lawsuit, or an unusually large one-time gain or expense. Valuation professionals take these items out so they can get a better view of management's expectations of future performance.

✔ **Making sure that wages, benefits, and rent reflect current market rates:** When a company does its due diligence in hopes of taking over another company, the potential buyer may find that the owners of the target company are paid wages and benefits either above or below market rates. Or the rent of the target company's property may not match market rates. If the acquiring company is going to replace that management or staff, or if it's not going to continue operating on the same premises on the same terms, the acquiring company may have to pay more or less to do so.

North American Industry Classification System codes — or NAICS codes — are a research tool to understand performance figures for various industries. These six-digit numeric codes are assigned by the governments of the United States, Mexico, and Canada to identify thousands of types of business establishments. The U.S. Census Bureau collects the data here in the States. You may hear the term *SIC code* — that's the older version of the system, but that data is still out there. For more information, go to www.census.gov and do a search for NAICS.

Other Considerations: Science Meets Art

Suppose you've examined all the financial documents and looked at all the numbers. That's the science, because those are real numbers that reflect real business activity. Now comes the art. The valuation professional taps his various research resources and relies on experience and judgment to build in risk variables for the company's depth of management, stability of industry, and diversity of product line and customer base (to name a few key measures) to get to the final answer. How does he do this? By getting more information. This section explains how that info comes into play.

Adding business and economic news

A generation ago, if you wanted to find out about how local, state, national, and international economic news affected companies in your town, you'd have to pick up the business section in your local daily newspaper or check out the *Wall Street Journal* every weekday morning. You might also have studied *Fortune, Business Week, The Economist,* or any other international business magazine that looked at the big picture. Then you'd have to do a fair amount of thinking to see how that news filtered down to what you were doing on Main Street.

But today, you live in a sea of information. Thanks to CNN, CNBC, local business weeklies, and Internet news organizations that specialize in various areas of business, gathering business and economic news is literally a 24/7 process that's targeted to businesses of all sizes.

Understanding business and economic news is crucial to the understanding of business valuation because marketplace events and trends can change a business's value on a dime. Some examples include the following:

- ✔ If energy prices are rising and you produce something that has to be delivered by car, truck, train, or plane, the rising costs can damage your ability to do business and therefore the value of your company. Transporting your product will cost you more, which will affect your overall expenses relative to that of your competition. That in turn will affect the price you charge your customer, unless you can pass along that added cost without complaint or find a way to mitigate the cost.

- ✔ The global economy — helped in large part by the Internet — means that the services and manufacturing you do may be done more inexpensively by a company in the Far East or Central Asia. Can you shift production to these cheaper locales if market conditions call for it?

✔ The U.S. housing market is currently in a freefall, and consumers are watching their spending more closely than ever. Your business can experience serious ramifications if it relies solely on consumer spending.

✔ Interest rates may be falling, but that means there's a risk for inflation. And inflation can force an increase in pricing so you can keep up with costs.

Folding in tangible assets

In this section, we're talking about physical assets owned by a business — a printing press, land, buildings, office furniture, computers, and more. These are *tangible assets,* assets of a physical nature, or those that can be valued based on pricing data that's accessible in the marketplace.

Every asset has a life cycle, and that's why age and depreciation need to be accounted for in the valuation process. In most cases, younger physical assets have greater value, especially when for mechanical items. Real estate has a depreciation process as well, but it can be an exception because even with market downturns, land and structures can appreciate in overall value over the course of time. As the old saying goes, they're not making any more land.

Drawing valuation conclusions with intangible assets

But wait — how do you determine the value of things you know are important but that you can't see, feel, or taste, such as the numbers on the balance sheet or profit and loss statement? What's the long-term value of a boffo brand identity? A knockout customer list? How about intellectual property — the sum total of knowledge encased in the minds of your brilliant workers? What about management's singularly extraordinary ability to manage costs and production? And how many dollar signs can you attach to that secret project going on in the lab? These are *intangible assets* — nonphysical assets that in these times may actually account for the bulk of some companies' value.

Why are intangible assets so valuable now versus 25 or 50 years ago? Look no further than the computer on your desk — or in your hand. Technology — particularly personal technology — has made it easier to create intense cultures of innovation within companies of all sizes. The faster you can think, research, and communicate, the faster you can develop, manufacture, and introduce products to the public. That's real value.

Intangible assets come in two flavors:

- ✔ **Legal intangibles:** These are mainly trade secrets that include customer lists, trademarks, brand names, patents, and copyrights. Legal intangibles generate legal property rights defensible in a court of law.

  The value of trademarks, brand names, patents, and copyrights is a function of the additional cash flow (over and above a "normal" cash flow) that can be generated by virtue of protection of ownership and the application of the asset.

- ✔ **Competitive intangibles:** These are assets that humans primarily bring to an enterprise. Here, we're talking about the value of good management; efficient business processes; smart, innovative thinking; and pretty much anything that goes under those headings.

  This is inherent goodwill and is the result of the determined value of the business, minus the net asset value of the business.

In the end, the intangible value of most businesses is the value of the cash-flow stream over and above the net asset value. And this difference includes all the various intangibles. Most of the time, the intangibles are so interconnected to the overall operation, reputation, and so on that they aren't valued separately or on a stand-alone basis.

Chapter 4

Approaches and Methods — Basic Theories of the Valuation Process

. . . .

In This Chapter

▶ A step-by-step review of the valuation process

▶ How risk plays a role in valuation

▶ The three primary approaches of valuation: asset, market, and income

▶ The key formulas that get experts to valuation

. . . .

*O*kay, so what's the difference between an approach and a method to finding the value of a particular business? Think of an approach as the expressway you need to get to the right town, and think of a method as a way to get to the right address. Each approach has several methods. We explain the major ones in this chapter and note some additional techniques that people use.

Although you may never put pen to paper — or finger to calculator — in working these mathematical and analytical formulas, you want to understand them, particularly if you're working with a qualified expert.

No two businesses are exactly alike, even those in the same business operating across the street from one another. Having said that, comparing similar companies can help you identify efficiencies and best practices that boost long-term value. Larger, more complex companies — and the increasing number of companies that consider intangible, intellectual assets the number one source of their value — may need to apply slightly different valuation methods and nonnumerical analysis to get to the bottom of things.

Adjusting financials — once more with feeling

As you're applying various methods or approaches to the valuation process, you need to have a clean view of the company's financials first. Adjusting financials is a critical step. You need to watch for plenty of items when you're adjusting financials; if you see anything you don't understand, ask a trusted advisor such as a Certified Public Accountant. Adjust for the following:

✔ **Inventory:** Calculate the inventory turn ratio or days' inventory ratio for all the years that you have financial statement for. The trends in these ratios may indicate either an improvement or a slacking off in cash management. Sharp reductions in turn or increases in days' may indicate a sudden downturn in sales, a new product line that's stocking up, or obsolete inventory because a product line was abandoned, among other things.

Comparing the ratios to industry norms may offer valuable insights into the quality of cash management and potential risk. Always ask to see physical inventory records to see whether they correspond to the book numbers. Take a look at inventory adjustments, too; sometimes companies make inventory adjustments when their financial data doesn't agree with the numbers collected in physical inventory. If you see these adjustments happening, ask why. They may indicate a management problem in the warehouse, but they may also point to unreliable financial data.

Be sure to ask how inventory is valued — LIFO (last in, first out) or FIFO (first in, first out). LIFO inventory accounting assumes that the last goods purchased are the first sold and that what remains in inventory at the end of the year are goods that were purchased first (and possibly bought at lower prices). FIFO inventory accounting assumes that the oldest remaining items are the first sold. Depending on the business and what constitutes its inventory, you may find a lot of undiscovered value within the inventory.

✔ **Receivables:** Granted, this is money coming in the door, but you need to find out whether any amounts in receivables can't or won't be collected by the time of sale. Comparing the inventory days' ratios for each of the financial periods being analyzed provides valuable information about the quality of the receivables. And comparing the ratios to industry norms provides a perspective on how well the business is being managed relative to its competitors and helps you see the business in terms of relative risk. Also ask to see an accounts receivable (AR) aging report to determine the quality of receivables. Look at the write-off history and whether the business has any AR insurance in place.

✔ **Office equipment, furniture, and fixtures:** As with most hard assets, the purpose in valuation is to discover what they're worth right now, not their book value, which doesn't account for depreciation. You need to determine whether to price these assets at market value, replacement cost, or liquidation value. If the company is healthy, market value probably will be your choice. If not, it'll probably be liquidation value An independent appraisal of the assets may be required, depending on whether the assets are an integral part of the funding of a deal.

✔ **Factory equipment and tools:** Older manufacturing businesses may have equipment on the factory floor that's in good working order but decades old. Unless the equipment is specialized and supplies a very lucrative product line, most of these assets are generally heavily depreciated. An independent appraisal of the assets may be required, depending on whether the assets are an integral part of the funding of a deal.

✔ **Real estate:** This category is easy for most individuals to understand. Company-owned real estate is valued similarly to residential real estate — it's almost always sold at market value. If a company has added sensible improvements and maintained its real estate well over the years, this category can be a source of great value . . . in a healthy real estate market. If the evaluation is being performed for a sale of the business, consider whether the seller may benefit from selling the real estate separately from the business.

✔ **Year-to-year numbers:** One of the ways to judge consistency in a company's financials is to divide the dollar amount of any item on the balance sheet by the total assets for that year. See whether those numbers are generally within a certain range or if they vary wildly. Do the same for items on the liabilities or stockholder's equity side of the balance sheet. What if you see a lot of variance? You need to ask questions.

Not all companies need to go through a detailed valuation process. Generally, the smallest of small companies (businesses with less than $1 million in annual revenues is a guideline most valuation experts agree on) can rely on database information and rule-of-thumb measurements that go a long way to setting a range to negotiate price on any business.

One of the best places to start for help in understanding a particular business category's valuation is the most recent edition of *Business Reference Guide: The Essential Guide to Pricing a Business,* by Tom West (Business Brokerage Press). For almost 20 years, West has published this growing alphabetical index of some 500 types of businesses that includes rule-of-thumb pricing information and negotiating tips based on where that business category stands at that particular point in time.

A Step-by-Step Overview of the Valuation Process

If any of the following information sounds familiar, that's good. We like to reiterate important ideas because doing so helps keep them stuck in your head. Here we take a minute to go over each critical step of the valuation process. Individuals can cover these steps, but they're more sensibly done by valuation experts:

1. **Figure out why you want to value a business.**

   Do you want to split it up in a divorce, pass it down to the kids, divide it between siblings, or sell it for top dollar to a total stranger? (See Chapter 2 for more situations that can trigger a valuation.)

2. **Gather all your company's or a target company's existing (and hopefully audited) financial statements and look them over to get a view of the business's health.**

   The real number crunching starts a bit later. (For info on key financial statements, go to Chapter 8.)

   If you're putting a value on your own business before a sale or some other transaction, you have to be just as tough on your own numbers and operations as you'd be on a company you were planning to buy. If you can't be that coldly objective — and most business owners can't — bring in a skilled person who will be.

3. **Look outside for objective, factual resources on valuation.**

   Look for industry-based information that shows comparable valuations for similar businesses, their costs of operation, and various news and trends that may affect value in the future.

4. **Adjust the numbers.**

   This step is the beginning of the extensive number crunching that continues throughout the valuation process. You adjust financial statements not to commit hanky-panky but to compensate for any expense or accounting behavior not in line with the norms of competing businesses. See the nearby sidebar "Adjusting financials — once more with feeling" for some common adjustments.

   Most business valuations are based on pre-tax earnings. That fact is particularly relevant among small businesses because an owner's own tax decisions are generally closely linked to the business and can skew the process of valuation. A new owner may not make similar tax decisions to the old owner's, so pre-tax earnings provide a generally even playing field.

5. **Use the right business valuation method — or methods — to calculate the value of your company or a target company.**

   This step is the focus of this chapter. You or your valuation expert will choose one or more valuation methods to complete this process.

6. **Look at all the assumptions and calculations you've made thus far and assign certain discounts and premiums.**

   These discounts and premiums are based on anything from the timing of the sale to future anticipated activities in the business's active markets.

7. Write up the report.

We go into some detail on what a typical valuation report looks like later in the book, but generally, this material should be gathered up and composed into a final document so it can serve as a guide for future action.

No single "correct" valuation on any company exists. Remember that valuation is all about self-interest. Self-interest goes beyond a dollar figure; it involves your particular circumstances for buying or selling a business, your knowledge (full or incomplete) of the target company, and who else will be affected by the reason for the valuation.

Risky Business: Gauging Circumstances for the Best Results

Risk is an important question in the whole subject of business valuation and has a direct bearing on the result of the valuation. *Business risk* is anything that can thwart a positive earnings forecast for any company, large or small, public or private. It's any event or item — inside the company or outside in the world at large — that can affect sales, the cost of sales, administrative or operating expenses, or at worst, innovation and growth. In other words, business risk is anything that can lower the potential value of a company. Sometimes risk is general, literally outside the control of individual companies. It can include the following:

- The general course of the economy, either up or down
- Consumer and business spending that supports all businesses and industries
- The health of the lending and investment banking industry
- Innovations or failures within competitors inside an industry

But sometimes risk is very, very specific to the company itself. Such risks can include the following:

- Poor managerial and financial stewardship of the company
- Failures in marketing, advertising, and other customer-gathering and retention activities
- Lackluster product or service development
- High turnover at the staff level and poor control of institutional knowledge

In this section, we discuss both the approaches and methods to finding the value of a business.

TIP

Avoiding stupid valuation mistakes

Believe it or not, professionals can make these mistakes as easily as business owners or their various representatives who've never attempted the process. Keep the following questions in mind when reviewing your own valuation process or the valuation done for a target company:

✔ **Were the numbers adjusted?** You also hear the phrase *normalizing the financials* for the financial adjustment phase. Remember, adjusting the numbers is all about tweaking and sometimes adding back amounts that won't continue when a company changes hands—the pay levels for top management relative to current market rates, the benefits in place for the workforce that may be over or under common offerings in the business, and so on. Excessive amounts paid before a sale may continue afterward, leading to higher costs.

✔ **Was the method correct?** If the main source of a company's value is its intangible assets

and a valuation professional uses such tangible methodologies as book value, you have a problem. Make sure that the methods fit the business.

✔ **Were all the skeletons pulled from the closet?** Dishonest businesses hide things, honest businesses sometimes forget things they should mention, and some valuation professionals forget to mention things. Smart valuation means that you need to keep an eye open for lawsuits, product problems, and other signs of past — or future — trouble in a business.

✔ **Did the valuation professional know what he was doing?** Due diligence applies to the hiring process as well. Check your valuation expert's track record and references, and keep up that process during the early stages. Does the expert visit the business, ask the right questions, and when time to do so, aggressively crunch the numbers?

Understanding the different approaches

The three top associations for valuation professionals — the American Society of Appraisers (ASA), the Institute of Business Appraisers (IBA), and the National Association of Certified Valuation Analysts (NACVA) — agree on three major approaches to business valuation:

✔ The Asset Approach

✔ The Market Approach

✔ The Income Approach

Some approaches are definitely more appropriate than others. The purpose of the valuation influences the ways the business must be valued, and so does the level of risk that business currently faces. That's why valuation experts choose one or more approaches over others. The following sections cover these three major approaches in more detail.

The wonderful world of color ... oops ... earnings

Numbers are sort of like paint on a canvas: Mix them one way, and you get a particular shade. Mix them a different way, and they change. Valuation experts use a lot of different shades of earnings and other financial data in their work because they want those numbers to tell them specific things. *Accounting For Dummies,* by John A. Tracy, CPA (Wiley), and related books can tell you more about the basics of accounting, but for now, here are some definitions of key earnings measurements that are woven into many valuation projects:

✔ **Normalized net earnings:** Also known as *normalized earnings,* these are earnings results that have been adjusted (there's that word again) for unusual one-time issues, non-GAAP (generally accepted accounting principles) practices, discretionary expenses, or cyclical moves in the economy.

✔ **Earnings before taxes (EBT):** EBT is a way to compare companies in different tax jurisdictions. Here's the formula:

EBT = Revenue – Expenses (excluding tax)

✔ **Earnings before interest and tax (EBIT):** EBIT is essentially a company's operating earnings before deducting interest and tax payments. It's a purer look at a company's ongoing ability to profit, and it can make for easier comparisons across business lines and other companies. Here's the formula:

EBIT = Revenue – Operating Expenses

✔ **Earnings before interest, taxes, depreciation, and amortization (EBITDA):** This measurement gets a lot of mileage during earnings season for public companies. It's a controversial favorite: Analysts use it to compare profitability between companies and industries because it eliminates the effects of financing and accounting decisions, which allows some companies to hide a lot (remember Enron?). Here's the formula:

EBITDA = Revenue – Expenses (excluding tax, interest, depreciation, and amortization)

✔ **Net cash flow:** Cash flow is the lifeblood of a business because it measures a business's ability to pay its expenses on time while continuing to grow the operation. Here's the formula:

Net Cash Flow = Cash Inflows – Cash Outflows

✔ **Free cash flow:** This figure is the amount of cash that a company has left over after it has paid all its expenses and purchased all the capital assets it requires to maintain the business. How do you get there? Start with a company's operating cash flows (net income plus amortization and depreciation) and then subtract capital expenditures and dividends:

Free Cash Flow = (Net Income + Amortization + Depreciation) – (Capital Expenditures + Dividends)

Keep in mind that young, fast-growing companies may have negative free cash flow because they typically run up expenses before money starts coming in the door.

The Asset Approach

Also known as the Cost Approach, the Asset valuation approach is based on your finding the fair market value of assets (the easiest ones to value are tangible assets) and deducting the liabilities to determine the net asset value or the net worth of the business. *Fair market value* is the amount that a willing buyer would pay to a willing seller in a free market for any piece of property, including a company.

Asset valuation methods include the following:

- ✔ **Book value:** In all honesty, book value really isn't a valuation method, because book value shouldn't be confused with fair market value — and that's really why we mention it. The fair market value can be notably higher than the book value because the book value is based on the historic value of assets — primarily tangible assets. Equally important, book value essentially ignores goodwill, and for many small businesses, goodwill can be the biggest asset.

  Book value isn't a good measurement for evaluating a business before a sale, even for an industrial company that's all about hard assets. Assets get depreciated over the years to a value of zero, but in reality, such equipment and other assets may still be valuable to the organization — depending on the quality issues associated with those assets, their value may actually go up. Yet it's surprising to note how many companies believe that book value actually describes the full value of the business. Book value is included in a valuation report for the sake of completeness, but beyond that, it has limited use.

  Here's the formula for book value, which in some circles is called a business's *net worth:*

    Book Value = Total Assets – Total Liabilities

  Using the *tangible book value* calculation, intangible or soft assets are deducted from the total assets. *Economic book value,* on the other hand, includes intangible assets and allows assets to be adjusted to their current market value.

- ✔ **Adjusted book value:** This figure is the book value amount after assets and liabilities have been adjusted to market value, which involves comparing assets of similar companies or obtaining an asset appraisal (in use) from an accredited asset appraiser.

  Why use it: This method should be included in a valuation project for going-concern businesses (ongoing businesses, without plans to close in the immediate future) because it serves as a reality check of the other methods and tells you where the bottom of the value is for businesses with inherent goodwill. If some of the other valuation approaches indicate a value lower than the adjusted book value, the adjusted book value or orderly liquidation value may be a more appropriate valuation of the business.

There's no actual formula for adjusted book value; you simply have to adjust book asset values to fair market values.

✔ **Liquidation value:** This calculation is somewhat similar to the book value calculation, except the value assumes a forced or orderly liquidation of assets rather than book value. In practice, the liabilities of the business are deducted from the liquidation value of the assets to determine the liquidation value of the business. The overall value of a business that uses this method should be lower than a valuation reached by using the standard book or adjusted book methods.

Why use it: The word *liquidation* suggests that this is a process confined to businesses that are closing, are closed, are in bankruptcy, or are in industries that are in irreversible trouble. However, this method may also be the indicated method for a business that's a going concern but that isn't putting its assets to good use and may be better off closing down and selling the assets. Sometimes you hear the term *orderly* liquidation value, and you often see it applied to companies that are closing and selling off machinery, office equipment, and other tangible assets in a piecemeal fashion over time.

For more info on going-concern value and liquidation value, flip to Chapter 3.

The Market Approach

With the Market Approach, you're comparing your company or a target company with other, similar companies. You can use comparisons to similar publicly traded companies or to actual sales transactions or similar businesses.

You must make comparisons with caution. Comparing a small privately owned business with a publicly traded company without adjusting for size and tradability is inappropriate. Likewise, comparing a business with $100,000 revenue to a multimillion-dollar business concern is inappropriate.

Another important issue that may detract from the usefulness of comparisons is that the comparables are obtained from databases that track completed transactions. You may find too few comparable transactions to base an opinion on. In addition, some of the databases don't disclose the terms of the transactions, and the terms may have an upward or downward effect on the price at which transactions close.

These valuations are frequently expressed in ratio form. You can use several ratios for this method of valuation, and as the importance of intangibles continues to grow, you'll probably see new methods evolve in the future. Here we list the most commonly used measures:

✔ **Price-to-revenue ratio:** This is expressed as the market price of the business divided by the revenue.

Why use it: Even if a company hasn't posted a profit over the past year, it always has revenue. This valuation measure is frequently applied to younger companies or businesses in high-growth industries. Also, depending on how the financials are normalized (and how earnings are calculated), the number most easy to verify may be the gross revenues of a business.

✔ **Price-to-earnings ratio:** The P/E ratio is expressed as the market price of a business divided by earnings.

Why use it: Earnings are the lifeblood of a company — without earnings, it can't continue over a long period of time.

✔ **Price to EBITDA:** This ratio is expressed as the company's share price divided by its earnings before interest, taxes, depreciation, and amortization.

Why use it: Using EBITDA improves comparability among businesses because it removes expenses that are or may be somewhat subjective.

The Income Approach

The Income Approach is probably the most common and appropriate valuation approach in most cases. Essentially, you're trying to analyze the future economic benefits you're anticipating from a business — better known as income — into a single amount in today's dollars, the term also known as present value.

You can say this another way: The Holy Grail of valuation based on income assumptions is the determination of future earnings, also known as the *future benefit stream,* or in other words, "big profits I expect to pocket if I buy this company." (If you don't want to see evidence of a company that's going to grow and make more money from year to year, why would you buy it?)

Valuation based on income and cash flows tries to project a company's future cash flows based mainly on historical financial data added to smart analysis of the company's current operations and plans for the future — anything expected to enhance the amount of money coming in the door. This past financial data should be audited data that has come from a respected accounting firm that's willing to sign its name to its work, if possible. That gives you accountability for those results. However, the Income Approach is suited for less-accountable data also because the approach gives you the ability to take into account the higher potential risk associated with an unaudited income stream.

In the smallest of small companies — and surprisingly, in some larger ones as well — don't be surprised if you run into financial data done by someone's Uncle Morrie. Uncle Morrie may be a crackerjack accountant and as honest as the day is long, but it's best to have a CPA with some experience auditing the finances of your particular industry doing your figures before you turn them over to a buyer. If sellers want a higher price, they need to think like buyers and make a more professional presentation of their financials.

Calculating risk and its relationship to present value

Companies with smart growth plans, solid financial controls, and good leadership build value. Knock out any of these three attributes, and the three-legged stool wobbles.

The evaluation of risk and its relationship to present value is what valuation professionals — and some of the smartest minds at the biggest companies in the country — get paid to do. They look for signs of solid management, but they also look for trouble. Ironically, trouble isn't always a turnoff, because trouble often can be managed and overcome. Risk isn't necessarily a bad thing if adjustments are possible.

Whether you're buying a business outright or a stock in any company as a personal investment, you need to determine whether that company's potential future reward outweighs the potential risks of getting in. This fact is true whether the company is a high-flying Internet startup or a corner family restaurant.

If you're buying a business outright, you should also come to the process with an idea of how to limit that business's risk in the future — art can trump science in this part of the valuation process (for more on the art of valuation, see Chapter 3).

You always have to monetize the future in the present to see if it's worth jumping on board. *Present value* is the central question of valuation; the simple definition is the current value of one or more payments to be received or paid in the future. The more interesting question is why present value is important. When you're buying or selling a company, you're literally buying or selling the future. Why would anyone buy a company that has no positive prospects after the end of this week, month, or year — or in five years? Valuation is focused on the concept of present value because you need to put an actual price tag on that future if you want to profit as a buyer or a seller.

In valuation terms, a *discount rate* is a rate of return on investment used to calculate the present value of a series of cash flows to be received in the future. More colloquially, a higher discount rate can be applied to particular assets that have a higher degree of risk — read that as *questionable value*.

Using discount and capitalization rates and income valuation methods

Some people describe a discount rate and a capitalization rate as separate concepts; others use the terms interchangeably. We'll just say that both concepts are the result of the *build-up* method in valuation. That means a valuation professional uses a variety of factors — hard numbers as well as judgment calls based on industry research — to "build up" a variety of numbers and reach a critical piece of information: whether it's smarter for a potential buyer to sock her funds in this business or simply invest the money elsewhere. In the context of business valuation, a *discount rate* gives that answer before certain tax, cost-of-capital, and cash-flow adjustments are made. The *capitalization rate* is the final measurement that comes after those final adjustments.

The discount rate can alternatively be called a *required rate of return* — what you're expecting the investment to yield, considering how risky it is. As such, it's essentially a measure of the risk of an investment. It's determined by building risk factor on risk factor until you've considered all the potential risks in an investment.

What kind of numbers go into calculating a discount rate? A valuation professional builds up a discount rate by starting out with a risk-free rate (usually the T-bill rate) and gradually building risk factors onto the risk-free rate until all the risk factors related to the business being valued have been taken into account. Here's how it works:

1. **The first addition is a market risk premium over the risk-free rate, to bring the rate to what can be expected from an investment in a publicly traded company (with average industry risk).**

2. **The second adjustment is an adjustment for industry risk (some industries trade at a higher market risk premium than others because of industry risk).**

3. **The next risk premium relates to the size of the business.**

4. **Thereafter, the valuation professional adds or deducts premiums for company-specific information that was uncovered during the analysis of the business.**

Consider an example of how the resultant discount rate is used. You have a business in your sights that you want to invest in and you know that your annual return from this business will be $100,000. You do some research and figure out that 33 percent is a standard capitalization rate for other businesses this size that operate in the same industry — that 33 percent is your capitalization rate here. So you do the math:

$$\$100,000 \div 0.33 \approx \$300,000$$

That $300,000 is the actual value of the investment. Should you pay $300,000 for that business? See whether you can get it for less.

When determining discount and capitalization rates, you have the option to use either the build-up method or the capital asset pricing model (CAPM) method. (We get to those methods shortly.) If you're valuing the company on a debt-free basis, you can convert the discount and capitalization rates to their debt-free equivalents based on the company's weighted average cost of capital.

The following sections cover the most common income valuation methods.

Capitalization of Earnings Method

The Capitalization of Earnings Method reflects the previous calculation: It takes an earnings number from a particular period and computes the value of the entire investment when divided by a particular capitalization rate. Here's the formula:

Income before Depreciation, Interest, and Tax (IBDIT) ÷ Cap Rate = Value

This basic method determines the value of a business's capital asset pricing and your strategy for negotiation. However, keep in mind that this method assumes that the business will grow at a stable rate every year or won't grow at all.

Discounted Cash Flow (DCF) Method

The DCF Method calculates the present value of future expected cash flows using a selected discount rate. People usually use it when a company's earnings growth is different from year to year (the company may be growing exponentially, or it may be unstable for a variety of reasons, good or bad). DCF analysis is usually applied to companies that are rather young or companies that are experiencing high growth. (Note that young businesses that are still experiencing variable growth may also be more risky.)

Each of the company's individual cash flows is discounted to a present value by using a discount rate over a discrete number of periods. At the end of the period, usually when it's assumed that the company's earnings have stabilized, a terminal value is calculated by using a capitalization rate. All the various values are summed to arrive at an overall value of the cash-flow stream.

Management of the business to be valued should provide the future cash flows and the assumptions they're based on, and the valuation professional should carefully and critically assess them. If you're assessing your own business, make every attempt to approach the process with a good dose of realism.

Here's the DCF formula:

$$DCF = CF0 \times \text{the sum of } [(1 + g) \div (1 + r)x] \qquad \text{(for } x = 0 \text{ to } n)$$

where *DCF* is discounted cash flow, *CF0* is today's cash flow, *g* is expected growth, *r* is the expected rate of return, and *n* is the number of periods (which is usually not more than three to five years).

However, you're not done yet. What you've done so far with the discounted cash flow doesn't include the prospects of the business after the discrete period years, and you sincerely hope that the business will continue on into the future. At this point, you need to make an educated guess regarding what may be expected as a long-term growth rate into the future and then use this information to determine the terminal value at that time. The terminal value can be determined by using the Gordon Growth Model, as follows:

$$\text{Price} = I \div (R - g)$$

where *I* is the annual cash flow at the end of the discrete period, *R* is the risk or the discount rate, and *g* is a constant growth rate into perpetuity. This calculation gets you to something called a *terminal value* at the end of a period when the company's growth rate is expected to become stable.

Consider the methodology examples you see here as the most common, but realize that many more techniques can reach valuation conclusions based on particular industries and situations. In many valuations, you see a professional use more than one approach and methods within that approach to test valuation from a number of perspectives.

Weighted Average Cost of Capital

The WACC Method can help a company calculate the cost of raising money. The calculation involves multiplying the cost of each element of capital, such as debt (loans and bonds) and equity (common stock and preferred stock) by its percentage of the total capital and then adding them together. The final figure, the weighted average cost of capital (WACC), is a rough guide to the rate of "required return" per monetary unit of capital.

Take a look at the formula:

$$\text{WACC} = [Ke + Kd(\text{D/E})] \div [1 + (\text{D/E})]$$

where Ke is the desired return on equity, Kd is the desired return on debt, and D/E is the debt/equity ratio.

Excess Earnings Method

We're not exactly in love with the Excess Earnings Method. In fact, some people like to call it the *Etch A Sketch Method.* This method gets a lot of attention for the valuation of companies with significant intangible assets, but it's also earned a fair amount of controversy. Here's how it works:

1. **The market value of net tangible assets is multiplied by a rate of return appropriate to these assets to calculate earnings attributable to tangible assets.**

    Net tangible assets are calculated first, and then an assumption is made about whether those tangible assets should provide at least a basic return on investment, such as 10 to 15 percent.

2. **This earnings figure is deducted from total earnings to calculate an earnings figure attributable to intangible assets.**

    After that return is calculated, the difference between that return and the company's actual cash flow is the amount of cash flow attributable to intangibles.

3. **These intangible earnings are divided by a capitalization rate for intangibles to calculate an estimated value for the intangibles.**

    You now have the value of the intangibles — in very, very rough terms at least. We talk much more about the debate over intangible assets in Chapter 5.

A lot of potential for inaccuracy arises with the Excess Earnings Method, particularly among neophytes. The level of subjectivity is very wide. What rate should a net tangible asset return — 10, 15, or 20 percent? A delivery truck has a different expected contribution than a piece of machinery on the plant floor, and depending on which one you pick, it has either less or more of an impact on the intangible calculation. A question also arises over what capitalization rate to use for intangible assets, and most people place that rate at a high level.

The IRS developed the Excess Earnings Method during Prohibition to compensate distilleries for putting them out of business during the Volstead Act. More sophisticated techniques have evolved since then.

So why use it? A lot of people love this method because it's a relatively easy one to do. But leave it to the IRS to be a wet blanket: The agency once thought the method was okay to use, but now it denounces it because depending on the calculation, some firms can create much more value than they're entitled to. Yet some people are still attracted to this method when they're reporting higher earnings than they normally do.

But back to the capitalization rate. When you hear the term *capitalization of income,* it's the way the economic worth of a company is estimated by computing the present value of average annual net income that the company is expected to produce in the future.

Projecting future income isn't just a matter of numbers — it involves applying certain assumptions about the risk and reward of a particular business investment. As you see in the preceding computation, a cap rate requires research and comparison with other similar companies — but the computation works for stock investments, machinery, or any asset.

Another way to explain the capitalization rate is as the yield necessary to attract investors to a particular investment, given the risks associated with that investment. And in the world of investing in businesses or in securities, the greater the risk, the greater the potential for reward.

What are some of the nonnumeric risk factors that get built into capitalization and discount rates that valuation professionals apply? We list a few here:

- ✔ Strong product lines
- ✔ Talented management
- ✔ Strong customer base
- ✔ Dominant market share
- ✔ Great financial controls
- ✔ Low employee turnover (and for some valuations, no unions are a plus)
- ✔ No hidden liabilities that may blow up into expensive lawsuits
- ✔ Financial ratios that exceed other companies in its industry class

We try to give you some better insight on valuing intangibles in Chapter 5.

Chapter 5

The Challenge of Valuation in a Knowledge Economy

*B*usiness valuation was a lot easier 50 years ago. In the days before computers, the Internet, and armies of people working as consultants, valuation was linked much more clearly to countable items: tools, machinery, facilities, office furniture, units produced, you name it.

Those countable items may still exist within a company, but a higher value is often placed on the brainpower within a company — not only the traditional intangibles of patents and brands but also the strategic focus of a firm, its product development process, and the attractiveness of its leaders and their ability to produce talented future leaders just like them.

Today's economy may be called a knowledge economy — but exactly how do you value knowledge? The truth is there are many ways to value all kinds of assets. But as knowledge and skills gather more importance in companies, the valuation of these intangibles is worth discussing in depth. Read on.

Moving from a Hard-Asset to an Intangible-Asset Economy

No matter how you feel about former Federal Reserve Board Chairman Alan Greenspan, he definitely had a way with a line. In 1999, he told an audience in Grand Rapids, Michigan, about this major change in the U.S. economy:

"The quintessential manifestations of America's industrial might earlier this century — large steel mills, auto assembly plants, petrochemical complexes and skyscrapers — have been replaced by a gross domestic product that has been downsized as ideas have replaced physical bulk and effort as creators of value. Today, economic value is best symbolized by exceedingly complex, miniaturized integrated circuits and the ideas — the software — that utilize them. Most of what we currently perceive as value and wealth is intellectual and impalpable."

This transition in the U.S. economy hasn't happened overnight, but it has had a profound impact on how experts view the value of businesses ranging from factories to software developers. The point is that in recent years, people have come to realize that the intangible assets of a business may be the most valuable of all.

Reviewing types of assets

Here's a review of all the assets that may be totaled up in the valuation of a business:

- **Tangible assets (real property):** These are things of value that can be physically touched. Examples of tangible assets include buildings; industrial, commercial, and municipal land; building improvements; and easements.

- **Personal property:** This term refers to machinery, equipment, inventory, motor vehicles, trade fixtures, furniture, computer equipment, and other items that can be sold.

- **Intangible assets:** Intangibles are the opposite of tangible assets: assets that aren't physical in nature. In many cases, intangible assets are ideas. Examples include intellectual property (patents, trademarks, copyrights, formulas, blueprints, designs, and so on), brand recognition, and goodwill.

Goodwill is an intangible asset that gives a company a competitive advantage, such as a good marketplace reputation or great employee morale. You see goodwill on a balance sheet as the amount by which the company's purchase price exceeds its net tangible assets.

You may see the words *definite* and *indefinite* applied to intangible assets. An indefinite asset is something like a brand name, because it stays with the company and can't be sold easily. A *definite* intangible asset is something like a patent, which can be sold to another party or company that wants to produce the item.

- **Intellectual capital:** This is pure knowledge linked to specific people who work in the enterprise and the enterprise's ability to capture that knowledge so that it doesn't travel outside the company.

The leading tangible and intangible assets that companies want to value include Internet domain names; trade names and trademarks; franchise, license, and royalty agreements; customer contracts; computer software; proprietary technology; and intellectual property, which we discuss in the next section.

The central identity of an asset is its capability to generate a return. The Internet has changed the face of business, and the world often seems overrun with companies that choose to outsource their production of things you can touch. We believe that the old formulas and approaches to valuation still hold for the companies that trade mainly in intangible goods. Profit proves the value of a company, regardless of where that company's most valuable assets lie.

Recognizing the increasing value of intellectual property

Since the start of the Internet era in the early 1990s, the bulk of corporate value has been sliding from the tangible-assets column — so-called "bricks and mortar" assets — to the intangible side. According to Baruch Lev, a professor at New York University's Stern School of Business, intangible assets now constitute up to two-thirds of corporate market value in the United States. For some firms, such as biotechnology companies, intellectual property may account for more than 60 percent of total value.

Here's a little more evidence for the increasing value of intangibles: In a December 2008 story, *Business Week* chief economist Michael Mandel wrote, "The war between the intangible and tangible sectors of the U.S. economy is over — and intangibles have won." He pointed out that since the economy went into recession in December 2007, the industries that produce or distribute physical or tangible goods — including construction, manufacturing, retail trade, and transportation — have lost 1.8 million jobs, including 60,000 in the auto industry and its dealer network and 300,000 in residential construction."

Industries in the intangibles sector, including education and healthcare, don't produce any tangible goods and have only a few basic real assets contributing to their value, but those industries alone have gained roughly half a million jobs between December 2007 and December 2008.

The government isn't terribly good at measuring the full job impact of intangibles and the qualities that go into producing jobs. Mandel points out that intangibles aren't well measured by the gross domestic product figures produced by the Bureau of Economic Analysis:

"However, intangibles do produce jobs. Consider the last business cycle, which ran from March 2001 to December 2007. Over that stretch, health and education alone added 3.5 million jobs, roughly 63 percent of all the net jobs produced by the economy. Altogether, the intangible sector accounted for about 75 percent of job growth. By comparison, the tangible sector, led by manufacturing, lost some 1.8 million jobs over the same period."

Mandel and many other economic experts are coming to see that intangible value goes beyond longtime intangible standards such as goodwill and patents. Whole industries are now built around ideas and human skills, and in a digital world in which information travels in bits and bytes rather than in physical form, that trend will continue.

Determining the Value of a Company Based on Ideas

In recent years, the value of an idea-based company has been a very pertinent question. Companies such as Enron once were media darlings because they seemed to amass tremendous market capitalization and make great money despite having very few tangible assets. Yet in 2002 — the year after the 9/11 attacks — the country was sinking into recession, and it was tougher for Enron to hide the fact that it had little underlying value to support its popularity. As was later revealed, deceptive tactics had propped up the company. By the late 1990s, much of Enron's portfolio was shrinking, and its assets were being paired with other figures to make the numbers look better.

However, there's plenty of debate over the valuation of these assets. Intangible assets are revolutionizing most markets, yet accounting professionals are still trying to find a way to value those assets consistently. Even though new accounting rules on intangibles went into effect in 2001, *The New York Times* said in a September 2007 article that official accounting rules still "give intangibles a wide berth." In this section, we discuss the significance of seeking detailed data when dealing with intangibles.

The importance of real, documented income

A company based on ideas may not make money in its first year or two, but eventually it has to; otherwise, it's simply not a company that you should buy.

Patents are valuable — if you can defend them

Intangible value is a line that keeps moving as technology keeps moving forward, and as intellectual property increasingly moves the economy, protecting that property becomes an ever-more-expensive part of staying in business.

In recent research, James Besson and Michael J. Meurer of Boston University School of Law reported that starting in the late 1990s, publicly traded companies saw their patent litigation costs outstrip patent profits. Besson and Meurer concluded that many patents are worthless to organizations because of the pace of advancing technology and the sheer cost of defending the patents in court.

To make that point clear, here are a few thoughts from Warren Buffett, one of the world's richest men and a financial guru best known for his insistence on verifying the actual value of anything he buys:

> "Your goal as an investor should be to purchase, at a rational price, a part interest in an easily understandable business whose earnings are virtually certain to be materially higher five, ten, and twenty years from now. Over time, you will find only a few companies that meet these standards — so when you see one that qualifies, you should buy a meaningful amount of stock. You must also resist temptation to stray from your guidelines: If you aren't willing to own a stock for ten years, don't even think about owning it for ten minutes."

Now, granted, Buffett was talking about investing in the stock of a company, not buying the company outright. But really, what's the difference? Anyone who buys a stock is buying at least a piece of a company; the thought process that gets you there shouldn't be any different. You can lose your shirt by making a bad decision about value in either case.

We should note that during the go-go 1990s, when the first Internet boom had investors jumping in with both feet, Buffett stayed out. People laughed because he bluntly stated that he "didn't understand" most of what the tech industry was doing — and in the end, he avoided losing a fortune.

In 2008, he sounded a similar warning to investors such as housing finance giants Fannie Mae and Freddie Mac about investing in *derivatives* — complex financial instruments that played a central role in that year's market crisis. "I know the people that run these companies, and they don't have their minds around what is happening," he said.

To get an overall look at what's happening in the world economy and what will eventually happen in your neighborhood, watch smart global investors like Buffett. These big investors understand value and have a lot to teach the little guys.

Lessons from the tech wreck and the credit crunch

The first decade of the 21st century may be remembered as one in which businesses and investors ignored proper valuation at their peril. Trillions of dollars were lost in consumer and business markets during 2008, and although economic factors were a major part of the problem, most experts believed that assets ranging from real estate to stocks tumbled after lax valuation practices left said assets even more exposed.

The lesson to take away from these events is very simple: Proper valuation keeps the chickens from coming home to roost. If you plan to buy or sell a business, do your homework so that you know exactly which factors make the business more or less valuable, and understand how local and world economic events beyond your control can affect your plans.

Particularly with regard to intangible assets, it's important to work with people who are familiar with your target industry and can trace actual income to those intangible assets.

What strategic buyers and lenders want to see

A *strategic buyer* is a person or a company that wants to buy a firm because the firm fits nicely with the buyer's strategy. If the acquired company were to do everything that the buyer expected, it would provide a new direction for the buyer's business to go in or just a nice little product niche that could stave off competition.

As intangibles grow in importance, strategic buyers should demand considerably more detail on what those assets are worth in the marketplace. Likewise, sellers are going to be asked to create significantly more detail on that front. Just be prepared.

Like buyers, lenders want to know their money is being invested in a company that has real assets and real growth possibilities. As we write this book, the United States is navigating its way through one of the worst credit crises since the Great Depression. A global economic slowdown brought about by the U.S. housing-lending crisis is redefining the way that lenders look at prospective borrowers on both the consumer and business sides. More than ever, lenders demand solid financials and provable income — especially when dealing with intangibles. Any income that companies can't prove won't be used as a basis for lending.

For info on how risk-taking investors measure the value of an unproven company in the first stages of its life, check out Chapter 21.

Reaching Intangible Value

There's little doubt that intangible assets have some very solid value. What would Coca-Cola be without that brand name and more than 120 years of marketing savvy? Little more than some brown sugar water in a shapely bottle.

So-called *cloud software* — software that's built, housed, and accessed only over the Internet — never rolls off an assembly line. It isn't a disk that a computer user can hold in his hand. But is it still a potentially valuable asset? You bet. In this section, we discuss brand value and how it's related to consumer behavior.

Taking a stab at brand valuation

As more of the products that people want leap into the intangible realm, accountants, corporate finance officers, and investors may conduct in-depth analyses by using three traditional value approaches: cost, market, and income. We discuss all three approaches in the following subsections.

An accountant or valuation professional needs to use a variety of methods to value an intangible asset.

Cost approach

The *cost* approach to valuation involves calculating what it'd cost another business to duplicate the asset from scratch. In the cost approach, you estimate current costs or calculate the current value of all the historical expenses of creating the brand.

Market approach

The *market* value calculation involves comparing the past sale transactions of the intangible that needs to be evaluated (such as a brand name) and making a stab at a similar value. Real estate agents use this approach when they recommend a selling price for your house.

The biggest hang-up is finding good data to use for the comparison; intangible assets don't produce a lot of tangible comparison data. Some people may have put a price tag on the Coca-Cola brand, for example, but valuing the leading submarine-sandwich chain in a city may be a much bigger challenge.

Income approach

The *income* approach allows you to measure the future benefits (sales, earnings, or savings) that the intangible asset in question will deliver to a business, estimating when the business will first receive those benefits and for how long. This approach shows businesses how much of their income is generated by a brand and other intangible assets.

With regard to intangibles, you can break the income approach into several possible methods, though gathering data for each method is something of a challenge:

- ✔ **Discounted cash-flow method:** This is used to value some of the most widely known intangible assets, such as technology, software, customer relationships, noncompete covenants, strategic agreements, franchises, and distribution channels. In this method, the value of an asset reflects the current value of the projected earnings that the asset will generate, taking into account the revenue and expenses of the asset, the relative risk of the asset, the contributions of other assets, and a discount rate that reflects the time value of invested capital.

- ✔ **Relief-from-royalty method:** You use this method to value trade names and trademarks. This method assumes that the value of an asset is equal to all future royalties that would have to be paid for the right to use the asset if it were not acquired. A royalty rate is selected based on discussions with management regarding the importance of the asset, the effectiveness of constraints imposed by competing assets, the ability of competitors to produce similar assets, and the market licensing rates for similar assets. The royalty rate is used to compute the expected revenue generated or associated with the asset. Then the hypothetical royalties are discounted to their current value.

    Royalty rates for trade names and trademarks vary widely, depending on the nature of the proprietary property, its role in the business, the specific industry, and the marketplace.

- ✔ **Comparable guideline/industry transactions method:** This one's used to value Internet domains and names of products such as newspapers or magazines. This approach requires comparison data, which can be tough to find, so premiums or discounts may be applied to the asset given its attributes, earnings power, and other factors.

- ✔ **Avoided-cost method:** This method is for valuing various kinds of technology. This method relies on available historic data. The value of the intangible asset is based on the costs that the acquiring company avoids by obtaining an existing, fully functional asset rather than building or assembling one. Valuation professionals gather data on employee salaries connected with the development of that technology, as well as on related expenses such as overhead, administrative, travel, and meal costs.

Why it's important to value intangibles in a downturn

Intangible Business, a London-based brand consultancy, maintains that understanding the value of intangibles is particularly important when the economy is bad. Here's why:

✔ **Maximizing value:** Valuing assets when the economy goes into a downturn allows you not only to maximize what you have but also to spot opportunities outside the company.

✔ **Maximizing use of the brand:** It's particularly critical to get the most marketing muscle out of a brand in tough times. Also, if you find that you do have to sell intangibles in a crunch, you won't risk a fire sale.

✔ **Improving target planning:** Understanding the value of a brand helps your organization set realistic targets for income, profit, supply-chain management, and staff morale.

✔ **Improving asset performance:** Understanding the true value of intangible assets strengthens the commercial application of those assets, according to Intangible Business.

✔ **Maximizing investment in the brand:** Without constant investment to maintain their value, brands falter. Valuation helps determine the right amount of investment to produce maximum results.

✔ **Restoring investor confidence:** Today, intangible assets must make their way onto a balance sheet. Sick brands depress share prices, whereas healthy brands do the opposite.

Recognizing customers as valuation drivers

Marketing consultants live for this stuff, but increasingly, new business metrics allow business owners to put a value not only on the number of customers they have but also on how those customers behave. A *business metric* is a customized system of measurement that allows you to figure something out, such as what people are spending with your company in certain situations.

Brands are worth little or nothing unless humans are clamoring for the products, so getting the most buying behavior out of every group of customers you have is a valuation issue. You may have heard about the 80/20 rule, which states that 80 percent of your business comes from 20 percent of your customers. As you consider ways to make your business more profitable for sale or ways to make a business that you're planning to buy more profitable, it makes sense to find out about the various metrics for measuring customers' behavior — what they spend, why they spend, and when they don't spend.

One of the current buzz phrases, *balanced scorecard,* is a way to present a whole bunch of metrics at one time so that you can get a complete picture of how customers are behaving.

Big companies typically have more money and better equipment to measure what their customers — and noncustomers — think and do, but don't let that fact discourage you. Sometimes, tracking customer behavior can be as simple as asking a few good questions at the register or during a sales call. Also, some online survey companies allow you to query customers — in exchange for a coupon or some other small item of value — about how well or poorly you're doing.

If you're trying to improve the value of your business, or if you're looking for a business that you can make more valuable, talk to marketing experts at your local community college, or read all you can about computerized ways to track customer behavior in your chosen business and find a way to chart that behavior over time. You may even want to exercise a little brand loyalty and check out *Consumer Behavior For Dummies,* by Laura Lake, or *Branding For Dummies,* by Bill Chiaravalle and Barbara Findlay Schenck (Wiley).

Preserving Your Knowledge Business for the Future

Accept this fact: All businesses are knowledge businesses. As intangibles become more dominant parts of what companies of all sizes do for a living, you need to become more sophisticated about how to use the knowledge in your business to generate value. Even the most traditional manufacturing business needs to have a Web presence, for example, because increasingly, the Web drives traffic from both first-time and repeat customers.

Also, if you want to sell the business someday and you don't necessarily want to stick with that business as the new owner's employee, you need to think through how you'll package the knowledge that you've acquired throughout your history for eventual sale along with the company. If you know what you're doing, you can price that knowledge at a premium.

Shaky times: When the founder's brain leaves the building

Many major businesses throughout the world are run by personalities — people with identities that are inextricably linked to the brand value of their companies. Richard Branson of the Virgin umbrella of companies — 360, at this writing — certainly is one. So is Steve Jobs, one of the founders of Apple, Inc.

It's great to have an identity and a well of knowledge that are virtually synonymous with the business. But if a company is tied to intangible assets that are linked to one person, the danger to the company of that person's resignation, death, or disability becomes greater.

Jobs is an interesting example, because as we write this book, speculation is swirling about the state of his health. Jobs beat pancreatic cancer in 2004, only to have rumors surface in late 2008 that he may be ill again. In January 2009, after an announcement weeks before that a "hormone imbalance" was affecting his weight, Apple said Jobs would take a six-month leave of absence because his medical condition was more serious than first thought. Jobs was no more precise than that about his condition. By the end of that month, the U.S. Securities and Exchange Commission announced it would investigate whether Apple had intentionally kept information from shareholders.

Most companies fear a leadership vacuum when the chief executive officer gets sick. At Apple, the speculation seemed to have an unusually serious effect on the company's stock, as well as on its customers, who were setting chat rooms on fire around the globe. Because Jobs is not only CEO but also the primary driver of the company's line of ingenious products — the walking embodiment of the Apple brand and mystique — fears about his death or incapacitation had company watchers wondering what would happen to the Apple brand after Jobs.

Consider the aftermath of Walt Disney's death in 1966. Although the Disney company saw significant success at its theme parks over the next 18 years, its film and animation units drifted until Walt's nephew, Roy Disney, unseated Walt's son-in-law, Ron Miller, and brought in Michael Eisner and Frank Wells to reenergize the brand. Under that new leadership, the company's undervalued brand was reinvigorated.

What owners need to do: Planning ahead

Owners and founders can't help being synonymous with the value of their businesses at all stages of its growth, but they have to develop a means of creating parallel value that can continue with the organizations after they're gone. As we state throughout this book, this situation is why long-term transaction planning is so important.

A succession plan is not something that you create merely in case of disaster. Creating one is a value-building exercise in itself — proof that when the intellectual capital of certain people is removed from the organization for any reason, the organization can sustain itself under existing management or new owners.

Creating business value means capturing and sustaining knowledge for next-generation management and owners.

Part II
Getting Familiar with Valuation Tools, Principles, and Resources

The 5th Wave   By Rich Tennant

"The investors liked our business plan — particularly the in-depth assesment of our competition, which is who they've decided to invest with."

In this part . . .

Although we don't drown you in numbers and computations, we do get a little deeper into the valuation process in this part. We talk more about what various experts do throughout a valuation and what you should know about a company's financial data going into the process. We also introduce a key resource that many people use as a starting point for a business valuation: rule-of-thumb data.

Chapter 6

Getting Familiar with a Typical Valuation Report

*W*e've said it before and we'll say it again: Valuations aren't driven by bricks and mortar sitting on a piece of land. They're driven by the reason someone wants to acquire a business or get rid of one. An asset's value is ultimately driven by the rationale for a transaction. And the goal of any valuation (regardless of the purpose) is to answer the question "What would happen in the market?"

In this chapter, we discuss the basic elements of a business valuation report, with the understanding that no two reports, like no two business valuations, should ever be the same. The best valuation reports tell a story about the history of a business, its pros and cons, and most importantly, its potential.

Understanding what a finished product should look like is always helpful before you start a process, so this chapter also lays out the general elements of any business valuation report that you'd pay for from a business valuation consultant or appraiser. Reports can vary in length and complexity based on the complexity of the job. Here, we give you a very basic starting point so you can see how reports present the essential information of valuation.

Note: This chapter, like most of the book, is focused on working with a valuation professional in determining what a business is worth. But in watching the habits of appraisers, accountants, and estate and tax attorneys, you should be gaining insight, too. So as you read, put yourself in the shoes of a trained valuation professional each step of the way — you'll start to figure out which facts to focus on and which questions to ask.

What a Valuation Report Is Supposed to Do

A good valuation report, like any piece of quality research, should open your mind to possibilities you've already considered and maybe a few you haven't thought about. As we mention throughout this book, putting dollar signs in your eyes isn't the job of a quality valuation professional. Nor is it her job to search in every corner for value or for data, events, or hidden matters that may take value away.

A good appraiser's job is to provide a third-party, objective opinion on what would actually happen if the subject company were for sale on the open market. You get a median valuation as the result, but if the appraiser or valuation professional is doing her job, you get what's known as a *range of values,* a compilation of opinions based on various methods of valuing those assets.

Always ask valuation professionals how many different methods they may potentially use to value your particular business and how they'll communicate those results to you.

A valuation report may contain very good news for you and your company or for the company you're hoping to buy. Or it may contain some bad news that sends you back to the drawing board but prevents you from making some expensive mistakes in the end.

Outlining a Typical Valuation Report

Every valuation professional may have a particular style, but most valuation reports follow a certain structure. We cover each section of the report in greater detail in the following subsections. For now, though, take a quick look at the setup:

- ✔ Cover
- ✔ Valuation summary (including assumptions and limiting conditions)
- ✔ Table of contents
- ✔ Executive summary
- ✔ Valuation summary
- ✔ Valuation assignment
- ✔ Economic outlook
- ✔ Industry outlook

> ✔ Business overview (including cost of capital, discounts, and premiums)
>
> ✔ Conclusion of value
>
> ✔ Appendixes (charts, footnotes, glossaries, and more)

A valuation report has no set number of pages. The length depends on the complexity of the assignment and the valuation possibilities based on the valuation goals being sought.

Cover

A cover's a cover, right? Well, in addition to looking at all the key information about the valuation firm, its contact information and where it's located, and its cool logo, you need to check one piece of key information and make sure you understand it: the date. Know whether the printed date is simply the date when the report was turned over to you or whether it reflects the official date of the valuation.

You need to be very clear about all the critical dates in any valuation you commission. The valuation date is critical because if this report is being done for tax reasons or eventually becomes evidence in a lawsuit or divorce action, the time sensitivity of the analysis becomes all the more important, depending on the circumstances of the case.

We talk a lot in Chapter 7 about planning for a sale or any other valuation-related transaction. Depending on what your plans are, when you do the valuation is a critical step in the process. Valuation isn't just about the dollar sign at the end of the transaction — it's also about timing.

Valuation summary

Unlike mystery novels, you don't have to flip to the end of most valuation reports to figure out what happens. You can pretty much flip past the cover and the table of contents, and then, boom — you find the number you've been waiting for. It looks something like this:

> The fair market value of XYZ Co. is $1.2 million based on a weighting of income and market valuation methods.

Note the phrase "weighting of income and market valuation methods." This particular company was valued based on the income approach and market-based comparisons. This fact may not be true for every business, which is why you need to do your homework about what kind of valuation approaches and methods best fit a business in your situation. Talk over these choices with a valuation specialist. We cover approaches and methods in Chapter 4.

Your report will probably also indicate a high/low range for the value of the business, based on various valuation approaches and control premiums and special situations (including minority ownership, if it applies in your case).

The rest of this section of the report usually delivers the following kinds of information.

The assumptions and limiting conditions of the business

This section is a statement of assumptions and conditions on which an appraisal is based that the appraiser may or may not have verified. A standard valuation may contain a statement that describes items such as the following:

✔ That the title and legal description of the business are correct

✔ That the property is free and clear of liens

✔ That the current management and ownership have been verified and declared responsible for the business

✔ That the factual information received from others in the course of creating the report is reliable

✔ Notes on the illustrative material

✔ Any environmental impact statements that may be relevant

✔ That all licenses necessary to operate the property have been obtained

✔ That there is evident compliance with zoning and land use regulation

Executive summary

Everyone likes summaries. The executive summary enables you to see the critical points in the valuation process.

Purpose of the valuation/ownership structure

This section tells you the assumption of ownership upon which you're basing the valuation. If this business is a target company and you want to own 100 percent of it, that situation requires certain assumptions and valuation methods of its own. Of course, if you're valuing a portion of the ownership instead of 100 percent (if you'll have a business partner or two, or if you'll own jointly with a spouse or other family members, for instance), you'll see more details on what discounts or premiums have been added to the computations to affect that total valuation.

In the business valuation context, discounts or premiums are facts that either enhance or diminish the salability of a business and, therefore, the amount of value.

Major mistakes that show up on valuation reports

Understanding potentially big gaps in a valuation report is important — after all, you're paying for it. Such problems may include the following:

✔ Failing to state the date of the valuation and the date the report was prepared; both may be critical in a court proceeding

✔ Leaving off — or failing to consider — the purpose of the valuation

✔ Not listing the standard of value for the valuation (fair market and so on)

✔ Never doing a proper site visit

✔ Not detailing proper assumptions about the business and the purpose of its valuation at this time

✔ Not detailing the industry and the marketplace trends the company will be affected by, as well as its current and future economic prospects

✔ Not reviewing all valuation methods necessary for this particular situation

✔ Not defining the kind of earnings used in computation, if using the income approach

✔ Not going far enough with guideline company data, if using the market approach for comparison

✔ Failing to apply the proper discount or capitalization rates necessary for the valuation methods chosen

✔ Failing to disclose all sources of data used for comparison

Standard of value

The standard-of-value section can be combined with one of the opening sections. Regardless, you need a statement of the standard of value used to create the valuation. Fair market value, fair value, strategic value, and intrinsic value all result in different value conclusions based on the type of company being considered. (For info on standards of valuation, see Chapter 3.)

The subject of valuation and standard of value also helps determine whether you need to take various discounts, including discounts for lack of control and lack of marketability, as in the case of valuing minority interests in a company.

If you've had your business valued in recent years, keep in mind that the same standard of value and methods may not apply based on your goals for this valuation. In other words, let the goals and the current structure of the company govern which methods to use to complete the valuation. Don't make decisions based on decisions you made before.

The valuation date

This section covers the particular date the valuation was done. All valuations must be set on a particular date to allow the valuation professional to freeze a company's conditions and financials at a moment in time.

Valuation assignment

Yes, describing the assignment after seeing the numbers may seem a little backward, but admit it — you wanted to see that dollar figure first, right? This section of the report talks more about the features of the company itself.

The valuation key assumption

In a report that aims for clarity, you see something here called the *valuation key assumptions*. Granted, you may want to value a business because you're thinking of selling, but valuation professionals think a little differently. They look at all the assets you have and make an assumption based on what they think is the best way to monetize those assets. The valuation professional may state here that the sum total of assets would be best sold as a whole — as in a sale of the company outright — or may state that the assets would attract more cash if sold separately.

The assigned valuation date

We start this chapter by discussing how important the valuation date is. Who sets the date? Optimally, you or your representative does.

Competent valuation professionals don't set the date because it's not their job to decide the critical facts of the valuation, and the valuation date may be among the most critical. Timing issues should be the purview of buyers and sellers, not people who value companies.

In other words, companies that are planning to go on the block immediately may want the most recent numbers for the company figured into their valuation picture, particularly if those numbers are perceived to enhance the value of what they're selling. Companies that want to obtain bank financing or equity participation in their business may want to set different timelines.

If a valuation professional offers to help you set the valuation date, be wary. Qualified valuation professionals typically insist on a written recommendation from the client or the client's attorney specifying the exact valuation date. That way, they never have to redo the assignment; if the date is wrong or changes for any reason, the client or the client's attorney then must start the process all over again.

As we often note, dates can be a critical factor in the valuation process. Divorce, estate, and gifting issues are examples in which valuation dates certainly matter. As for the ordinary buying and selling of companies, the date doesn't matter as much, but a date must be set at some point. For example, the initial valuation of a company may be based on the last full year of financials for analysis in a report, but eventually, the year-to-date performance of a company will have to be communicated to be part of the report or not.

A smart buyer or a banker considers any data more than 90 days old to be outdated.

Economic outlook

Don't hire any valuation professional who doesn't watch how world and domestic economic factors affect your industry. Anyone can watch business channels and read as much as possible about the general state of the economy, but a business valuation professional has to know how to apply that macro view to the micro world of your business.

Today the most successful companies — even ones that are tiny right now — are global, thanks to the reach of the Internet and what it enables even the smallest companies to do. Even the smallest manufacturer can develop a supply chain that reaches all the way to Central Asia or the Far East. A small consultancy can have clients halfway around the world.

When various segments of the world economy experience either good times or downturns, valuation professionals can't turn a blind eye to those trends. They must pay full attention to anyone a company is doing business with or competing against.

In a valuation report, you should see detailed notes on how the economy is playing out, both in general and in particular in your sector of business. You'll probably see economic terms such as the following:

- ✔ **GDP:** The *gross domestic product* is the value of all the goods and services produced within a given year. The GDP is a crucial way of measuring how free businesspeople feel to invest in their businesses and increase production.

- ✔ **Interest rates:** People watch the Federal Reserve Board closely for a reason: It sets the general course of what borrowers will pay at all levels of the economy. Banks, businesses, and ordinary individuals find it easier to borrow and increase their spending when credit is looser; when credit is tighter, they slow down. Valuation professionals should bring this trend down to the level of the client who has to borrow in a particular economic climate.

✔ **Commodity prices and exchange rates:** If a business works with particular raw materials, such as metals, foodstuffs, or energy products, it needs to know how costs for those particular items will affect the cost of production in the business's area. Likewise, exchange rates — a reflection of the value of world currencies — can have a detrimental or a positive effect on a company's operations overseas. Valuation professionals need to know where these trends are heading and whether those measurements will increase or decrease valuations over a stated term.

✔ **What Washington plans to do:** Political and policy considerations are also important drivers of the economy. What the president and the nation's legislators hope to do with regulatory, tax, and energy policy is crucial to business. Again, valuation professionals need to know how federal legislation will affect state legislation that deals specifically with the business in question.

✔ **Key measurements:** Depending on the size of your business and its industry, you probably follow a market indicator that measures how your sector of the economy is doing. These indicators may include the following:

  • **The NFIB *Small Business Economic Trends* report:** The National Federation of Independent Business produces a series of research reports that describe how small companies feel about their businesses right now.

  • **Industry-specific indexes:** Pick an industry, and you'll find an index. Many trade publications have developed their own economic indexes to measure economic activity.

Equally important, a valuation professional must understand how your competitors are doing. If you don't get the sense that a valuation professional is asking enough annoying questions about who your competitors are, how they're doing, and whether they're gaining on you, he's not working to learn enough about your business.

✔ **The state of capital spending:** Capital spending is a driver of economic growth. You want to see whether companies anticipate spending more to make investments in their business. Even more important is seeing where they're going to make those investments.

✔ **The state of business financing in general:** Most businesses need to have some relationship with credit. As we write this book, sources of credit are very tight. In preparing to buy or sell a business, a valuation professional needs to keep the overall credit environment in mind.

Industry outlook

Valuation professionals are supposed to shine the cold searchlight of truth on the state of the subject company's industry. To value a company properly, it's important to know what the leaders in the industry are doing, what their products are, and what their growth prospects are. Valuation professionals use news stories, database material, and a host of public and private company data to create this story.

As with the rest of the valuation assignment, the industry story isn't told in a snapshot view of what's going on during the latest year of business. You should see comparisons of revenue and operating profit growth for the industry over a certain period or whatever is appropriate in the context of that industry so you can get an idea of possible three- to five-year prospects going forward.

Other factors you see in the industry outlook section of the report include the following.

Growth prospects

The valuation professional's job is to give you an opinion on where your company stands on that growth path, but doing due diligence on that front is your job as well. If you're a thoughtful participant — or potential participant — in an industry, you owe it to yourself to know something about that industry's growth prospects and where the business in question ranks. Otherwise, how can you really trust the information other experts are providing you?

Potential threats and benefits for the overall industry

If the company being valued is a manufacturing company in a particular industry, such as computers or toys, you'll likely see a comparison made to the overall growth of manufacturing businesses in the United States (or internationally as well, if that's a necessary point of comparison).

Some valuation firms develop their own proprietary systems and formulas to further analyze this issue; others simply report what they're seeing in the news and from other trade sources that closely follow the industries. One is not necessarily better than the other.

Business overview

Yes, you may know the business you're in, but you want to see how the valuation professional describes what you do. You want to know how much they know about you. This section explains the parts of the report's business overview.

The *median value* is just a convenient midpoint; it doesn't represent the revenue multiple for any actual transaction. It indicates that half of the revenue multiples are below the median value and half are above. Median values depend on the attributes of the firm and the outside data points an expert uses to value it.

Your overall financial performance

The overall-financial-performance section usually consists of a one-year summary of your target company's financials, but the report also makes many references to the company's financials over a multiyear period. It may be accompanied by a chart of three to seven years of the company's financial performance.

Using outside professionals can be invaluable in discovering what your business is worth, but try to identify and make friends with people who own businesses similar to yours who aren't competing directly with your company. Buy them a meal or coffee and talk to them about what they hear similar businesses are going for in your area. If you don't feel you can just call someone up (you really should get over this fear, by the way), try joining a chamber of commerce or an industry association that serves your type of business. If nothing else, you'll get to know your competition even better.

How financials were adjusted/normalized (and for what purpose)

Valuation professionals adjust financial figures to accomplish certain goals or to facilitate certain valuation methods. These adjustments may be for one-time nonrecurring expenses such as a rare lawsuit or maybe capital expenditures from a flood or fire.

The adjustments are typically derived from control adjustments. Put in simpler terms, one of the tax advantages of owning a privately held business is the ability to run certain expenses "through the business." Owners may have family members on the payroll who aren't essential to the operating of the business. Or they may be burying certain personal items that aren't essential to day-to-day business operations. Examples include the following:

- Cars and car insurance (also boats, airplanes, and vacation homes)
- Personal travel and entertainment
- Country club dues
- Healthcare for family members

When maximizing deductions for tax purposes, these control adjustments are common. As long as taxpayers are using them properly under the U.S. tax code, all should be well. But potential sellers should be prepared to open up their books because, many times, these control adjustments are major factors in getting to the cash flow used for the income approach. If people are playing fast and loose with how they're preparing their taxes because they're being overly aggressive with running personal items through the business, they probably need to take a year or two to clean up the financial statements before a sale or valuation. If you want a buyer to pay you for cash flow that isn't readily apparent on the books, you need to be willing to show where "the bodies are buried."

Owner's compensation

Assuming that this company is a small business with a single owner, the owner's-compensation section is where you see the company's top salary benchmarked against that of executives at similarly sized companies in the same field. If this salary is above the range, it may be valued outside the expense side of the company's normalized financials: If the business changes hands, a new chief executive walking in the door may not need to be paid as much. In larger firms with more top officers, you may see a broader benchmarking of salary data.

And what happens if a business owner isn't paying herself a fair market wage for the size of her company or business? That in itself may indicate poor stewardship of the company you may be planning to buy. And that's another important reason to analyze compensation.

Conclusion of value

The scope and depth of the valuation assignment determine how many valuation methods the professional employs in the valuation of the company. The report's conclusion-of-value section devotes space to why each method was used and what computations were used to establish the standard of value.

You should see a narrative description of each method, along with a chart of the computations used in each method.

Methods examined and accepted/rejected

This section discusses the approaches and methods considered and rejected (and reasons why), as well as the approaches and methods considered and accepted to provide a reasonable conclusion of value.

Explanation of weighting each valuation method

Weighting is an indicator of importance — a ranking. Some valuation methods weight certain methods to reach a conclusion of value. Other reports do not. That decision depends on the school of thought or philosophy of the individual appraiser.

The next stop may be discounts and premiums. That depends on the scope, depth, and purpose of the assignment — and may also depend on the appraiser's philosophy. In some instances, the discount and premiums are calculated within the method. And in some cases, they're applied after determining the overall value. If they appear after the conclusion of value, the professional sets numbers for the following:

- ✔ **The firm's control premium:** This premium represents what an interested suitor — or existing shareholder — would pay to get majority control of a firm.

- ✔ **The firm's marketability discount:** This discount, a factor that actually decreases the value of a company, is tied to various factors that make a business tougher to sell.

Marketability discount is a natural issue for private companies because their shares do not trade on public markets and their value isn't set publicly on a daily basis. Experts can apply various methods to come up with the discount that must be applied, including the restricted stock method, the IPO method, and the option pricing method.

You may also hear about the *liquidity premium* — it's an extra reward that investors demand for tying up money in the firm for a longer period of time than they may otherwise choose.

Appendixes

Here you see specific information describing the expert and the valuation firm he works for, notes on exhibits and charts, and other descriptive material you'd see in any report. Some valuation firms list a specific glossary in the appendixes to make sure everyone understands the terms discussed throughout the report.

Chapter 7

Meeting the Supporting Players in the Valuation Process

In This Chapter

▶ Discovering situations in which you may need experts

▶ Knowing the kinds of experts who can be useful in a business valuation

▶ Seeing how valuation experts are trained

*W*hether you end up doing the valuation yourself or enlist help is up to you. Yet we're big believers in getting help, as long as you do your homework beforehand and get the *right* help. We're not saying that you have to bring in a squadron of experts to do a simple valuation, but you should consult certain professionals before you do anything based on your situation. In fact, in a lot of situations, you definitely don't want to try this at home. This chapter focuses on the key professionals in this process, what kind of situations they fit, and how to hire the best people.

Your business finances and personal finances are inextricably linked. If you've never been in business, this fact is one of the first things you find out. So what does that have to do with valuation? When you start thinking about business valuation, your number one objective is to know not only how the value of your business affects the course of your business strategy but also how it influences your personal finances, including the people you may need to hire along the way. No one ever went into business to get poor, so your valuation strategy has to complement any particular tax, estate, or retirement strategy you've built. If you've never thought about this stuff, then start. We talk much more about the link between business and personal finances in this chapter and throughout the book.

Getting Help in Valuing Your Business

As some people whined through grammar school, high school, and college, "Math is hard!" But valuation goes beyond math. It's the assessment of a business's hard and intrinsic assets to determine its moneymaking power in the hands of the same owner or a new owner years from now. Not all those items can be totaled up on a calculator (we get more into that issue in Chapter 8, where we discuss financial statements).

Business valuation occurs when offers or deals are on the table, of course, but business valuation is best used as an ongoing strategic tool to determine the best time to expand, contract, enter, or exit a business. Valuation can be necessary in light of many other circumstances — such as succession, divorce, death of a founder, or erosion in markets — that may signal a good time to sell or liquidate a business. Keep in mind that "sale" reasons for an owner may indicate a "buy" opportunity for the right outsider.

But back to the need for help: Why bother with experts? Very few people can keep their business and personal finances at their fingertips. Small-business people are busy and often distracted. A trade-off occurs in focus between business finances and personal finances, as well as in the lifestyle issues that necessarily fill your time — family, friends, and sometimes even leisure. People who have the skills to toggle among all these areas with all the information they need to make the right decisions are rare.

People with the right money skills may still lack a quality essential to the valuation process: objectivity. Asking an owner to value his business objectively is a bit like asking a parent to identify which of his kids is smartest. Most entrepreneurs are too close to their businesses to value them without bias, so you need detached experts and sources of information to rely on. This is why the valuation process rests on the shoulders of people who understand not only the financial aspects of your business but also its future value and what effect a sale or other transaction may have on your estate, your retirement plans, or your plans to get involved in a new business.

Here's a quick list of the people who commonly participate in the business valuation process. We list them in alphabetical order — Hollywood style — so you don't get the idea that one is more important than another. Having all these professionals show up in a single deal is rare, but it happens.

- ✔ Accountants and auditors
- ✔ Appraisers
- ✔ Business brokers
- ✔ Business consultants
- ✔ Business intermediaries
- ✔ Divorce and family-law attorneys
- ✔ Employee stock ownership plan (ESOP) attorneys
- ✔ Estate attorneys

✔ Financial planners and advisors

✔ Tax attorneys

Generally, you can break this list down into four categories based on the type of help you need. The Big Four are

✔ Appraisers

✔ Accountants

✔ Attorneys

✔ Brokers

We discuss the Big Four in more detail later in this chapter. First, though, you need to know how to pick out the best people to help you.

Recognizing situations that call for valuation experts

Almost more valuation situations exist than one can count, but here are the most common situations that require the help of professionals who are familiar with valuation processes:

✔ **Everyday sales and purchases of businesses:** Valuations are made at the time when businesses are bought and sold — or when companies plan to merge.

✔ **Purchase price allocation:** *Purchase price allocation* is the process of assigning fair values to all major assets and liabilities of an acquired company as part of a merger or purchase. This issue should be addressed early enough to ensure that all the parties understand the deal and that there's a meeting of the mind on how each party will be affected from a tax perspective.

✔ **Estate and gift taxes:** This situation involves establishing the fair market value of gifts and bequeathed assets that may fall under the scrutiny of the Internal Revenue Service.

✔ **Marital dissolution (better known as divorce or annulment):** This situation involves valuing assets that will be split between a couple.

✔ **Employee stock ownership plans (ESOP):** An ESOP is a tax-qualified plan that an owner can use to meet her goals in business succession, diversification of assets, estate planning, or property settlements in a divorce, or as an exit strategy from a business.

- ✔ **A company's liquidation or reorganization:** Valuation occurs when a company fails or is forced to file for bankruptcy protection (also known as *reorganization*).

- ✔ **Buy/sell agreements:** Buy/sell agreements are made between partners or co-owners, spelling out the circumstances and terms under which shares of the business or partnership will be transferred to one owner from the other.

- ✔ **Stockholder disputes:** In public companies, stockholders may take issue with the pricing of various assets in merger or sale deals, and valuation may be required as a defense in court.

- ✔ **Financing:** Lenders want proof of the value of assets as collateral if they plan to loan a company money.

- ✔ **Ad valorem taxes:** For most people, ad valorem taxes involve a garden-variety method of computing property taxes on residential and commercial property. Yet businesses like to confirm that they're not being overtaxed, so the frequently do valuation for this purpose.

- ✔ **Incentive stock options:** Accounting regulations require more rigorous valuation of incentive stock options to hold up in court when employees and shareholders dispute their value.

- ✔ **Initial public offerings:** Before public stock can be issued, investors like to see the certification of value of both tangible and intangible assets in a company.

- ✔ **Damages litigation:** When lawsuits are filed for any number of reasons, both defendants and plaintiffs may need assistance with valuation.

- ✔ **Charitable contributions:** For tax reasons, people may need to put a valuation on various assets donated to charitable institutions.

- ✔ **Eminent domain actions:** If a property owner finds her land or facilities condemned by the government, she definitely wants to challenge the government's fair-value estimate of that property before she agrees to an amount.

Finding the experts you need

Keep in mind that good professionals know other good professionals. For fledging entrepreneurs, the best professionals in the valuation process may come from the following sources:

- ✔ **Professionals you're already working with:** If you're working with a tax expert such as a Certified Public Accountant (CPA) or a tax attorney, start talking to that expert about people who are best qualified to help you with various stages of the valuation process.

- **People you network with:** Granted, valuation is something you don't want to broadcast too loudly — unless you really want someone to know that you're planning to buy or sell a business. Start working with discreet people you trust in professional or industry groups and even in alumni groups in which you're active.

- **Local professional associations:** Local societies for attorneys, financial planners, appraisal organizations, and accountants typically list specialists in various disciplines.

Seeking the qualities your experts should have

As you begin the valuation process, it helps to understand the concept of self-interest when you're bringing in experts to help you value your business. These experts are professionals with their own interests at heart: They're in business for themselves.

They also need to understand your motivations for valuation, and they need to demonstrate the following traits:

- **Independence/objectivity:** As much as you want to see an asset grow in value, you need professionals to appraise and value those assets without bias. That means that in reviewing your financial statements, interviewing executives, and eyeballing the physical aspects of your business, they need to rely on recognized standards of value — not merely on your influence because you're paying them.

- **Confidentiality:** Even if you're paying for honest, unbiased advice, you need to make sure that your goals are protected from people on the outside who could interfere with your plans. The professionals you bring into the process need to gather and process information legally, but they also need to be savvy about your need for discretion and confidentiality.

- **Industry awareness:** Experts need to know the current market backward and forward. There's really no single correct price for a business, but the experts have to price your assets fairly, relative to the market.

- **Clarity about fees:** Cost isn't the only factor involved in selecting professional help, but an understandable fee structure is key.

- **Clarity about dispute resolution:** The best valuation processes may not be dispute-free. Before you enter into any professional agreement, discuss how both sides will handle disputes and differences if they happen. You ask not because you anticipate trouble but because you want to prevent it.

One point about disputes over valuation: Many professional-services firms write specific language about arbitration or mediation into any contract you sign to hire them. This language may mean that you won't be able to sue the firm later for results that you find inadequate. Arbitration is a common dispute-resolution technique in many industries, so make sure you understand the process.

As you zero in on the valuation process, certain experts who do very specific things. The next section introduces a few.

Appraising What Appraisers Do

Appraisers are trained to analyze and set the value of a particular kind or category of asset. The best appraisers aren't utility hitters; they're specialists who not only have specific training in finance and accounting techniques but also have deep experience in certain industries or ownership situations that call for valuation, such as divorce, lawsuits, or bankruptcies.

Why can't the CPA who does your taxes do a business appraisal? He may have a sharp eye for figures, but in most cases, appraisal is a separate discipline. Appraisal involves many of the same basic financial skills that accountants and other finance majors are trained in, but appraisers also need other skills. They need to be able to do the following:

- ✔ Read and dissect a balance sheet so that they can compare and analyze various assets for current and future value
- ✔ Behave like detectives, questioning officers, management, and staff members about the current and future value of various assets
- ✔ Measure the value of both tangible (physical) and intangible (idea-based) assets
- ✔ Function under significant time pressure in many cases
- ✔ Write clear, extensive, detailed reports on findings
- ✔ Be able to defend their findings in court if they're challenged

Most chief financial officers (CFOs) and accountants don't have the time or the skills to do what qualified appraisers do. Nor are they truly independent of the organizations being valued. A CFO is to an appraiser what a police chief is to a crime-scene investigator: The top financial officer of a company oversees the big picture on valuation, whereas an appraiser gets called in to go over financial evidence with a fine-toothed comb. Simply put, appraisers strap on the gloves and do the detail work.

Where rule-of-thumb valuations come in

The purchase of even a simple business can get pretty complex, and in all financial transactions, people have a natural need to simplify what's going on. (Hey, that's the hallmark of a *For Dummies* book: making the complex simple!) So in the valuation world, where things can get mighty complex, you hear the phrase *rule-of-thumb valuation* a lot.

A *rule-of-thumb valuation* is a guideline that people use in a particular industry or line of business to value a company when it's bought or sold. The greatest thing about using rule of thumb is that it's a great way to jump-start your valuation research. You can get up to speed on businesses in a particular industry so that your research and work with professionals can continue in more depth.

In Chapter 9, we work with some examples from the annual *Business Reference Guide*

(Business Brokerage Press), by leading valuation author Tom West, to show you what rule-of-thumb valuations look like. Jim also adds his own commentary. *Business Reference Guide* is a leading encyclopedia of rules of thumb on valuing businesses ranging from private accounting firms to wireless communication franchises.

You'll also hear the term *benchmarking*. In the context of valuation, this term means everyday costs and expenses particular to a category of business, such as the kind of wages people get or certain performance measurements.

Rules of thumb are guidelines, nothing more. Throughout this book, we talk about working with experts who can help you with valuing a business for a variety of scenarios.

In reality, most appraisers don't get called in to do what they do for companies with less than $1 million in revenue, because local standards of value or written guides provide benchmarks for these kinds of deals.

Before you hire an appraiser, know exactly what you're going to need to appraise. Individual appraisers generally specialize unless they're in a rural area, where they may have to know and evaluate several kinds of businesses. If you have a rural farm-implements dealership, bring in someone who knows that business, not someone who just does real estate or retail stores. If you have a variety of assets to appraise, however — such as intellectual property, land, property, and equipment — an appraisal firm or valuation practice may need to subcontract out your job.

How appraisers are trained and certified

Most business appraisers have four-year college degrees with majors in accounting or finance. Their career paths can take several forms. These individuals may eventually operate as independents, but they may initially join appraisal firms or sign on as full-time or contracted experts with law firms that need valuation services.

One of the most important reasons for appraisers to join an existing firm is for continuing education. New graduates generally don't have a specialty, but over time and with funded education, they develop one, and that specialty boosts their value in the marketplace. (See, careers can be valued as well.)

New college graduates with a background in finance need class time and work hours to qualify for a particular valuation certification. According to the American Society of Appraisers (ASA), such certifications include the ones we list in Table 7-1.

Table 7-1	Main Certifications for Valuation Professionals	
Appraisal Organization	**Professional Designation**	**Requirements**
American Society of Appraisers (ASA)	AM — Accredited Member	College degree and two years of appraisal experience; must pass four courses and an exam and perform peer review of appraisal reports
	ASA — Accredited Senior	Same requirements as those for the AM designation, plus three years of experience
	FASA — Fellow	Same requirements as those for the ASA designation, plus election to the ASA college of fellows
Institute of Business Appraisers (IBA)	CBA — Certified Business Appraiser	College degree, completion of one appraiser course and exam, peer review of two appraisal reports, and completion of at least two appraisal assignments
	MCBA — Master Certified Business Appraiser	Same requirements as those for the CBA designation, plus ten years of business practice experience, credit for published writing or lecturing, and references from four other MCBAs
	FIBA — Fellow	Same requirements as those for the MCBA designation, plus election to the college of fellows on the basis of leadership and contributions to the appraisal profession

Appraisal Organization	Professional Designation	Requirements
National Association of Certified Valuation Analysts (NACVA)	AVA — Accredited Valuation Analyst	Business degree, completion of analysts exams, and two years of experience or completion of at least ten business valuations
	CVA — Certified Valuation	College degree, completion of Analysts One course and exam, and CPA certification
American Institute of Certified Public Accountants (AICPA)	ABV — Accredited in Business Valuation	AICPA membership, Business Valuation license, completion of one-day exam, and involvement in ten business valuations
The Canadian Institute of Chartered Business Valuators (CICBV)	CBV — Chartered Business Valuator	College degree, completion of six valuator courses and exams, and two years of full-time experience

What appraisers cost

Business appraisers primarily charge based on the complexity — and the time constraints — of the valuation required. If you're looking for a rough estimate, a rule of thumb is a basic starting point (For details, read Chapter 9).

Business valuation isn't all about green eyeshades and sweat equity. As in most industries, computerization has made a huge difference in business valuation, bringing tons of information to valuation experts via databases and making critical computations easier. Ask a potential valuation professional how much of her work she does on a computer and whether the computer frees her to do more onsite work or other hands-on tasks.

For business valuations tied to specific situations, however — potential purchases or sales, divorce valuations, partnership dissolutions, and so on — the appraiser spends much more time analyzing corporate figures (which may require an audit by a CPA), inspecting assets, and talking with executives about those assets. Depending on the size of the company and the challenges to be met, the fee for the appraiser can easily be thousands of dollars — and sometimes tens of thousands of dollars.

Some valuation professionals charge fixed fees based on particular types of valuation assignments, but you aren't limited to that fee if the process takes longer for any reason. Know in advance what may "unfix" a fixed-fee arrangement.

Appraisals that are certified by the appraiser usually cost more because they tend to be more detailed. A certified appraisal may include items such as the following:

- ✔ An overview of local, national, and international economic factors that affect this particular company and its industry, and what factors may affect the company and industry in the future
- ✔ A review of five years' worth of financial statements, as well as a review of tax returns and other financial documents for clarity and accuracy
- ✔ A balance-sheet analysis and review of the depreciation schedule, including adjustments for machinery, equipment, and other assets to come up with fair market value
- ✔ A detailed presentation of the valuation of a company based on several valuation methods that a future buyer or seller may demand
- ✔ Onsite visits to gather data and present findings

Anyone hiring a business appraiser should talk to at least two or three prospects to get an idea of his fees and his work process (which we cover in the next section).

How to examine a business appraiser's work process

Work process is all about the assignment — the actual thing or company that needs valuation.

The size and scope of an appraisal assignment determine the appraiser's work process in establishing the fair market value of a single asset or a whole company. Size and scope define the time that the appraiser needs to spend on the job, as well as the number of assets and related issues that she needs to review as part of the valuation process.

The simplest valuation assignments don't require a face-to-face meeting; a phone call and a few keystrokes into a database later, a very general dollar amount emerges as the value of a particular company. But when the company's revenue exceeds $1 million and the reasons for doing the valuation are more complex, the assignment requires the following tasks:

- ✔ Extensive research of the company's industry and its prospects
- ✔ Interviews with company officers
- ✔ Onsite visits to see the physical facilities and assets being valued

✔ Exchange of information with company attorneys and tax experts

✔ Creation of reports and presentations on intermediate or final findings

✔ Possible after-valuation activities, including testifying in court or in deposition, usually priced as a separate item

The best valuation efforts are planned and comfortably scheduled for the scope of the project. When interviewing valuation professionals, ask them how long a typical valuation process takes and what they consider a rush job; otherwise, you may end up paying more for a quick valuation that doesn't give you as much depth as you need. Of course, smart valuation professionals know their limits and communicate them.

What to ask a prospective business appraiser

Much of how your valuation will go is determined by the questions you ask a professional before you hire him. Here are some basics:

✔ What's your specialty? (Ideally, you've checked this information beforehand, but let the prospect describe his expertise to you.)

✔ What are your training and certification?

✔ What basic information will you need from me to estimate the job, and what kind of information will you need from me on an ongoing basis?

✔ What do you think the features of this appraisal will be, and how long could the appraisal take?

✔ Is there a cost range you're prepared to offer at this time? If not now, when?

✔ Will you need to call in other experts to complete the valuation based on the assets I need you to value?

✔ How much experience have you had in valuing companies like mine (or like the one I want to buy)?

✔ I have specific reasons for valuing this company. Have you dealt with those circumstances in other valuations you've done?

✔ What did you find out about my company and me before we got here?

✔ Offhand, do you know what valuation methods you might use in computing fair market value for my company?

✔ How will we deal with each other during the valuation process, and how will I be apprised of your progress?

✔ Can you show me an example of what a finished appraisal report will look like? Will you meet with me and my colleagues when you're done and present those results?

✔ What happens if I have a problem with your results? What dispute-resolution process do you typically follow?

Beware of any valuation professional who automatically dismisses any valuation as "simple" without asking pointed questions about what you're trying to do.

Taking Account of Accountants

Granted, most people generally know what accountants do, but accountants are key to the valuation process for one critical reason: They're part of an essential checks-and-balances system that you need to guarantee the integrity of your results.

Accountants find themselves in a variety of roles and subspecialties, but here are the major work areas for accountants who are involved in the practice of valuation:

✔ **Public accountants:** They do basic accounting, auditing, tax, and consulting activities for individuals, companies, government entities, and nonprofit organizations.

✔ **External auditors:** These are the detectives of the accounting profession. Their job is to certify the integrity of an organization's or an individual's financial results. The specialty of forensic accounting (which we cover later in this list) also falls into this category. In most cases, auditors hold the CPA designation.

✔ **Internal auditors:** Internal auditors work inside a company (usually a large company) to verify the effectiveness of the organization's internal controls and to check for mismanagement, waste, or fraud. Their job is to ensure the integrity of the company's records and financial systems. Subspecialists may audit a firm's technology, environmental, or compliance functions.

✔ **Management accountants (also called cost, managerial, industrial, corporate, or private accountants):** These people record and analyze financial data for the companies that employ them. They prepare financial reports for stockholders, creditors, regulatory agencies, and state and federal tax authorities. They also prepare the reports that outside valuation professionals will review.

✔ **Tax accountants:** These are perhaps the best-known variety of accountants. They confirm that a company's or individual's tax filings are completed with accurate and truthful information and are compliant with local, state, and federal tax guidelines.

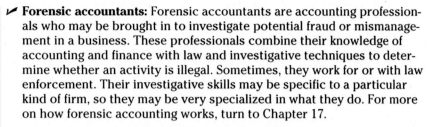

✔ **Forensic accountants:** Forensic accountants are accounting profession-als who may be brought in to investigate potential fraud or mismanage-ment in a business. These professionals combine their knowledge of accounting and finance with law and investigative techniques to deter-mine whether an activity is illegal. Sometimes, they work for or with law enforcement. Their investigative skills may be specific to a particular kind of firm, so they may be very specialized in what they do. For more on how forensic accounting works, turn to Chapter 17.

Blame it on *CSI:* In 2007, *U.S. News & World Report* ranked forensic accounting as one of the 20 hottest jobs in the country.

Assuming that they're doing their jobs correctly, accountants are critical in verifying that a company's finances, assets, procedures, and controls are exactly what they say they are on both sides of a transaction.

Accountants also get training to do business valuations. In fact, over the past 20 years, many more have sought certification to provide those services within their firms. The American Institute of Certified Public Accountants (AICPA) has drafted a new set of operating standards to make sure services are uniform. Go to the AICPA's Web site at aicpa.org for more information.

For most small-business people, accountants are indispensable parts of their advisory team, not just on valuation issues but also on all aspects of business planning. For many small businesses, the outside accounting firm is the company's finance and planning brain trust, so questions about a firm's approach to valuation services should be part of the hiring mix.

How accountants are trained

In the past 25 years, the specialization boom in general business training has extended to financial jobs. Whereas Bob Cratchit may have been a typical accountant more than two centuries ago, simply recording transactions in and out of a business nonstop on a daily basis, today's accountants are prepared not only to handle numbers but also to interpret and position those numbers strategically for the future of the business.

In most larger businesses, the CFO's job has gone from being largely a background position to a key strategic post. Before, CFOs were primarily the guys — and most *were* guys — who told the chief executive officer and the board whether any money was available to do what they wanted to do with the business. That situation has changed significantly in the age of Enron. Businesses that have high transparency — numbers that a person can make sense of quickly — get high marks for honesty and reputation.

Today's CFOs may have used their accounting skills during tours of duty in marketing, planning, information technology, and many other departments in a typical company. The need for financial controls has become much more prevalent on all levels of a business.

Dare we say it? Have accounting skills become sexy in the 21st century? At the very least, they've become much more critical to a business's reputation and identity.

If the Enron era has taught American business anything, it's the importance of the need for financial controls. Good financial controls in any business, large or small, are critical to any business valuation. If the numbers can't be trusted, it's difficult to put a fair price on the business.

Today's accountants get their training at all levels. Many start with basic bookkeeping courses in high school and move on to two-year and four-year accounting degrees at the college and university level, which prepare them for entry-level jobs in government, corporations, and dedicated accounting firms.

Accounting training has moved up the specialization scale in most recognized college business programs, particularly at the master's level. The most highly ranked Master of Business Administration programs in the country have a recognized finance track that goes beyond basic accounting into training in dealing with domestic and foreign assets. As the business world has gone global, accountants need to be able to manage the finances and assets of global industries.

How accountants are certified

According to the U.S. Department of Labor, any accountant filing a report with the Securities and Exchange Commission (SEC) is required by law to be a Certified Public Accountant (CPA). This requirement includes senior-level accountants working for or on behalf of public companies that are registered with the SEC.

CPAs are licensed by state boards of accountancy. Any accountant who passes a national exam and meets the other requirements of the state where she practices can become a CPA.

The Department of Labor reports that as of 2007, 42 states and the District of Columbia required CPA candidates to complete 150 semester hours of college coursework — 30 hours beyond the usual four-year bachelor's degree. CPAs don't have an easy certification process. All states use the four-part Uniform CPA Examination prepared by the American Institute of Certified Public Accountants (AICPA).

The CPA examination is tough; fewer than half of those who take it each year pass every part they attempt on the first try. Candidates aren't required to pass all four parts at the same time, but most states require candidates to pass all four sections within 18 months of passing their first section.

The CPA exam is now computerized and is offered two months out of every quarter at various testing centers throughout the United States. Most states also require applicants for a CPA certificate to have some accounting experience, but requirements vary by state or jurisdiction.

For CPAs, the AICPA offers the option to receive any or all of the Accredited in Business Valuation (ABV), Certified Information Technology Professional (CITP), and Personal Financial Specialist (PFS) designations:

- ✔ The ABV designation requires the completion of a written exam and at least ten business valuation projects that demonstrate the candidate's experience and competence.
- ✔ The CITP designation requires the achievement of a set number of points awarded for business technology experience and education.
- ✔ Candidates for the PFS designation also must achieve a certain level of points based on experience and education, pass a written exam, and submit references.

Other certification programs are available to accounting specialists in auditing, tax preparation, government accounting, and forensic accounting.

What accountants cost

We're going to sound like a broken record again: The cost depends on the job you're paying an accountant to do. Most accountants are like attorneys in that they charge by the hour rather than a fixed fee for a particular task. Some require an annual retainer to serve your business and add specific fees based on regular tasks or jobs that crop up suddenly.

Even tax preparation — which used to be a steady, fixed-fee business — has moved away from that pay structure due to the complexity of many individuals' finances. To a certain degree, retail tax preparation firms such as H&R Block have kept those fees low.

As we indicate earlier in this chapter, valuation training is now part of life at many accounting firms, and if you think you'll have a need for those services, they should be part of your shopping process. Any time you hire an accountant, list every possible service you may need and ask him to explain whether you can negotiate pricing based on that package of services and what activities still need to be priced à la carte.

The dominance of computer-based financing programs such as Quicken have made it possible for most small businesses to track their own finances, which is definitely a good thing. But computer-based programs really provide basic bookkeeping. Unless you have specific training in finance and tax issues, it's probably better to turn those numbers over to an accounting professional, not only for tax reasons but also to help determine a growth and exit strategy for your business.

How to examine an accountant's work process

Depending on their assignment, accountants may see you once a year and work with your numbers intensively for a few weeks at tax time, or they may be regular contacts year-round. If you have an accountant working within your business, that contact can be daily. But most small businesses work with outside accountants either annually or quarterly (for those that are incorporated and want assistance filing their quarterly reports).

Do you really need an accountant? If your business is small and relatively uncomplicated and all you need is someone to handle your tax filings, you may want to consider hiring an enrolled agent instead — someone who's trained specifically by the IRS to handle tax returns. The good thing about experienced CPAs is that they tend to have more experience working with financial planners and estate specialists in helping you form an overall financial plan.

With computerization, most accountants never have to walk into your offices to do their job, and with the Internet, you may never need to walk into theirs. Digital tracking, shipment, and computation of financial data has made the whole accounting and financial planning process simpler and more widespread, and accountants have their own computer programs that help speed their jobs along. Although accountants definitely burn the midnight oil at tax time, their volume of business is now significantly larger thanks to the digital revolution.

What to ask a prospective accountant

Because this book is about valuation instead of overall accounting tasks, we base our suggested questions on how an accountant will factor into your valuation strategy (if you want to find out more about accounting, we'll refer you to *Accounting For Dummies,* by John A. Tracy, CPA):

✔ What are your qualifications and training?

✔ Based on my size and type of business, what kinds of valuation services do you recommend, and when should I have them done?

✔ From a tax and accounting perspective, what can be done over the course of time to boost the value of my business?

✔ What experience does your firm have in valuing sole proprietorships, corporations (C and S), partnerships, and companies with significant operations outside the United States?

✔ What valuation methods would you apply to my operation if I were to put it on the block tomorrow?

✔ Tax planning is great, but what can you do to help my business grow? Will you help me set benchmarks that measure how my business is doing and when I should either quit or sell?

✔ Will your firm offer advisory services for my personal finances as well as my business finances? Can you also do legal referrals?

✔ Will you work with computerized files, or can you still work with paper documents and paper receipts (the old shoebox method)?

Hiring Advocacy: Attorneys

Attorneys are paid advocates. They may work in any of dozens of specialties. In the context of business valuation, they may have nothing to do with the actual appraisal work that goes into a valuation ordered by you or another party, but it's their job to make sure that valuation findings are legitimate and that they serve your best interest.

Several legal specialties are prevalent in valuation:

✔ **Estate attorneys:** These folks help you formulate wills, trusts, and other power-of-attorney documents that guide both your personal and business lives. They have the skills to work with accountants and other personal finance professionals to create a seamless financial strategy that serves your personal and business lifestyles. They care about business valuation because the business is what's funding your family and your future.

✔ **Divorce attorneys:** Divorce attorneys administer the breakup of a marriage and, often, the breakup of a business. Although those who specialize in family law may defer to other attorneys and accountants who are more immediately familiar with your business and personal finance strategies, they should have basic training in coordinating any movements with your business assets in divorce court.

- **Tax attorneys:** Tax attorneys understand state, local, and federal tax codes. They handle tax challenges from the government and devise legal planning strategies that minimize the taxes that a business has to pay. They need to care about valuation because assets are taxed based on value.

- **Bankruptcy/liquidation attorneys:** The valuation question comes into sharp focus in troubled companies. Bankruptcy attorneys help clients get fair market value on assets that must be sold to repay debt, court settlements, and other amounts.

- **Corporate attorneys:** These people help entrepreneurs draw up papers to establish the structure of a business, which can be important for how assets are valued.

In the context of valuation, attorneys may assist in the following tasks:

- Purchase or sale of a business

- Separation of property during a divorce

- Creation of an estate plan

- Ownership assignment of assets in a prenuptial agreement

- Creation of ESOPs

- Structure and draft partnership agreements

- Defense of clients in litigation challenging the value of a company, organization, or partnership

- Drafting of wills, powers of attorney, and various directives affecting the future of a business after the owner is incapacitated or deceased

- Defending tax challenges from local, state, and federal authorities

How attorneys are trained and certified

Attorneys are trained at law schools with a typical three-year course of study, though some colleges offer graduate training to create dual graduate degrees in the law and other areas, such as JD(Juris Doctor)/MBAs, better known as a combined law degree and MBA degree. Other attorneys may also train as accountants and gain a considerable amount of expertise in calculating valuation.

Most lawyers, however, come out of school with very little direct training in business and certainly not in valuation. For those attorneys, such training generally takes place after employment; they may train through apprenticeship at their law firms or seek outside training in the certification programs we mention in Table 7-1, earlier in this chapter.

Attorneys really aren't certified in the practice of law; rather, they're cleared for the practice of law by taking the bar exam of the state in which they plan to practice. Attorneys may elect to train for certification in valuation.

What attorneys cost

Unlike valuation experts, attorneys typically charge by the hour, not by the job. Market rates, the attorney's prominence, and the complexity of the assignment affect the fees, which can total hundreds of dollars per hour. It's not possible to give a price range for attorney fees for any particular aspect of a business transaction, which is why you need to quiz attorneys about their fees when you interview them.

How to examine an attorney's work process

An attorney's work process very much depends on the assignment. If an attorney is a specialist in family law and the issue is the splitting up of the family business in a divorce, the assignment will require not only a valuation of the business (likely contracted out to a valuation professional) but also the attorney's advice on how the business will be split based on that valuation and supervision of the negotiations going forward. If the divorce is a relatively friendly one, that friendliness may save thousands of dollars in attorney fees.

When you consider an attorney to handle a dispute, ask whether any part of the process could be contracted out to a licensed mediator. Most law firms recommend local licensed mediation firms if both parties are inclined to do their own talking. The mediator records the results. This process is generally cheaper than having attorneys handle negotiations.

What to ask a prospective attorney

Hiring an attorney can be daunting, particularly if you anticipate that this person will be advising your business over a long period of time. But it can be even more difficult if you're dealing with a stressful situation such as bankruptcy or divorce. Here are some general questions to ask a prospective attorney before you hire her:

- ✔ What is your approach to your specialty?
- ✔ How do you work with valuation? Are you certified to judge valuation questions, or do you need to subcontract with experts?

✔ Do you have an opinion on how my company should be valued?

✔ Do you deal with companies in my situation often? Is there anything different about the way you'd handle my business?

✔ What is your fee, and is there a way for me to control expenses?

✔ What other experts do you need to bring into the process?

✔ What do I need to do in this process?

✔ What timetables do I need to be aware of?

Brokers: One-Stop Valuation and Sale Services

Business brokers are unique among valuation players because they may or may not represent your interests. Take a step back and think about the meaning of the word *broker*. A real estate broker can work for you — if you hire him — or work against you if he's working for the opposing buyer or seller.

Whenever you work with any kind of valuation expert, you always need to understand whether that expert's interests mesh with your own. Business brokers are one-stop valuation and sale services for businesses. They do the following things:

✔ Help buyers and sellers of privately held business complete a buy or sell transaction

✔ Help clients price and market a business, including providing valuation services

✔ Specialize in particular industries, which allows them to get closer to particular valuation questions

✔ Work with both sides of the transaction in preparing a property for sale, bringing in potential buyers, facilitating due diligence, and negotiating with both parties

Brokers may also hold real estate licenses in case their clients need to market real estate assets.

In some states, businesses can be sold only by registered real estate agents. Be aware that if the business broker you work with does not have a real estate license, the real estate may have to be marketed by another professional.

Brokers like to close. That's true of all brokers, even reputable ones. Disreputable ones make big promises they can't keep. Steer away from those who are fuzzy on fees or those who promise that they can get your asking price without doing a full valuation of your assets. Also, if your broker can't explain in simple language how she would perform your valuation, move on.

People hire business brokers for most of the same reasons that they hire real estate brokers: They're busy and don't want to be bothered with all the details of selling a business themselves. Business brokerages generally work on private transactions in excess of $1 million in annual sales and operate mainly locally or regionally, which is what you want — brokers who really understand your local market. You may be able to get good recommendations through your attorney or accountant.

Here's what business brokers do:

- ✔ Value your company
- ✔ Identify prospects and market your company to them, including the creation of brochures and other relevant marketing materials
- ✔ Help you set a price that makes sense for the market
- ✔ Negotiate the deal, prepare the paperwork, and help you close

Understanding how a business broker will work for you is particularly important. Is the broker packaging your business for sale to an established group of leads that he has in his files, or is he attempting a sale effort to buyers who make particular sense for you?

How business brokers are trained and certified

Most business brokers are trained through industry associations such as the International Business Brokers Association (IBBA) and the American Business Brokers Association (ABBA). You may ask whether a broker has a related financial background or specific training in valuation or accounting. The IBBA also accredits business brokers with the title of Certified Business Intermediary (CBI).

You definitely want to know whether your state licenses these types of brokers, because not all states do.

What business brokers cost

Like most brokers, business brokers charge a percentage of the total sale price. Fees can run as much as 10 percent for a company selling for less than $10 million or a few percent on companies selling for more. You need to check whether the fee is based on the overall amount of the sale or whether other fees are charged à la carte.

Also find out whether there's any chance that you'll be charged if the business doesn't sell after a certain period. In states with no licensing or limited licensing for business brokers, checking makes sense.

How to examine a broker's work process

Like other professionals, a broker's work process very much depends on the assignment. Is the broker just going to list the business on a business-for-sale Web site? Or is she going to create a market by launching a controlled auction? What if the seller is sensitive to confidentiality and wants to approach only a few hand-selected buyers? Many factors, such as the company's size, industry, and confidentiality, determine a marketing strategy for selling a company. Understanding the marketing strategy the broker follows, or finding out whether the broker is experienced in crafting different marketing strategies, is a crucial factor in choosing a broker.

When you consider a broker, ask for a proposal that includes the specific services that will be provided and the marketing strategy that will be employed.

What to ask a prospective business broker

When you're hiring any professional, always come armed with a list of questions. If you don't like an answer you receive for any one of these questions, you may want to consider looking elsewhere for a broker:

- ✔ Aside from your certification, what training do you and your staff have in all areas of the business sale process?
- ✔ What's your success rate in closing deals, and can you document it?
- ✔ What's the full range of services you provide?
- ✔ May I speak to the owner of the brokerage?

✔ How will you market my business, and how will I be kept informed of that progress?

✔ How long is your typical engagement with a client? May I see the contract you require clients to sign?

✔ How do you charge for your services?

✔ Will you work with my attorney or tax professional?

✔ How will we communicate?

✔ What if I'm unhappy with the offers you present to me?

✔ May I see examples of brochures, Web sites, and other marketing materials that you've presented for clients?

Chapter 8

Understanding Financial Statements

*I*n the first part of this book, we tell you that valuation isn't all about the numbers. But frankly, neither you nor a valuation professional can do valuation without the blasted things. We're going to make an assumption that you're not experienced in accounting (and point you toward a great title to rectify that situation: *Accounting For Dummies,* 4th Edition [Wiley]). But all we really focus on in this chapter are the basic sources of financial data necessary to measure the financial performance of a business and, therefore, the numbers necessary to do a valuation.

We talk about how important these numbers are in judging the short- and long-term health of a company you're considering buying or investing in. The chapter's a good primer for starting a business from scratch as well.

These reports are easy to get if you're looking at a public company, but for private companies, you usually have to present yourself as an interested party in a possible transaction, and very likely, you'll have to sign a confidentiality agreement to get access to this information in the due diligence process, which you find out about in detail in Chapters 12 and 16.

If you're starting a business and haven't received any training in finance, marketing, or any other aspects of starting a company, consult your community college system to see which basic courses it offers. Reading is a good companion to hands-on coursework, and best of all, you may be able to deduct the cost of the courses from your taxes!

Gathering the Financial Data You Need

Optimally, you need three to five years' worth of financial statements from the target company to do various calculations and adjustments to test the company's financial health and prospects. Here are the basic financial statements and records that you (or your valuation professional; refer to Chapter 7) need from the target company:

- ✔ Balance sheet
- ✔ Income statement
- ✔ Cash-flow statement
- ✔ Statement of retained earnings

These documents aren't the only ones you need to craft a full valuation of the company, of course — we get into those documents at several points in the book — but they're the foundation of any company's valuation process.

If you're considering starting or buying a business and you use an experienced Certified Public Accountant (CPA) to do your personal taxes, why not set up some time with her after the April 15 tax deadline to discuss basic business recordkeeping? This meeting is a good way to discuss which business structure is best for you to choose, as well as to review the basic financial statements and filings you'll need to make when you're in business. You can discuss setting up financial recordkeeping on your computer as well.

Looking into Support Data

We bring the point into sharper focus as the book goes on, but beyond the basic financials, the kind of company you're looking at defines the kind of additional data you need to establish the value of the company. That's when market data, transactional information, and consumer and supplier intelligence become important. Following is a small sampling of other data that smart valuation professionals gather.

External data

External databases are a great place for prospective business owners to research the industry they're considering entering or buying into. This is where individual business owners can start developing the knowledge necessary to work with all the professionals in the valuation process:

- ✔ **News databases:** These databases may be useful to detail outside analysis on a target company, as well as events and developments affecting the fortunes of the industry in which the target company operates.

- ✔ **Business databases:** These databases contain critical and detailed information on companies and their suppliers. Even if the target company is a small, private competitor that isn't listed, these resources can be good sources of background information on which to base decisions.

- ✔ **Valuation databases:** In Chapter 9, we discuss so-called rule-of-thumb databases that help you get a general idea of how categories of businesses are valued. They don't replace professional valuation as a way to correctly value a company, but they're an excellent starting point for understanding the factors that determine value in various kinds of companies.

Business databases are generally expensive, so check with public and university libraries where you have access to see whether you can do a search for free.

- ✔ **Trade journals:** Like business and news databases, trade journals may provide a sweeping overview of an industry, but because these journals often cover their industries microscopically, they can have an advantage over more general databases.

Internal data

Certain internal data may or may not be disclosed prior to due diligence. Typically, the seller provides a summary of key financial and business data in its offering memo, but these numbers represent the tip of the iceberg of what you or your valuation professional need to dig for.

When you're in the due diligence phase, this information needs to be available in full detail so that the numbers can be verified. For example, an offering memo may mention payroll as a percentage of sales, so you have a rough idea of that information going in. But you need to know that it's surface information. You start asking the tough questions and crunching those numbers during due diligence.

Here are key examples of that data:

- ✔ **Sales and customer spending data:** This information helps you understand the quality of customers that an organization has — how long they've been doing business, how creditworthy they are, and why they spend, for example. Smart valuation professionals representing buyers talk to customers and even competitors of a target business to gather this intelligence.

The bigger the organization, the more detailed the valuation process is. For businesses worth less than $1 million, you'll probably be leaning on rule-of-thumb estimates for value. For businesses above the $1 million level, get advice from your existing tax and estate expert on how detailed the valuation should be to keep your costs and time commitment reasonable.

✔ **Any history of lawsuits or legal challenges over internal or external practices at a company:** It's not enough to know just that a company was sued and then won, lost, or settled the case; you also need to know why the company was sued and how it handled the suit. Legal problems can linger for new buyers as well.

✔ **Payroll and employee turnover data:** Payroll typically is an organization's number one expense, so understanding the employee base from the standpoint of pay, benefits, and placement is critical. Yet payroll goes beyond what a company pays people. Keeping great talent within an organization is a major valuation issue, but protecting company secrets when employees leave is important, too.

✔ **Product evolution:** Is a steady stream of new products, services, and enhancements coming out of a company over time, or does it cling to old successes? Research and development (R&D) is part of every organization; even a restaurant updates its menu and prices from time to time. If a company isn't constantly working to update its offerings and tracking that process, you should be suspicious.

Taking a Look at Financial Statements

To determine the value of any business, you need to have access to that business's financial documentation. If you're valuing a public company, a company's financials are generally accessible because the law requires it. For private companies, however, you need to be at a relatively serious point in a negotiation before a potential seller will open its books to you. But no matter whether you're looking at a public or private company, you need to see the balance sheet, the income statement, a statement of retained earnings, and as much supporting documentation behind these financial results as possible.

The balance sheet

Also called the *statement of financial condition,* the *balance sheet* summarizes a company's financial position at a specific time. In simplest terms, it tells you what a company has, what it owes, and what's left for the owners. This is often expressed as a formula:

Assets = Liabilities + Shareholders' Equity

Public company annual reports: Basic training in financial analysis

The U.S. Securities and Exchange Commission (SEC) requires that public companies make public disclosure of all the financial documents that we refer to in this chapter. Although private companies don't have to make this disclosure, they have to have a system set up for sharing documents if a buyer comes sniffing around.

Because you're at the start of your valuation education, dissecting a public company's annual report is good general training in understanding valuation at any company. Just remember to ignore all the pretty pictures and words in the front of the annual report and turn to the back where all the boring numbers are. Look for the following:

✔ **The 10K:** This document, filed with the SEC, contains a detailed explanation of a business (it's often packaged with the annual report). It offers a more detailed view of financial statements than does an annual report. It allows you to see the amount of stock options awarded to executives at the company, as well as a more in-depth discussion of the nature of the business and marketplace.

✔ **The 10Q:** This is the quarterly version of the 10K. If the company is planning a merger announcement, changing its dividend policy, facing a lawsuit, or worse, it may not issue a press release but rather slide it into the 10Q.

Why analyze a balance sheet? It's the doorway to the inner financial workings of a company. The numbers contained in this statement give important smoke signals of whether business is good or sliding into trouble.

The balance sheet includes assets, liabilities, and stockholder equity. Read on.

Assets

There are two classes of assets — current and long term. Current assets are those that can be converted into cash during a stated period of operations, known as the *operating cycle.* Long-term assets are those that are seen as usable for more than one year, and they're depreciated annually based on their expected useful life.

What falls under current assets? Items that are liquid — which means they can be sold quickly. They include the following:

✔ **Cash:** You've heard it before — cash is king. Cash as stated on a balance sheet is money that can be accessed quickly, such as money in a cash box in the office or hopefully inside a bank. Cash held in long-term reserve to buy company shares or extinguish other debt is considered separate from this category because it's earmarked for a specific purpose, not a general one.

Keep in mind that there's no one single format for presenting consolidated financial statements at any company. What you see here are general structures, and depending on the company and industry it's in, the level of detail will change.

- **Marketable securities:** This is money in short-term bank certificates of deposit or government obligations (such as bonds) that can be accessed within a one-year period of operations. You may not be able to get your hands on it today without a penalty, but you'll definitely be able to do so within a few weeks or months.

- **Accounts receivable:** This is money that should be coming in the door within a short period of time. Accounts receivable are amounts billed to your customers for the goods and services you create. All accounts receivable should be labeled separately for accounting purposes (not every account receivable appears on the balance sheet because it's mainly a summary), but a potential buyer or investor will definitely want to see a list and aging report of all of your accounts receivable. This information can tell a lot about the quality of who you're doing business with.

- **Inventories:** These are goods (mainly physical items) that are available for sale, items already on the assembly line, and raw materials not yet part of the manufacturing/assembly process.

- **Prepaid expenses:** This might not sound like an asset, but it is. Prepaid expenses are the result of a business making payment for necessary goods and services to be received in the near future. This is stuff like prepaid rent for facilities and business insurance.

What falls under long-term assets? Obviously, assets that may need more than a year to liquidate fall under long-term assets. Here's what they include:

- **Investments:** These go into two categories on the balance sheet — short term and long term. Generally, long-term investments are those that a company plans to keep for more than a year (the definition is actually true for individuals, too), and they may consist of stocks or bonds of other companies, real estate, and cash set aside for a specific project or reason. Long-term investments also include money that's held for a pension fund. Short-term investments are those in non-cash accounts that can be liquidated within a year. These may include marketable securities or specific properties meant for short-term resale.

- **Plant assets:** These are also called *fixed assets.* They include plants and equipment as well as land, buildings, machinery, and other items intended to be used in business operations over a relatively long period of time. These are generally not assets you'd rush to convert into cash — their value comes from the goods and services they produce for sale in the business.

✔ **Intangible assets:** Our favorite. These are assets you can neither see, taste, or touch, and they consist mainly of valuable rights, privileges, or other advantages and perks. This category of assets can be the whole ballgame as far as the value of some companies goes, particularly technology companies that produce ideas that travel digitally (see Chapter 5 for details).

Sometimes the most valuable intangibles in a business don't land on the balance sheet. We're talking about internally developed brands, trademarks, and copyrights.

✔ **Other assets:** This is a bit of a catchall category. When any company prepares a balance sheet, it finds assets that can't be classified easily under any of the categories we've stated. What falls into this category? Pay advances made to company officers, the cash surrender value of life insurance on officers, the cost of buildings in the process of construction, and the miscellaneous funds held for special purposes.

Liabilities

Liabilities are what a company owes. Company obligations come in the following forms:

✔ **Current liabilities:** Current liabilities are those you'll pay off or otherwise discharge within your normal operating cycle or within your operating year. This is likely to include amounts owed to trade creditors in accounts payable. Other current liabilities may include income taxes and payroll, as well as utility bills, payroll taxes, local property taxes, and other services.

✔ **Long-term liabilities:** These are generally notes, bonds, and mortgages — debts that usually take more than a year to pay off. Of course, if you have long-term debt that's coming due within the operating year, you need to move it to the short-term debt column.

✔ **Deferred revenues:** Customers sometimes make advance payments for merchandise or services, sometimes in exchange for a discount or other incentive. Revenues are booked when merchandise or services are actually delivered.

✔ **Provisions for legal settlements:** These are reserve amounts to cover potential losses from court disputes that aren't yet official.

Stockholders' equity

Also called *owners' equity* or *capital, stockholders' equity* is in essence the net worth of the company from an accounting standpoint. It's the third stage of the balance sheet.

Why footnotes are important

Good reading glasses are a necessity in understanding financial reports. In any set of financial statements, it's critical to read the small print in footnotes throughout. There's a lot of good stuff in there, such as

✔ **Big changes in accounting policies and practices:** In both private and public corporations, accountants are generally brought in to do the taxes and certify that the company is operating under generally accepted accounted principles. There are, however, situations in which outside accountants and finance executives have to issue warnings and clarifications on their results, and you should keep an eye out for such notes. This may be a key smell point for trouble in an organization, or it may be important when judging trends over several accounting periods.

✔ **Taxes, taxes, taxes:** Footnotes can provide significant information about a company's current and deferred income taxes on the local, state, federal, or international level.

✔ **Pension data:** As you may know, retirement obligations are considerable responsibilities at most companies. Footnotes can tell you about the assets and costs of these plans and whether they're overfunded or underfunded and why. Why is this a valuation issue? Retirees can have a significant claim on a company's assets if their plans aren't backed up, and state and federal governments may have to get involved.

✔ **The handling of stock options:** Recent news reports on the handling of stock options within many public companies are a cautionary message for companies of all sizes. Investors and potential buyers need to know what stock options have been granted to officers, staff, and employees and how those stock options will be accounted for in the company's results.

Say you started a business and your initial investment was $25,000. That amount is recorded in a capital account, also referred to as an owners'-equity account. In publicly traded companies, outstanding preferred and common stock also represents owners' equity.

The income statement

The *income statement* helps you zero in on the quality of revenues and earnings in a business. Also called the *profit-and-loss (P&L) statement,* this document helps you see first the amount of revenue (also referred to as "sales" in some businesses) brought in by a company over a period of time as well as the cost of sales, operating expenses, and taxes that whittle down that total to what hopefully will be a positive number at the end: a company's net earnings or profit.

Stock and the private company

When a company goes public — that is, when it offers its stock for sale on the public markets — a lot of fanfare and considerable preparation surrounds that day. But for more than 90 percent of the companies operating in America, there's never going to be an initial public offering (IPO) date because most companies don't want to go public.

That said, the issuance of private stock in a company is a serious matter and deserves the right expertise going in. Simple business structures like sole proprietorships don't have to consider this issue, but if you plan to incorporate, you should consult a tax expert, an experienced incorporation attorney, and possibly an estate attorney on how many shares you should issue and allocate to the various owners of the business or keep in the corporate treasury.

This is a unique issue for every company, and it should be tied to your growth plan. For instance,

some states price their incorporation fees on the number of shares of stock a company issues, so that may drive the decision in concert with an owner's desire to bring in other investors or possibly go public at some point.

The bottom line? Even if you're a sole business owner who plans to stay in full control of your business for a lifetime, you may decide to do things differently later. You may get married and have kids you want to involve in the business someday. You may involve partners or other owners in growing the business. Circumstances always change.

So if you incorporate or create a partnership, a share of stock isn't just a share of stock. It's key to your planned — and sometimes your unplanned — possibilities for your business in the future. Get the full range of help you'll need to make stock decisions wisely.

Profit is also expressed in a different way. Operating profit is sometimes called *earnings before interest, taxes, depreciation, and amortization (EBITDA)*, *earnings before interest and taxes (EBIT)*, *net profit*, *cash flow to equity*, and so on. Cash flow to equity is the calculation that tells investors how much money they'd receive if the company decided to distribute all the net earnings for the period. This really doesn't happen — companies tend to reinvest profits back in the business — but if you watch or listen to the stock market report on TV or radio, you'll hear commentators comparing current per-share results to year-ago results as a way of saying earnings have gone up or down.

The income statement explains the route to the bottom line of any company and what got it there — not only annual increases in revenue but smart money and people management that allowed the company to hang on to every penny of profit at the end of the day.

You need to know where the IRS is concentrating its efforts in any given year. Since 2001, IRS investigators have been triggering audits at companies over the handling of their employee pension plans and executive compensation — stock options and severance agreements, specifically. Always ask whether a target company has been audited and why.

Income statements are structured like a funnel. At the top you see the gross revenues of a business. As you go down, you see those numbers get smaller as you deduct costs and operating expenses that were needed to generate that big number at the top. By the end, you get to the spout and see how much is left — the net earnings for the period. Obviously, if nothing drips out, that's a loss.

So that's the picture. Following are the numbers you see on the way down the income statement.

Revenues

Revenues are the receivables of a company, generally what's paid by customers in exchange for a company's products or services. Depending on the business, however, it can include other gains for the period. The revenue segment of the income statement includes the following:

- **Net revenues:** Again, this depends on the structure of the company and its operations, but some companies accept returns on certain products or allowances of some sort, so those are subtracted from the gross revenues and expressed as net revenues.

- **Cost of goods sold (COGS):** This is the total expense of manufacturing, creating, and delivering a product. It includes the cost of raw material and production. Typically, these costs are *variable costs* (that is, they're a function of sales).

- **Gross profit:** Gross profit is the cost of goods sold subtracted from the revenue. Here's a common formula that expresses it:

    Gross Profit = Total Revenue – Cost of Goods Sold

- **Gross margin:** This is the ratio of gross profit to sales revenue. It's a measure that shows how efficient a company is at turning raw materials into income. For a retailer, it measures their markup over their wholesale price. Here's the formula:

$$\text{Gross Margin} = \frac{(\text{Revenue} - \text{Cost of Goods Sold}) \times 100}{\text{Revenue}}$$

Expenses

The expenses section of the income statement notes several critical expense categories (some are semivariable costs; some are fixed costs):

Acceptable debt

Is debt bad? Boy, is this a controversial topic! Although a solid credit record is a good thing for people and businesses to have, it's best for businesses to think in terms of how they can fund their operations from money they make doing what they do.

How do you know when a company has too much debt? Generally, if a company has solid cash flow and a return on investment (ROI) that's significantly greater than the percentage it is paying on borrowed funds, it's probably going to be okay.

✔ **General and administrative expenses (G&A):** These expenses are tied to the overall running of the company, not to specific product lines.

✔ **Sales and marketing expenses:** These are promotional, advertising, and other selling costs (for example, sales commissions) for the entire company, though some organizations break these down among divisions.

✔ **Depreciation or amortization expense:** Depreciation happens to virtually any hard asset in a business subject to wear and tear — furniture, vehicles, machinery, computers, you name it. Companies spread the cost of these assets over the periods in which they're used.

✔ **Research and development expenses:** Check to see how much the company is investing in R&D and whether that's paying off in building the business.

Earnings

In earnings, you're finally getting close to figuring out the bottom line. Again, there are some intermediary steps:

✔ **Operating income:** This is the first stage of earnings you see when you subtract all the operating expenses from gross profit.

✔ **Operating margin:** Here's another important ratio. This measures what proportion of a company's revenue is left over after paying for variable costs of production such as wages, raw materials, and other related costs. Here's the formula:

$$\text{Operating Margin} = \frac{\text{Operating Income}}{\text{Net Sales}}$$

✔ **Income before taxes:** This comes after the company deducts any interest paid on its outstanding debt, which is the amount of earnings on which the company expects to pay taxes.

✔ **Taxes:** These are the taxes a company has paid to local, state, and federal officials.

✔ **Net income from continuing operations:** This is the net profit that comes from continuing business activities. It's the amount earned by a company before any adjustment for preferred dividends, discontinued operations (such as divisions that have been sold or closed), and extraordinary items (such as unusual costs from natural disasters or things that rarely affect operations).

✔ **Profit margin:** This is yet another critical ratio — a measure of how good a company is at cost control. The higher the net profit margin is, the better it is at converting revenues into actual profit. Here's the formula:

$$\text{Profit Margin} = \frac{\text{Net Income (continuing or net)}}{\text{Net Sales Revenue}}$$

Net income

Net income is the big one — the amount of profit left over after taxes and all expenses. If you see this amount in brackets, it's not a profit — it's a loss.

✔ **Earnings per share:** This is net income divided by each share of stock in the organization. It's a useful measurement to compare results quarter-to-quarter or year-to-year.

✔ **Shareholder dividends:** Many companies pay dividends to shareholders on an annual basis. If any dividends have been paid during the reporting period, they're noted on a per-share basis here.

Statement of retained earnings

A *statement of retained earnings* represents a company's earnings since day one, minus any money deducted or distributed to the owners of the company. If retained earnings keep going up over the course of time, it indicates that company officers are electing to put more earned income into the business to support operations. The more self-generated investment, the less need a company has to rely on outside financing to grow the business.

GAAP (generally accepted accounting principles) is the main framework of guidelines for the U.S. accounting industry. It governs how accountants and other finance professionals prepare financial statements.

The balance sheet, the income statement, and the statement of retained earnings — these are the major financial road maps in any company, and valuation professionals use several years' worth of those numbers not only to compute how the company has performed over past years but also to project how it may behave in future years. They make such projections by adjusting those numbers (see Chapters 3 and 4 for more on such adjustments).

Activities boosting valuation

Numbers reveal behavior. So what exactly is value-building behavior in a company? Here are some ideas:

- ✔ A strong management team with longevity

- ✔ Hot products with plenty more in the pipeline — research and development spending that's paying off

- ✔ Customers in a love affair with the company

- ✔ A plant and equipment in top shape

- ✔ Consistent upward trends in revenues and earnings — no big swings or extremes

- ✔ Low employee turnover and high marks for its workplace

- ✔ A wide variety of customers without anyone accounting for more than 5 percent of the company's sales or earnings

- ✔ A history of an appropriate level of advertising

Cash-flow statement

The third piece of financial data necessary for valuation is the cash-flow statement — again, it should cover a period of years. For many people, the words *cash flow* trip off the tongue, but nobody realizes the true meaning of the concept until he's in business for the first time: Cash flow is both food and oxygen to a business. Without it, companies die.

A company's cash-flow statement explains its relationship with the outside world. It shows several things:

- ✔ The flow of cash into the company through the sale of goods and services

- ✔ The flow of cash into the company from investment (sale of stocks and bonds)

- ✔ The flow of cash from the company to vendors, employees, and other activities representing investment in the company's own growth

The good news that everyone's looking for in a cash-flow statement is the news that the company can finance its own spending with money it makes from operations. An income statement can tell you whether a company made money, but a cash-flow statement tells you whether the company had a bloodstream of cash keeping it going.

The sources of information for the cash-flow statement are the balance sheet and the income statement.

In accounting terms, cash isn't just about the greenbacks. *Cash* refers to cash and cash equivalents, including currency, bank deposits, U.S. Treasury bills, money market accounts, and commercial paper. So what's *not* cash? Stocks, bonds, and other securities.

The cash-flow statement's bottom line shows the net increase or decrease in cash for the period. The statement is divided into three parts, indicating cash flow from three types of activities:

- ✔ **Operating activities:** This section is all about cash generated by the day-to-day operations of the business — incoming revenue from the sale of goods or services and most kinds of outgoing payments. What it doesn't include is principal paid on or received from loans.

  No transaction is considered to be cash flow unless cash was actually received or paid; amounts in accounts receivable or payable don't qualify. Any cash activities appearing on the company's income statement qualify for the operating-activities section of the cash-flow statement. The same is true of cash activities related to accounts receivable, inventory, accounts payable, and movements in asset values that have a *contra account* (an account that offsets another account) on the income statement and on the balance sheet.

- ✔ **Investing activities:** Investment of cash and cash equivalents creates more cash for use in the business. Investing activities can include the purchase or sale of property and equipment, the purchase or sale of securities and related investments, and loans made to other businesses.

  Interest and depreciation are classified as operating cash flow, as are net gains or losses on investments.

- ✔ **Financing activities:** This section is all about the company's liabilities and shareholder equity, noting how the company obtains its capital and enhances the value of its stock. A company can issue bonds, pay back debt, pay dividends, and issue and buy back its own stock.

Stock buybacks happen in both public and private companies. Stock buybacks are notable tactics in business valuation because they involve a company's realizing that buying back stock is an advantageous strategy. This can happen for a number of reasons that are unique to the company itself.

Figuring your cash flow

Two methods allow people to compute cash flow: the direct and indirect methods. The *direct method* is pretty much what it sounds like. All cash-flow information is pulled from cash receipts and payments that cover the following:

✔ Cash from customers

✔ Interest and dividends received by the company

✔ Cash paid to employees and suppliers of goods or services (including suppliers of insurance, advertising, and so on)

✔ Interest paid

✔ Income taxes paid

The *indirect method* involves pulling information from the balance sheet and income statements based on changes noted in both. Instead of reporting the total cash received from customers, an indirect statement lists only the change in cash received from the previous period. This method pulls information from the following sources:

✔ Net income

✔ Depreciation and amortization

✔ Deferred income taxes

✔ Interest income

✔ Change in accounts receivable

✔ Change in accounts payable

✔ Change in inventories

What a cash-flow statement looks like

Most cash-flow statements contain two sets of figures: source of funds and use of funds. Here are the elements that may appear under both headers:

Source of Funds

Beginning cash

Sales services income

Sale of assets

Customer deposits

Loans made to other companies

Contributed capital

Total cash in: _____

Use of Funds

Salaries

Other operating expenses

Payments for the company's own loans

Capital expenditures

Tax payments

Total cash out: _____

Cash management is a serious issue for all companies, particularly for young ones that may not be bringing in much — or any — revenue. If you don't have specific training in company accounting or managing business funds, talk to a trusted accountant or advisor about how the following issues work:

- ✔ How the target company manages its cash

- ✔ How the company deals with cash shortfalls when customers pay late or in other circumstances that affect the flow of cash into the business

- ✔ What the company does with excess cash

- ✔ What kinds of accounts the company uses to hold any excess cash and whether it uses efficient, low-cost methods to do this. Are those funds allocated in properly insured accounts?

 One of the best ways to maximize cash flow is to have effective on-time-payment and collection strategies for customers. Companies that have the cash flow to do so may negotiate specific discounts and other advantages for paying bills early. Be aware of these practices in the companies you're looking at; they're a sign of good business practices.

Ratios and formulas for valuation

New ways of number crunching are born every day, so what you're about to see are some of the most common valuation ratios used today. In the real world of business valuation, there are considerably more-complex ratios that allow people to deal with specialized situations, and as the book continues, you get to see a few of them. The vast majority of these ratios never see the inside of an annual report, but you may see them referenced in outside resources like stock listings and analysts' data on particular companies.

But you should understand some of the most basic ratios used in valuation so you have a base of knowledge to work from. We're sure you've already seen a few of these and probably calculated a few.

Valuation ratios tell you whether the company is inexpensive or costly on an absolute basis. Your job is to find companies that are bargains relative to their profitability, growth rates, and financial strength. Remember Graham's purchase trigger: If you can find a stock with a value that's 50 percent above the stock price — buy.

Note: We mention some target numbers for these various formulas, but we're going to paste on a caveat: Just as valuation professionals use certain computations to fit the operation, target numbers for these formulas may vary based on the industry. And as much as it bugs us to say it, sometimes the appropriate answer for target numbers is "it depends."

Value Line is an easy-to-understand source of valuation data on public companies, but it's a good one to get familiar with. This investment research service is available online for a fee (www.valueline.com), but it's also available in most public libraries. Again, it's a good way to test out your valuation knowledge.

Price-to-earnings ratio (P/E)

The price-to-earnings formula is

$$P/E = \frac{\text{Share Price}}{\text{Earnings per Share}}$$

Where to find it: P/E is a ratio included next to most individual stock listings online or in daily papers. Also, you can find annual P/E ratios in Value Line, including comparisons to other stocks within an industry. Its main source is in the company's income statement.

If the P/E Ratio of a company is less than its industry average P/E, the company is selling at a discount valuation to its peers. When you hear someone refer to a "low P/E," they're referring to an investment that may be worth a look because it's priced lower than other companies in its industry (also known as its *peer group*).

Some people think buying a stock with a 15 P/E is better than buying one with a 40 P/E because the latter company's earnings are so much further below its stock price. Sometimes people do get too excited about a company, but others may find that it has the potential to support such a valuation. That's further proof that the truth may not rest solely in the numbers.

Price-to-sales ratio (P/S)

Price-to-sales is a way of valuing companies that aren't earning money or are so young they're practically in the startup phase. In the technology sector, many acquisitions have been based on P/S because buyers want to know that revenues are headed up. Here's the formula:

$$P/S = \frac{\text{Current Market Capitalization}}{\text{Last 12 Months' Total Revenues}}$$

Where to find it: You can find the market capitalization by multiplying the number of shares times the market price. The last four quarters of revenue are in Value Line or in the last four 10Q statements from the company.

Check P/S against the working capital ratios (later in this chapter) just to make sure that management is using the company's assets the way they should. It's a leap of faith that management will control costs and eventually produce earnings because the bottom line, not revenues, is what supports a company's value.

Price-to-tangible-book-value ratio (PTBV)

The tangible book value, or net asset value, is a rough estimate of what a company would be worth if it were liquidated. Here's its formula:

Tangible Book Value = Total Assets – Intangible Assets and Liabilities

You can use that calculation to find the price-to-tangible-book-value ratio (PTBV):

$$PTBV = \frac{\text{Stock Price}}{\text{Tangible Book Value}}$$

Where to find it: Book value is listed in the consolidated balance sheet portion of the balance sheet, or it's listed separately in Value Line.

If this calculation is below 1.0, then the company is selling below book value — technically below liquidation value. If this happens, you've found either the bargain of the century or a problem company, so take a fine-toothed comb to its operational history. Generally, though, a low PTBV ratio relative to the rest of that company's competitors is considered a positive sign for investment.

Price-to-tangible-book-value is one of the most controversial value ratios because investors like to argue whether the assets posted at their original (or "book" value) could be sold at roughly the same value today. Check the industry before you use a computation like book value; traditional rust-belt companies with lots of machinery may have a book value that's too high because its technology is obsolete.

You really need to understand the assets of a company before you rely on a traditional measurement like book value. Widen your collection of resources — read analysts' reports on the company if they exist, and if they don't, read voraciously about the industry.

Debt-to-equity ratio (D/E)

Companies need to borrow on a regular basis to fund short-term needs and long-term expansion. Like people, companies can create a good credit rating that stands them in good stead when it's time to borrow affordably for big events like mergers and acquisitions. But as the country has discovered with subprime mortgages and credit cards, debt can go very bad very quickly. Debt-to-equity (D/E) lets you look at a company's borrowing behavior. Here's the formula:

$$D/E = \frac{\text{Total Liabilities}}{\text{Shareholders' Equity}}$$

Where to find it: You can find the D/E ratio already figured in Value Line under your chosen company. But if you want to do it yourself, turn to the consolidated balance sheet in the annual report, look for the total liabilities and shareholders' equity, and grab the calculator.

The standard D/E ratio for most companies is 50 percent, meaning investors want $1 of equity for every 50 cents of debt so they won't lose everything in liquidation. Value investors like to see this number a little lower.

Companies take on debt for different reasons. The best reason is for expansion that will attract higher sales and earnings to pay off that debt in a hurry. The worst is to keep payroll and other basic expenses covered — that's a company in trouble.

Want another way to check a company's relationship with debt? Check out its corporate bond rating in Moody's or Standard & Poor's, the leading bond rating services. Provided the ratings services are doing their jobs, a good rating means you have nothing to worry about; a bad rating means you're taking a chance putting your money in this company.

Working capital (net current asset value)

Working capital is the amount of money a company uses to cover expenses from daily operations, ranging from the price of raw materials to finished goods and sales. Here's the formula:

Working Capital = Current Assets – Current Liabilities

Where to find it: Go to the current assets and current liabilities section of the consolidated balance sheets in the annual report. Current assets include cash, accounts receivable, and inventory.

Essentially, this measurement shows that a company's assets can pay for its liabilities and is a reflection that management has things under control. It's also a rough measure of liquidating value for a company should it close its doors today.

Current ratio

Again, you want to know that management has assets generating enough capital to fund liabilities. Current ratio is another way to gauge that. Here's the formula:

$$\text{Current Ratio} = \frac{\text{Current Assets}}{\text{Current Liabilities}}$$

Where to find it: The current ratio is always in Value Line, but if you want to figure it out yourself, gather your information from the balance sheet.

Consensus has a desirable current ratio at 2, meaning that there's no more than $1 in liabilities for every $2 of assets. A current ratio higher than 2 means that the company is controlling its inventory well and is collecting revenues quickly.

Quick ratio

If revenues were to stop or severely decrease for a period of time, could this company continue to pay for daily operations until they start again? Use the quick ratio to find out. Here's the formula:

$$\text{Quick Ratio} = \frac{\text{Current Assets} - \text{Inventory}}{\text{Current Liabilities}}$$

Where to find it: The balance sheet and, of course, Value Line.

Consensus is that a quick ratio of 1 or higher indicates that a company could meet those obligations.

Chapter 9

Using Rule-of-Thumb Valuations for Mom-and-Pop Businesses

In This Chapter

▶ Why rules of thumb are good starting points but never endpoints

▶ What general business valuation can tell you

▶ Ten examples from Tom West's *Business Reference Guide*

*T*he folks at Merriam-Webster Online have it right about the expression *rule of thumb,* which they define as "a general principle regarded as roughly correct but not intended to be scientifically accurate." We like that definition. It means a rule of thumb is intended to be helpful and educational but shouldn't be the final word on a decision, particularly one that involves a life's savings or the potential risk of tens or hundreds of thousands of dollars' worth of borrowed money.

This chapter deals with rules of thumb in business valuation and how people should use them. We have the privilege of introducing one of the leaders in researching and gathering business-valuation rules of thumb. Tom West is a founder, past president, and former executive director of the International Business Brokers Association (www.ibba.org), and for the past 18 years, he's been the author of the *Business Reference Guide,* an annual bible on pricing hundreds of categories of independent businesses and name-brand franchises.

In this chapter, we feature rules of thumb on ten specific kinds of businesses from data from entries West compiled for the *Business Reference Guide* and listings he features on his subscription Web site, Business Brokerage Press (www.bbpinc.com).

What Rules of Thumb Do in Business Valuation

Rules of thumb are starting points. You have to thoroughly investigate the rest of the information that you need on your own and with the right help, but here are some key points:

✔ The rules provide general price guidance on categories of businesses. In West's guide, the rules of thumb come in two formats that most valuation experts recognize.

✔ The rules provide buyers and sellers a ballpark figure on what average companies in a certain industry are worth.

The first rule of thumb for pricing a business is simply a percentage of annual sales. If the total sales of a business last year was $100,000, for example, and the multiple for the particular business was 40 percent of annual sales, the price based on that particular rule of thumb would be $40,000.

The second rule of thumb is a multiple of earnings. An earnings multiplier makes the most sense to prospective buyers because it directly addresses the buyer's motive: making money by achieving a return on investment.

What kinds of earnings are involved in this calculation? In many small companies, this multiple is commonly used against the *seller's discretionary earnings (SDE),* which are earnings before accounting for the following items:

✔ Income taxes

✔ Nonrecurring income and expenses

✔ Nonoperating income and expenses

✔ Depreciation of an amortization

✔ Interest expense or income

✔ Total compensation for one owner/operator after the total compensation of all owners is adjusted to market value

Earnings are also designated with earnings before interest, taxes, depreciation, and amortization (EBITDA). You can use EBITDA to analyze and compare profitability between companies and industries because it eliminates the effects of financing and accounting decisions. People use EBITDA in evaluating a company's ability to earn a profit; it's expressed as follows:

EBITDA = Operating Revenue – Operating Expenses plus Other Revenue

Earnings before interest and taxes (EBIT) is expressed as follows:

EBIT = Operating Revenue – Operating Expenses plus Nonoperating Income

West's listings are based on a consensus among valuation professionals who deal with those particular kinds of companies. With the basic information you gather through rules of thumb, you turn into a private detective.

Rules of thumb are best used as baselines. Every one of West's rules is nothing more than a general approximation of what you may pay for a particular kind of business based on general data about its category. The rules of thumb don't account for critical local details (such as the value of location); the effect of the local or national economy on that business; or most importantly, how an actual business in that category is owned and managed.

Valuation is not just about crunching numbers. It's also about asking the right questions — and then asking more questions. If you want to know more about selling a business or prospecting for one, we invite you to read Parts III and IV of this book closely.

2008 Rules of Thumb from the Business Reference Guide

The following examples are based on the listings in the online version of the *2008 Business Reference Guide,* with permission from Business Brokerage Press. We keep the examples short in the interest of space and *For Dummies* style, but they should give you an idea of what you see in some of the leading business categories to which entrepreneurs gravitate.

Full-service restaurants

Description: This industry comprises establishments that engage primarily in providing food services to patrons who order, are served while seated (via waiter/waitress service, for example), and pay after eating. These establishments may provide food services to patrons in combination with selling alcoholic beverages, providing carryout service, or presenting live nontheatrical entertainment.

Rules of thumb:

- ✔ 30 to 35 percent of annual sales plus inventory
- ✔ 2 to 2.5 times sellers' discretionary earnings (SDE) plus inventory
- ✔ 2 to 3 times earnings before interest and taxes (EBIT)
- ✔ 2.5 to 4 times Earnings before Interest, Taxes, Depreciation and Amortization (EBITDA)

Pricing tips from valuation professionals:

- ✔ "There are five critical criteria for restaurants to meet. First is location: busy location, high traffic, booming business in the area and finally mid- to high-income population. Second is rent: it should not exceed 10 percent of gross revenue. Third is conversion potential: can the restaurant be converted into another concept that will not compete with other restaurants within same particular center? Fourth is condition of equipment: are they National Sanitation Foundation (NSF) approved and in good condition? Since they are expensive, we shouldn't overlook that. Fifth is asking price: the most important is percentage of gross revenue, which shouldn't exceed 30 to 40 percent, that's what experienced restaurant owners/buyers look for; and the gross annual revenue shouldn't be less than $500,000 for a full-service restaurant, otherwise it should sell as an asset sale. If you have all these 5 criteria, the business will sell for market value."

- ✔ "Lease terms and liquor license are important factors that can affect the value. If the facility is relatively new and up to current codes, it can be sold as an asset sale even with negative cash flow."

- ✔ "Occupancy cost should not exceed 10 percent of annual gross sales. Restaurant operators tend to drag vendors out to 60–90 days. If cost of sales exceeds 35 percent, there is probably some skimming going on."

- ✔ "Currently a buyers' market: must be profitable or will sell for depreciated asset value only. Lease obligations are a large part of negotiations."

- ✔ "Two times EBITDA plus value of furniture, fixtures, and equipment (FFE) plus Liquor License plus Inventory"

- ✔ "Be wary of comparing industry statistics against smaller mom and pops who do not have equal purchasing power. Fuel surcharges are pushing costs much higher."

General information:

- ✔ "It is much better to buy an existing franchise rather than start one with no sales and high costs."

- ✔ "Most 'rules of thumb' regarding valuation of restaurants don't apply across the board. Each is very individual unless the restaurant is a franchise."

✔ "Very rare to find a restaurant that is absentee owned and profitable. Some can do it but must gross over $1.5MM."

✔ "Checking online reviews such as `Yelp.com` can provide insight to a restaurant's operations and success that an owner may accidentally overlook while profiling their business."

✔ "It's all in the lease! It's Location, Location, Location. Books must be well kept and make sense."

✔ "In a slow economy it is important for restaurateurs to sharpen their prices, service, cleanliness and don't stop advertising (just have to look for the best results)."

✔ "Don't do it, unless you can commit to seven-day work weeks and long hours."

✔ "When going into this business, in my opinion, you need to plan to be there a lot. There are two kinds of bartenders out there. The ones that steal from you and the ones that steal from you a lot."

Bars

Description: This industry comprises establishments known as bars, taverns, nightclubs, or drinking places that engage primarily in preparing and serving alcoholic beverages for immediate consumption. These establishments may also provide limited food services.

Rules of thumb:

✔ 35 to 40 percent percent times annual sales — business only plus inventory

✔ 2 to 2.5 times SDE plus inventory

✔ 2 to 2.5 times EBIT

✔ 2 to 2.5 times EBITDA

✔ 4 times monthly sales plus game revenue (net) plus inventory

✔ 4 times monthly sales plus liquor license and inventory

Pricing tips:

✔ "Main variable is the fair market value of the liquor permit, as some areas have a high number of available permits which results in the permit having no, or limited, additional value, while in other areas limited number of available permits may cause the permit to have a substantial value. One will need to research type of permit and its availability and if in fact a market exists for the permit itself. I have seen liquor permits being sold for as high as $150,000, which obviously impacts the value of the business."

✔ "The location, lease rate, and restrictions on the conditional use permit or liquor license will largely impact any given operation's value. As some licenses are valued at $75,000+, there is always some 'floor' value regardless of profitability."

✔ "Factor in liquor license, understand what equipment is actually leased, make sure the restaurant is up to code and salable before investing time."

✔ "Location, lease, and liquor license dictate the value of a bar. The concept is usually changed with a new buyer, and a significant investment is made to improve the premises."

✔ "Recently in the Denver market we have seen 50 percent of sales as a rule of thumb; more if easily operated (fewer employees)."

✔ "You really need to understand if the liquor and beer costs are in line and how much the establishment is selling versus food."

✔ "Drinking places, or bars or taverns, are always in high demand. The most important factors in assessing the value of the business are the location and the lease (how long remains), when and at what rate will the options be exercised, etc."

✔ "Discretionary cash flow [DCF] can be very different from deal to deal. There is one very important DCF item that should be identified: Does the bar or taproom have any vending? (Examples of this are video poker, tobacco, jukebox, pool tables, etc.) If the answer is 'Yes,' then the next question should be, is there a vendor arrangement, or does the seller own the machines? A vendor arrangement means that the vendor owns the machines and collects a portion of the proceeds. If the seller owns the machines, the seller collects all of the proceeds, and can use these funds to reduce their cost of goods sold (COGS) and labor considerably. In each case (with the seller as owner or the vendor as owner of machines), OFF BALANCE SHEET seller financing or vendor financing can be a very powerful source of funds.

"There are a few little things that can alter the valuation in a bar or taproom. Generally, these types of establishments derive a lot of revenue from draft beer. (COGS for draft beer 25 percent to 30 percent, gross profit 70 percent to 75 percent.) If the establishment is operating on an antiquated draft system, glasses may not appear clean, spouts look discolored . . . this could warrant a discount. Most states require that draft system/draft lines are cleaned weekly.

"A potential buyer should ask for vendor beer invoices to determine the 'popular' products of the establishment. This is important if the buyer has a potential age group in mind as the primary patrons. This is a forward cash flow assumption that should be acknowledged. If vendor beer invoices are not made available, check the trash dumpster on a regular basis, it is an excellent source of information.

"If liquor is being served, the pouring routine should be observed. Measured shot or free pour can materially change COGS. 750ML bottle yields 26 ounces, which is 14 shots at a 1.75-oz free pour, and 21 shots at a 1.25-oz measured shot. This difference could be the cost of 1.5 bottles. (Generally these establishments sell mostly beer/draft beer, but this scenario should be included in forward cash flow assumptions)."

✔ "You have to factor in the location, lease term or property sale, equipment, and the ease of someone taking over without having to put a lot of funds in."

General information:

✔ "State changes in gambling legislation are making these types of businesses more attractive where there has been an allowance of on-premise gambling."

✔ "Neighborhood corner locations will always be valuable."

✔ "Owners must understand this is a business and the purpose is to make money, not be a place to 'hang out.'"

✔ "You have to understand how liquor licensing works in your state."

✔ "High degree of owner involvement on a day-to-day basis. Ability to contain costs and prevent 'shrinkage.' Creating a customer-friendly environment which provides good value. Owner usually must have excellent people skills, not a business for introverts."

✔ "Number of licenses in town, length of lease, percent of food sales, percent of liquor sales, entertainment costs, if any. Watch for ratios that are out of industry standards."

✔ "Never trust the books. Check sales tax returns, bank statements, etc. Also, check the price points and compare to the actual COGS. Are the comps legitimate on the profit-and-loss statement (P&L)? Are COGS high due to the owner skimming, or are they giving the house away? We never address a value to skimming and never represent it to buyers. Experienced buyers will recast the financials using their own labor percentage, etc."

✔ "Food costs must be controlled. Lots of businesses fail due to ineffective food and liquor cost controls."

Gift shops

Description: This industry comprises establishments that engage primarily in selling new gifts, novelty merchandise, souvenirs, greeting cards, seasonal and holiday decorations, and curios.

Rules of thumb:

- 2.5 times SDE includes inventory
- 1.5 times SDE plus inventory
- 35 percent of annual sales includes inventory
- 3 to 4 times EBITDA

Inventory at cost plus FFE plus 1 to 2 times SDE

Pricing tips:

- "Inventory should be valued separately and include any costs associated with shipping inventory to the point of sale and preparing it for sale. Example: Beads are bought in bulk. They are heavy and require extra costs to ship and require time and cost to re-package and weigh into smaller sellable units."

- "Location weighs heavily. Products are very important in relation to value. Is the store a card plus gift shop? Does it carry high-end American crafts and upscale gifts, gifts plus toys? The mix is important along with profit margins."

General information:

- "Companies with multiple store locations have a much higher survival rate. Buyers will not pay for obsolete inventory."

- "You need to understand which segment of this industry you are working with (craft type). Also, are you working with the retailer, the distributor, or the manufacturer?"

Medical practices

Description: This industry comprises establishments of health practitioners who hold an MD (Doctor of Medicine) or DO (Doctor of Osteopathy) degree and engage primarily in the independent practice of general or specialized medicine (except psychiatry or psychoanalysis) or surgery. These practitioners operate private or group practices in their own offices (such as centers or clinics) or in facilities such as hospitals or health maintenance organization (HMO) medical centers.

Rules of thumb:

- 40 to 45 percent of annual gross sales plus inventory
- .05 to 1.5 times SDE includes inventory

- ✔ 2 to 3 times EBITDA
- ✔ 1.5 times EBIT

Pricing tips:

- ✔ "Very wide range of values depending on numerous characteristics. Primary care practices tend to sell for higher multiples (35 percent to 50 percent) than specialty practices. Need to be especially cognizant of current compensation range for medical specialty in question. Some specialties may think a cash flow of $200,000 is good, other specialties won't consider practice with cash flow less than $400,000. Payer mix/contracts is important. Revenue deriving from inpatient work (i.e., hospital work) may not count toward value as the hospital and not the selling doctor controls that revenue stream. Some specialties very susceptible to changes in technology. Stark Laws and Anti-Kickback Statutes can impact sales price/terms. The more specialized the doctor — or the more the practice relies on personal reputation of doctor — the harder to sell and lower value."

- ✔ "The transferability of the value from the seller to the buyer is essential! Excellent clinical technology, management systems and managers, and effective relationships add value. A successful transition is critical to transferring value from the seller to the buyer."

- ✔ "Entirely dependent on facts and circumstances of SUBJECT PRACTICE, e.g., specialty, percent ancillary services and technical component revenues, payer mix, etc."

- ✔ "1 to 1.35 times SDE plus inventory and accounts receivable are not included."

- ✔ "[. . .] SDE, EBIT and EBITDA multiples really no longer apply. The best current formula is 2.5–4 times (SDE minus compensation for owner labor). The 2.5 multiplier is for insurance-based practices, and the 4 multiplier is for the best of cash practices. Insurance reimbursement trends are downwards, hurting values significantly. The reason AGS, SDE and EBITDA don't apply is the owner might be active or passive. It is illogical to think that a practice with $1,000,000 AGS has the same value to ownership if the owner works there 50 hours per week or is an absentee owner; which is why you have to subtract the market-rate comp for owner labor prior to applying the multiplier. Many specialties have merely liquidation value or close to it because of shortages, the ease of opening a competing practice, and hospital income and overhead guarantees via forgivable loans in lieu of practice purchase. Value issues are very, very localized. Rule of thumb: the sale should pay for itself to the buyer within 5 years with profits above comp for labor."

✔ "EBITDA is most important; percent of Annual Gross Sales is generally irrelevant since profitability varies so widely. Rural practices are getting almost impossible to sell because of physician shortages. Watch out for big insurance reimbursement changes in 2008–12 due to Medicare changes and PPOs [preferred provider organizations] following their pricing. 501-C3 'not-for-profit' buyers will require formal appraisals. Maybe have to adjust value for lack of electronic health care record if it is needed locally within 1–2 years; $25,000–$40,000 per doc, reduces profits."

General information:

✔ "Pricing of professional practices is less amenable to 'rules of thumb' because of wide disparities in reimbursement, costs, physician manpower availability, and challenges of transferring the intangible elements of value to a successor owner, etc."

✔ "Billing turnaround is very important."

✔ "Be very careful about state licensure, state laws, and federal Stark, Medicare and Medicaid laws. Many docs don't know when they are in violation of laws that don't make sense. Use a specialist attorney on every deal to minimize errors and omissions (E&O). Many illegal medispas popping up now and trying to bail out via sales."

✔ "Labor includes physicians and support staff. This is a labor-intensive service business."

✔ "Heavy Medicare/Medicaid practices very susceptible to federal government payment structure from year to year. Depending on specialty and year reimbursement may be up/down considerably. Technology can also have significant impact on future practice earnings. Brokers should have familiarity with Stark and Anti-Kickback Statutes. Brokers should make sure that buyer/seller attorneys have medical practice transaction experience and knowledge of Stark and AKS."

Auto repair shops

Description: This industry comprises establishments that engage primarily in providing a wide range of mechanical/electrical repair and maintenance services for vehicles such as passenger cars, trucks, vans, and trailers; or engine repair and replacement.

Rules of thumb:

✔ 25 percent to 30 percent of annual sales plus inventory

✔ 2 times SDE plus inventory

✔ 1.5 to 2 times EBIT

✔ 2 to 2.5 times EBITDA

Pricing tips:

✔ "Most service centers need minimum eight bays to show higher revenues and strong cash flow."

✔ "Many auto centers with sales revenues under $500,000 per year have closed their doors due to little or no profit. Consumers are driving less due to the high price of gas and this directly affects sales revenues. Rents continue to escalate and it becomes increasingly more difficult to find good managers or top-line techs. Major auto dealerships are also becoming more aggressive in their service departments and have taken some of the sales revenues away from the independent auto centers. Conversely the auto centers with sales exceeding $1 million per year continue to show good profits and will benefit from the smaller auto centers who close their doors. The above multiples do not include inventory, at cost; the multiples do include equipment, FFE."

✔ "Rent can be added to the SDE if the seller also owns the building and is selling the building with the business. If the seller hires too many employees, it is sometimes possible to show the buyer why the business can be run with fewer employees, and add the soon-to-be-terminated employee's salary to the SDE."

✔ "Sometimes I will use 2.5 times SDE. This depends on if the business is located on a prime corner, how much equipment the business has, and how new the equipment is. A shop that has a very low SDE, or possibly is losing money, is able to sell for between $100K to $135K just for its location, build out, and equipment."

✔ "Smaller auto centers can be the most difficult to sell due to the very personal nature of the business. It is very helpful if the owner stays for 1 to 2 months to ease the buyer into the business especially creating a comfort level with the customers."

General information:

✔ "Good technicians are always hard to come by, but with a busy and nice looking shop it makes it easier to attract them."

✔ "Most auto repair shop owners focus too much on offering the lowest prices rather than providing excellent customer service. If you provide excellent customer service, customers are willing to pay for it. Most people think the number of bays is important. The number of parking spaces is a lot more important than the number of bays."

✔ "Eighty-eight percent of my automotive purchasers are buyers with no prior experience. The multiple on this type of business has dropped from previous years. Why? Lack of skilled technicians, overabundance of service centers, low unemployment. Most buyers in today's market are not looking for a business that falls under the heading of a low-paying job. Rule of thumb is applicable for Franchise or Non-Franchise Centers."

✔ "Demand for this service business has gradually decreased over the last four years. The smaller (Mom and Pop operations of $35,000 gross/month or less) are becoming non-existent in many larger cities."

✔ "Factors to look for: the gross profit of the business pre-wages, equipment leased vs. free and clear, management and certification of techs, percentage of wages, the length of lease and terms. The business should do a minimum of $30K per month in sales revenue (excluding smog Certs). Any special licenses required? Does the owner work as a mechanic? Things to add to value: volume exceeds $50K per month, the owner works only in administrative capacity, number of bays (minimum 6 bays), all equipment is free and clear, all mechanics have at least two years' experience, rent is eight percent of sales or less, strong manager in place, gross profit exceeds 60 percent. Things to subtract from value: owner is active as mechanic, monthly sales under $25K per month, appearance, location, most equipment on lease, the age of the equipment, lack of professional management, inexperience of mechanics, unable to expand in capacity or sales, rent high, short term lease."

Day-care centers for children

Description: This industry comprises establishments that engage primarily in providing day care for infants or children. These establishments generally care for preschool children but may care for older children when they're not in school and may also offer prekindergarten educational programs.

Rules of thumb:

✔ 40 to 45 percent of annual sales includes inventory

✔ 3 times SDE includes inventory

✔ 2.5 to 3 times EBIT

✔ 3 to 4 times EBITDA

✔ 2 times SDE includes inventory (most child-care centers are acquired with the real estate; the 2 multiple of SDE is after the debt service required to buy the real estate)

Pricing tips:

- ✔ "State laws, regulations and market rate have large impact on price."

- ✔ "Site location is critical; curb cuts and ease of access in/out of center is very important; proper side of road for traffic flow during rush hour; tenure of center, tenure of teachers and their level of secondary education; strong director/mgr very important; quality centers with consistent earnings achieve price points in the higher end of the price range than other centers."

- ✔ "Based on gross sale, is 2 to 3 times sales. Based on license capacity, it runs $10,000 to $14,000 per child."

- ✔ "Size matters. Licensed capacity less than 75 expect a 2.5 to 3 times EBITDA, over 100 expect a 4 +/– EBITDA multiple."

- ✔ "The larger the business, the higher the multiple of earnings. A 4 times multiple is the maximum for a large center (licensed for 100+). Smaller businesses, depending upon how well they are maintained, can achieve 2.5 times sellers discretionary cash flow (SDCF)."

- ✔ "Price is a direct effect of cash flow. The amount the business provides the seller needs to cover debit service and provide a return to the buyer. Banks look for a debit service ratio of 1.25 to 1.50. Price is also determined by the number of students and the income they provide to the school. For example, childcare centers sell from $10,000 per child (license cap) to as low as $6,000 per child. Price is also sometimes 2 times gross income."

- ✔ "Much of the value of a childcare center is based upon number of children enrolled, gross revenues, net operating income, and what percent of revenues are subsidized by the state."

- ✔ "Multiples of EBITDA vary depending upon the size of the operation and depth of management. The larger the operation, the higher the multiple. Smaller operations will sell for over 2 times EBITDA, while larger operations with competent management will sell for in the 3 to 4 times EBITDA range. Reconstructed EBITDA should include adjustments to fair market value (FMV) for arm's length transactions (salaries, rent, etc.)."

General information:

- ✔ "State and government programs can positively impact earnings but are not guaranteed long term; high staff turnover is a common trait; ones which have lower turnover rates are favored by buyers; high-quality centers with consistent earnings and good visibility and access demand highest price points."

✔ "First, the childcare industry is strong and important to the employment picture in areas where it is provided. In the adult-education business, it is important to have a trained work force."

✔ "There is need for both 'mom and pop' operations as well as larger 'institutional' type businesses. Each can serve their own niche and be literally right next door to one another. A good, clean, quality service provider can be profitable in almost any competitive environment."

✔ "Striking the right balance between quality and profit is critical to long-term success. Many parents will place cost as a secondary consideration to quality and reputation."

✔ "Check out licensing authority for complaints against the business. Understand frequency of rate increases. (Rate increases should be annual if only a couple of dollars.) Look at staff longevity to understand the caring nature of the business, which is critical to the reputation of the business."

✔ "Check to see if state-subsidized."

✔ "People look for unique program structure and location which they deem desirable (which vary by buyer). As birth rates stabilize and decline, program will be what keeps the progressive centers open and thriving in the future."

Dry cleaning

Description: This industry comprises establishments that engage primarily in one or more of the following activities:

✔ Providing dry cleaning services (except coin operated)

✔ Providing laundering services (except linen and uniform supply or coin operated)

✔ Providing drop-off and pickup sites for laundries and/or dry cleaners

✔ Providing specialty cleaning services for specific types of garments and other textile items (except carpets and upholstery), such as fur, leather, or suede garments; wedding gowns; hats; draperies; and pillows

These establishments may provide all, a combination of, or none of the cleaning services on the premises.

Rules of thumb:

✔ 70 to 80 percent of sales plus inventory (plants with on-site laundry equipment get a higher multiple; plants with over-the-counter sales of $35,000 get a higher multiple)

✔ 2.5 to 3 times SDE plus inventory

✔ 2 to 3 times EBIT

✔ 2.5 to 3 times EBITDA

✔ 2 times SDE for a poor unit, 2.5 times SDE for a so-so business, 3 times SDE for a good store, 3.5 times SDE for a hot unit with a good lease and equipment, and 4 times SDE for a real winner

Pricing tips:

✔ "70 percent of annual gross sales if equipment is under 5 years old. If equipment is between 6 and 10 years old, it will be 60 percent of annual gross sales. If equipment is over 11 years old, it will be between 40 percent and 50 percent of the annual gross sales."

✔ "Purchase price ranges from 70 percent of annual sales to 100 percent. Single stores with full garment pricing (no discounts, no coupons) and having monthly retail sales over $35,000 will achieve the higher multiple. Retail pick-up stores (no equipment) 25 percent to 50 percent of annual sales."

✔ "One can get 3 times cash flow (SDE) if the owner is a manager and does not perform a specific job such as counter, dry cleaner, or presser. If the owner does perform a specific job, such as dry cleaner, etc., the cash flow should include the owner's salary and the business would be valued at 2.5 times that cash flow."

✔ "Dollar for dollar (100 percent of sales) on a plant that has dry cleaning equipment and a single buck or double buck shirt unit, assuming all sales are over-the-counter, not from pick-up stores or hotels or other cleaners. 75 percent of sales for plant w/o shirt unit, and 50 percent of sales on pick-up stores, assuming sales are $125,000 or more."

✔ "75 to 100 percent of annual gross sales for complete retail plants, must be able to verify. Pick-ups (drop stores) go for 30 to 50 percent of annual gross sales. Routes vary greatly, but can sell for 25 to 50 percent of actual paid gross sales."

General information:

✔ "Stores that have no discount cleaners in the area are the way to go."

✔ "Dry cleaning analysts say Zoots faced an uphill battle from the start, trying to turn a mom-and-pop industry with razor-thin profit margins on its head.

"'Over the years, attempts to build large dry cleaning chains with company-run stores like Zoots have largely failed,' said Bill Fisher, chief executive of the Dry Cleaning and Laundry Institute, a trade group. Unlike fast-food chains that standardize all the food and cooking techniques, dry cleaners deal with thousands of different garments with unique issues on a daily basis." Source: "High Concept Cleaner in Tatters" by Jenn Abelson, *The Boston Globe,* May 13, 2008.

✔ "With approximately 30,000 dry cleaners in the United States, dry clean-ing is one of the largest industry sectors that is still recognized as a 'mom-and-pop' small business. Although the size of dry cleaners varies, most commercial dry cleaners are single-facility, family-owned opera-tions. An average number of five employees work at a plant. Commercial dry cleaning is not a high-profit business, with the median annual rev-enues below $250,000." Source: International Fabricare Institute (IFI), September 2007.

Coin laundries

Description: This industry comprises establishments that engage primarily in operating facilities with coin-operated or similar self-service laundry and dry cleaning equipment for customer use on the premises, and establish-ments that engage primarily in supplying and servicing coin-operated or similar self-service laundry and dry cleaning equipment for customer use in places of business operated by others, such as apartments and dormitories.

Rules of thumb:

✔ 3 to 5 times SDE plus inventory (higher multiple for newer equipment and long lease)

✔ 100 percent of annual sales plus inventory

✔ 1 to 1.5 times annual sales plus inventory

✔ 5 times EBIT

✔ 3 times EBITDA

"Generally 2.5 to 5.0 times annual SDE; depends on various parts of the U.S. — California, for example, sells between 4 to 5 times SDE, whereas in Nebraska it's 1.5 to 2.5 times SDE."

Pricing tips:

✔ "Coin laundry business is predictable. It does not jump up and down or respond to marketing as quickly as, say, a restaurant would. Having said that, the flat trend, old but functional equipment and slightly run-down interiors, get about 5 times the SDE; the newer equipment, crisp and clean interior with slight uptick in historical volume trend, tends to get high multiples. The annual sales number around $180,000 seems to be almost magical. Over that amount of annual sales, demand is huge, since they can be flowing around $100,000+ in profits."

✔ "Location and demographics. It's important to study the surrounding area for city planned changes or housing changes that may affect business performance."

✔ "Larger multiplier number used for newer equipment and long-term lease."

✔ "Depending upon the market or location of the Laundromat, pricing can actually range between 1 and 1.5 times gross annual sales."

✔ "Age of equipment a huge factor in price determining. Fold and wash service available?"

✔ "They typically sell for 100 percent to 125 percent of the annual sales. Location, age of machines, total appearance very important."

✔ "Typically laundries sell for between 55 and 65 times monthly net."

✔ "Net Income should = ⅓ of Gross Income. Sales price is 5+ × Net."

✔ "Coin-operated laundries typically based on a 20 percent return on capital."

✔ "Try and achieve a 25 percent return on capital; not including owner's salary."

✔ "Utility costs are the single largest operating expense in a coin laundry." Source: Coin Laundry Association.

✔ "Higher multiplier for businesses with newer equipment (3–4 years) and long-term lease (10+ years) increase business value."

✔ "Here are the steps used to calculate how many times the washers would have to be used to use all the water reflected in the water bill: (1) Get the water bills for the last year, (2) Since water bills are usually in cu. ft., you will have to figure out how many gallons of water were used (there are approximately 7.5 gallons per cu. ft.), (3) Find out how many gallons of water the particular washer type uses, (4) Calculate how many times the washers have to be used to use all the water based on the bill. That should give you the number of washes. Multiply that by the cost per wash. The national average for 'turns' is 5 — the number of times the washer is used. Dryer income is generally half that used of washer income, and vending income can produce 10 percent of total."

✔ "Historically, laundries have been priced to sell at some multiple of their annual gross. Primarily because of tradition, this multiple varies from one section of the country to another, but normally it's within the 90 percent to 150 percent range. [. . .] Variations on the annual gross formula include such rules of thumb as 12 to 18 times monthly gross, or three to five times annual net income (before taxes)."

General information:

"Location is very important. Good locations are in densely populated areas with high percentage renters and low-to-mid income."

"Rising utility costs are an issue. I would recommend an analysis of the cost per wash and dry load, to ensure a reasonable profit per turn."

"Population demographics within 1-mile radius should show high percentage renters (50+ percent), low-to-mid income, limited competition, larger family size."

"If it is too good to be true, run!"

"Listed below are many of the different points that will require additional cash before you get in the door."

- ✔ "A rent deposit, which may include up to three months' worth in some cases."

- ✔ "Utility deposits — in many cases, if you have never owned a business, they can be as much as $3,000."

- ✔ "Quarters for coin changer, which typically run somewhere between $1,000 to $3,000."

- ✔ "Soaps and supplies. If you're selling over-the-counter goods, you'll need an additional $2,000 or so."

- ✔ "You should have some cash set aside for marketing, and, coming out of the box, it will be about $2,000 and up."

- ✔ "Most laundries don't have security cameras, and I highly recommend you get them. That will range somewhere between $2,000 to $6,000."

- ✔ "Legal fees, which typically run $2,000 to $5,000, depending on how complicated things get, and I have never seen a deal go through without some spiders."

- ✔ "There will be some closing costs and/or bank fees, which will vary on each deal."

- ✔ "Miscellaneous expenses, which can include mops, buckets, cleaning supplies, paint to spruce up the place, new TVs, uniforms, and more. This normally falls into the $3,000 to $5,000 range."

Source: "Do You Have Enough Money to Buy an Existing Coin Laundry?" by Robert Renteria, WashProUSA, www.AmericanCoinOp.com, May 15, 2008

Bookstores

Description: This U.S. industry comprises establishments that engage primarily in selling new books.

Rules of thumb:

- ✔ 15 percent of annual sales plus inventory
- ✔ 1.6 SDE plus inventory

General information:

"Two surveys released over the past several weeks put the share of the consumer book market controlled by online retailers at between 21 percent (R.R. Bowker) and 30 percent (Fairfield Research), growth that has been fueled, in large part, by the expansion of Amazon." Source: "As Amazon Soars, Bookstores Creep" by Jim Millot, *Publishers Weekly*, April 2008.

"Average profit margin is 4 percent."

Bed-and-breakfasts

Description: This U.S. industry comprises establishments that engage primarily in providing short-term lodging in facilities known as bed-and-breakfast inns. These establishments provide short-term lodging in private homes or small buildings converted for this purpose. Bed-and-breakfast inns are characterized by a highly personalized service and inclusion of a full breakfast in the room rate.

Rules of thumb:

- ✔ 550 percent of annual sales includes inventory and real estate.
- ✔ 4.2 times gross room sales for small B&Bs (fewer than eight rooms), 4.5 for dinner-service inns (for businesses as opposed to real-estate-driven small properties).
- ✔ 8 times SDE includes inventory and real estate.

Pricing tips:

- ✔ "$50,000 to $100,000 per guest room. In the Midwest, the year-round larger inns are selling from $80,000 to $100,000 per guestroom. 3 times net operating income plus $20,000 to $40,000 for the aesthetics and tax benefits plus value of real estate and furnishings."

✔ "The larger inns are selling for 8 (w/o seller financing) to 10 times (w/ seller financing) adjusted net operating income. The base real estate value of the smaller B&B contributes to a large part of the value. In small, supplemental income B&Bs, their value is typically $25,000 to $50,000 more than the base real estate value as a house or other real estate use. There are probably more supplemental income B&Bs than cash flow inns of the 20,000+ U.S. B&Bs. Gross Rent Multiplier is in the 5 to 6 range."

General information:

"Innkeeping attracts educated, sophisticated and prosperous folks for whom many are seeking a bridge between career and retirement. While buying a B&B is a lot like buying a house, there are some differences. If you're more than 6 mos. from making your move, you should be reading the B&B books and magazines, attending a B&B seminar, visiting B&B's as a guest, vacationing in your area of interest, and volunteering your time at a local B&B to experience the 'feel' of innkeeping. Once you're within 6 mos. of moving, you should put your house up for sale and begin looking at B&B's for sale. If you slightly overlist your house, the worst that can happen to you is that someone may pay you more than you thought it was worth and you may move twice. We've had a number of B&B dreams crushed when the buyers couldn't sell their house during the time they needed to. Why let the past control your future?! If you're thinking about relocating to an unfamiliar area, you should consider renting in that area for a year so that you experience a full cycle of your dream spot — not just a 1 week vacation."

"An IRS Audit Technique Guide (Market Segment Specialization Program — MSSAP) is available for this type of business. It is an excellent source of information and is available at `bookstore.gpo.gov` (search under IRS-IRS Audit Technique Guides)."

"Breakdown of B&B's: The following definitions attempt to codify what is presently being used in the field. They are only approximations and will vary by region or individual innkeeper."

✔ "Bed and Breakfast Inn (B&B): Both a home for its owners and a lodging establishment usually operated at a higher level of professionalism than a home-stay. Some B&Bs have the word 'inn' as part of their name. A professional B&B meets all the appropriate tax, fire, building, zoning, and health requirements. Many B&Bs have been inspected by a state association or an inspection rating service such as AAA or the Mobil guides. The owners advertise and may legally post a sign. Breakfast is served to overnight guests and may be quite lavish. Many smaller B&Bs provide a part-time or seasonal occupation for their owners, who do most of the work, often with some help for housekeeping and other chores. Most larger B&Bs (eight rooms or more) require the full-time year-round attention of one or more owners. There is always a high degree of personal service to guests. Reservations may be made directly with the property or through a service. The inn may host events such as weddings or family reunions. Increasing numbers of inns also cater to the business traveler and have facilities to host small business meetings."

✓ "Country Inn: This kind of lodging property has all the characteristics of a B&B inn, but serves an evening meal in addition to breakfast. Some country inns serve dinner to overnight guests only, and the cost of dinner and breakfast is generally included in the room rate (called the Modified American Plan). A country inn with a 'full-service restaurant' serves meals to the general public. Generally, the owner or owners are actively involved in daily operations of the inn, and often live on site. To be a country inn, a property does not have to be located in a rural area, though historically, restaurants were added so travelers in remote locations could enjoy a good evening meal. Most country inns have 10 or more rooms."

✓ "Bed and Breakfast Hotel: These are properties in which the historic structure, unique decorating components, guest amenities, and breakfast offering provide the atmosphere of a B&B. Many of these properties formerly were standard hotels, apartment buildings, or other commercial structures in urban or rural areas; some have been built specifically as bed and breakfast hotels. Most of these B&B hotels have fewer than 40 rooms.

"No matter the type of property, innkeepers seek to provide the following to B&B travelers:

✓ "A high level of service with a personal touch from the owner or owners

✓ "Generous hospitality and good value

✓ "Unique ambiance and surroundings

✓ "Architecturally interesting or historic structure

✓ "Individually decorated rooms that are clean and comfortable"

Source: Professional Association of Innkeepers International (PAII)

"Smaller B&Bs (less than eight rooms) are usually real-estate driven."

Finding additional information

The *Business Reference Guide* isn't the only game in town, but it's the most basic guide for showing prospective small-business owners the ropes of valuation. Among other popular paid transaction databases are Pratt's Stats, BIZCOMPS, and Mergerstat (www.bv marketdata.com). The first two look at smaller transactions among privately held companies; Mergerstat tends to look at transaction data in public companies.

When you're looking for information on companies and business communities, you can't stop at databases. Here are other resources you should put on your reading list:

✔ **Trade journals:** Trade journals and publications follow the fortunes of the particular industry in which you either own a company or are thinking about buying one. If you've operated a company for years, maybe you already do a pretty good job of keeping up with industry news, but if you're looking to sell, it's best to do a lot of reading to keep on top of recent news on the state of the business and on the selling prices that comparable businesses are attracting.

✔ **Local business publications:** See whether you can look up your target company in the local press, online, or in print. If you can't find it, see what stories exist in the local industry or neighborhood where you hope to operate a business. The same applies to stories about how local lenders are behaving (are they lending money or not?). Finally, it's always a good idea to look at local and national stories on the economy to see how your potential customers are spending — or not.

✔ **Business books and Web sites:** If you're a first-time business owner, you need to become a student of the business operations process. Wiley publishes two particularly good books on the subject: *Small Business For Dummies,* 3rd Edition, by Eric Tyson, MBA, and Jim Schell; and *Accounting For Dummies,* 4th Edition, by John A. Tracy, CPA (Wiley). Also, for a great general overview of the business process, check out the "Small Business Planner" page of the U.S. Small Business Administration's Web site (www.sba. gov/smallbusinessplanner).

Part III
If You're Selling a Business . . .

The 5th Wave   By Rich Tennant

@RICHTENNANT

"In the interest of a future stock issuance, I highly recommend you NOT use your family name as part of your corporate identity, Mr. Defunct."

In this part . . .

*V*aluation is all about perspective. Which side of the deal you're on influences how you view the valuation of a company: yours or someone else's. In this part, we talk about your company. We focus on the sell side of a transaction, and our main advice can be summed up in one word: planning.

Think about it. Sellers don't want to be rushed into a transaction if they can help it. Even if sudden opportunities arise to sell — opportunities that are always welcome — the idea is always to be prepared, because preparation means you're likely to get an optimal price.

We also talk about how valuation research should be part of the seller's overall estate and succession planning for the firm, starting years (sometimes decades) before the sale of the company.

Chapter 10

Making Sure You're Ready to Sell

*T*iming is everything when it comes to a purchase or a sale of a company. This fact is especially true for sellers. The best possibilities for a higher valuation on the sale of a company come from planning in advance.

In reality, relatively few people have an exit plan in place for a company that they've either bought or worked hard to start years before. But exit planning is essential. You should do this planning three to five years in advance, and valuation is an important step in that process. Unless you know the value of your company inside and out — or the steps it will take to improve that value — you'll have a tough job making a convincing sale.

Preparation is the stuff of business opportunity. It means finding out everything possible about a business's operations and the specific markets you're interested in so you can grab opportunities when they happen. It means laying in the financial foundation — cash savings, liquid investments, or attractive financing — to afford those opportunities at the moment they happen.

Finally, it means conferring with particular experts who are familiar with your business plans, your finances, and your personal financial goals to make sure the opportunities you go after are absolutely the best fit for you. This chapter gives you the information you need to move in that direction.

Understanding Why Timing Is Important

Anita Roddick, the late founder of the cosmetics chain The Body Shop, viewed business opportunity this way: "I am aware that success is more than a good idea. It is timing, too."

Timing doesn't come only from luck or smarts, although they're both factors. Timing derives from an intimate knowledge of how a business works and of how to harness its repetitive patterns for the best effect.

Furthermore, you must look at the overall economy and the economy of the specific industry you're considering. You have to look at the quality of competing products in the marketplace. Then you must decide whether your particular place in the business cycle is best for staying in or selling.

Most owners wait too long to sell. Why? Poor planning and emotion, mostly. People without a game plan can't take advantage of opportunities when they happen because they're not emotionally ready to do so — and perhaps their families aren't ready, either.

Examining the Motivations behind a Potential Business Sale

Even in tough economic times, people believe that the sale of a successful business is a surefire ticket to retirement wealth or possibly a stake for a new venture. But particularly in the case of small businesses, owners sometimes forget that their businesses must overcome obstacles that many larger firms don't have on the way to a sale:

✔ A small business may be enormously profitable and very successful, but the owners have never bothered to create a financial reporting structure that woos potential buyers.

✔ Because private companies aren't required to make financials public as a public company does, benchmarking the values of a private company is tough without the aid of a database or a valuation professional.

✔ Potential sellers often don't consider due diligence on the attractiveness of their business in the current market before they try to sell.

✔ Emotional factors enter the picture. Founders may be reluctant to sell, and kids may have their own issues with the business that delay prudent actions at the right time.

Understanding buyers and what they want

You can't really develop a negotiating strategy for your business unless you really understand what kinds of buyers may be circling your company and for what reasons. Here are three primary kinds of buyers:

✔ **Financial buyers:** These buyers act a bit like investors in the stock market. They want to come in and spot value, and they'll spruce you up a little and sell. They like to see profitability and stability — or signs that profitability and stability are right around the corner. They're not looking to buy your company to merge it with another similar operation in your industry. They're not operators per se. They may even work out a deal to keep you in charge if they like what you're doing.

✔ **Strategic buyers:** These folks are already in your business or want a business like yours to complement what they already have. They're the buy-and-hold types. A strategic buyer can be a conglomerate or a big company already in your field that wants your company as a way to enter a new market or to add your products to a mix that's already doing well for them. But the purchase isn't just about products; it can be about people too. Management — particularly newer management that looks like it's on the verge of a turnaround — can be an additional attraction for a strategic buyer. Perhaps you have talent good enough to run their entire company someday!

✔ **Special-purpose buyers:** These buyers are typically private citizens doing private deals. A special-purpose buyer may be a father or mother who purchases a business for a son or daughter, or it may be a serial entrepreneur who has just sold a business and is looking for a new challenge.

Obviously, you want to see someone who knows your company well. You want to hear surprising insights from buyers, not questions that reflect ignorance about what you've done during your entire career.

Good buyers have more than the financial might to do a deal — though sellers do need to verify that ability. Good buyers also understand the emotional complexities involved in such a transaction. They should understand how an owner feels about leaving the helm of a business she has built, how she'd have her employees treated after she's gone, and what numbers would make the most sense to her.

Solid buyers are professional, knowledgeable, and empathetic to the issues of their target.

The Alliance of Merger and Acquisition Advisors reported in 2008 that many business advisors believe that although seven out of ten mid-sized businesses will transfer ownership in the next decade, at least 90 percent aren't prepared to do so. Why? They haven't kept up with the recordkeeping and documentation that qualified buyers want, nor have they made their businesses particularly salable.

Most experts suggest that small to mid-sized companies create a three- to five-year game plan before a sale or other major ownership transition (which we detail later). For now, this section looks at the primary reasons owners consider a sale.

Anticipating the owner's retirement

For business owners, retirement is either a welcome event or something they don't even want to think about. But all things must pass, and owners really do need to think about what a chance to step down — on their own terms — can mean for them.

We talk throughout the book about retirement and estate planning, and valuation is a key part of such planning. It determines virtually every aspect of an owner's retirement, from the timing of his departure to the amount of money he'll have available to support himself and his family members after work.

When you plan the sale of a company, you have more data to go on than rule-of-thumb estimates such as the one you always hear (that any company of less than $20 million in revenues should go for three to five times annual net profits at the time of sale). Without a clear, early look at valuation and specific actions taken to improve your entire operation and the timing of your exit, you're really just guessing.

The kids are taking over!

Business survival gets tougher for each succeeding generation (you hear a lot more about this topic in Chapter 11). And even though passing on a business to the next generation isn't always a sale situation that you find in the open market, owners must think of it in the same context as a sale process.

Even if the family members who take over the business from the owner have been with the company for a while and know it intimately, the current owner should speak with the family about the process of pass-down well in advance, and valuation should be part of the picture. As part of the long-term succession plan, the owner should have a professional value the company to determine whether the business should make certain operational, financial, or management changes before the targeted transition date to the new generation.

Most of all, that process should be transparent. If family is already working within the company, it's tough to do a valuation process without having everyone know about it, anyway.

Weighing the possibility of a merger or acquisition from a friendly suitor

If the owner of a family business expects — with good reason — that her company will sell at a premium if she decides to put it on the block, that's still a good reason to do an independent valuation so that the business has completed all value-building exercises before talks begin.

As we mention, owners sometimes have trouble seeing all the pitfalls and sometimes the hidden benefits of the companies they've created. A dream buyer may be waiting in the wings, so it makes sense to plug that possibility into the planning process, which includes professional valuation.

Changing market conditions are threatening a company's future

A proper valuation exercise doesn't stop at present value. It gives you an idea of whether a company will be viable in the next two to three years. A valuation expert can at least identify particular trends — both positive and negative — that may affect a company's future.

Knowing that the sun is setting on an industry or a particular type of product may be sad news if you've devoted your life to it, but selling to a larger and more viable competitor while prices are fairly high can make such a tough decision worthwhile. It can also help you with price strategy ahead of time.

Bringing Valuation into the Picture before You Bring In the Buyers

The scenario of planning three to five years beforehand gives a business owner time for ample thought and preparation on how she wants to exit her business. She also gets time to understand the myriad details that go into a sale and that must be worked out with the help of proper advisors in the linked areas of legal, tax, wealth management, business strategy, and, of course, valuation.

A preliminary business valuation is essential in the early stages of preparation to sell a company. You must know what your business is presently worth before you can take well-advised steps to improve its value.

Providing a reality check

Knowing problems ahead of time enables you to make repairs to a company's systems and, therefore, increase its valuation. Here we list only some of the items and issues to address before a formal for-sale sign goes out in front of a business:

✔ **Show profits and a steady growth trend not over months but over years.** A business must be doing those financials professionally throughout that time, preferably through normalized financial statements as time goes on. Even if you've never had to borrow for your business, approach the preparation and presentation of these numbers as if you were applying for a loan. Be sure to create pro forma data that adjusts for unusual or nonrecurring events and clearly identifies them.

Are financial statements *normalized* or *adjusted?* Either term is fine because they mean the same thing: Normalized or adjusted financial statements have been adjusted to eliminate unusual items or anomalies and to enable clear comparisons. People use the terms interchangeably.

✔ **Be in the right place at the right time — that is, have the right products ready for the marketplace at the time customers want them.** Keep up with innovation, manufacturing, and distribution, particularly leading up to a possible sale date. The better your company looks, the better the value of your company looks.

✔ **Forecast how the economy — and your particular business cycle — will impact your business by a particular sale date.** The best time to sell a business (much as when selling a home) is in a healthy economy with interest rates at reasonable levels, in case your buyer needs to use financing to acquire your company. Make sure you can predict these factors with some degree of certainty, either alone or with expert help.

✔ **Consider personal goals.** Your personal goals are a huge factor. Everything from retiring to starting a family may be grounds for selling a company. Getting your personal wealth planning in order before you do your business plan makes a great deal of sense.

One early conversation in a negotiation is about the make-or-break aspects of the potential deal. Some prospective buyers ask whether the potential sellers care more about the down payment or the purchase price, for example. Because few buyers can do all-cash deals, the seller's answer helps give shape to a potential offer in terms of cash, debt, and other considerations. Be ready with an answer in case a prospective buyer asks you this question.

Transparency: Preparing for a sale

Transparency, in a business sense, is a policy of sharing both good and bad news with fellow owners and shareholders, suppliers, customers, and potential buyers. It derives from the traditional definition of the word: to see through something. In recent years, it's gotten a lot of usage because of companies that tried to hide problems in their balance sheets, in their facilities, and in their direct dealings with shareholders and customers.

Do you want to attract the best buyers and business partners out there? Do you want to have an efficient deal process from overture to closing? If so, transparency is your first goal. It comes before valuation, and it certainly must come before negotiation.

The road to transparency involves carrying out the following tasks:

- ✔ **Auditing your financials on an annual basis:** Audited financials by a Certified Public Accountant willing to sign her name to her work is crucial if you're expecting to borrow money, seek investors, or in all but the smallest-company situations, secure a buyer. People want to know that numbers are for real before they'll sign a check, and they'll want to see several years' worth of audited figures, not just one year's figures.

  If your company has been somewhat informal in its accounting methods — even if you or your designated chief financial officer have been handling your tax issues for years with no problems — it's time to start pricing the services of reputable CPAs to audit those numbers. Because accountants typically price their services on an hourly basis and those rates are priced locally, plan for a significant bump in your professional services bills.

- ✔ **Streamlining your data systems:** Any number of well-run and asset-rich companies issue handwritten paper invoices and keep critical data on Post-it notes, but if you're looking to make a deal, 20th-century record-keeping has to go. Due diligence (see Chapters 12 and 16) involves plenty of questions and demands from potential suitors that require you — or their representatives — to chase data in your file cabinets, computers, and stockrooms. If particular industry standards require you to upgrade your computer systems or at least straighten out your "intuitive" filing systems into something an outsider can understand, that's part of your prep work before valuation can begin.

✔ **Adopting a warts-and-all disclosure policy:** Got dirty laundry? Problem customers? A division with results that you absolutely know are going to stink in the next three to six months? If you're opening your doors to potential buyers or partners, it's best to develop an organization-wide philosophy of how you'll handle and disclose bad news, not only to outsiders but also to each other. Bottom line: You need to get stuff out there first so it's not discovered during due diligence. The more bad news others discover before you disclose, the worse it may be for the final number on your deal.

Creating a disclosure culture is a very big challenge in a lot of private companies, particularly those with owners who rule with an iron fist. But if you're going to try to do a major transaction, you need candor in your financials, processes, and facilities for an important reason: Candor builds trust, and trust is necessary to making a successful deal.

Heading off problems to increase value

Clear up any problems within the business that make it less attractive to buyers. Whether such issues are related to customers, management, regulatory, financial, or legal, the time frame of three to five years represents a chance to clean up these problems.

Consider these steps to take to enhance your business's value:

✔ **Assemble a quality team of professionals to work with you throughout this process.** Not many owners have the experience to prepare a company for sale or shepherd it through the sale process. Working with financial planning or tax experts is a good first step in addressing your wealth-management goals, and it goes a long way toward defining the kind of transaction you end up doing. You can then work with the right valuation, legal, and business advisory specialists to determine your current business value and which tactics you can use to make your business more salable. We get to these strategies shortly.

✔ **Remember that price is secondary to the best deal.** A high offer for your company means little if buyers are mostly offering a promissory note rather than cash. A big part of why you're selling has to do with your ability to monetize your investment in the company. Make sure you can actually do that quickly instead of having to wait years for your money.

✔ **Understand that deals take time.** Deals are not done in a day. They may take a series of negotiations, and you have to allow a prospective buyer time to do proper due diligence. By the time you get serious about a particular buyer, it may take a whole year to get to closing.

✔ **Adjust that niche.** This point may sound obvious, but is your business as attractive as it could be? If you steer your company into a market niche that is destined to leave it less vulnerable to competitive attack, it's a salable point for the company.

✔ **Turn off the perk spigot.** To normalize financials, valuation experts eliminate items such as payments for company cars and other corporate perks. It may be a good idea to cut back on those nonessential expenses as you get closer to a sale. Even though they're legal, they cut into profitability, and that's what you want going into a sale: a highly profitable company.

✔ **Take a serious look at salaries.** You have to do a real balancing act: trimming above-market salary levels to match comparables at public companies without chasing away talent. Obviously, you're not going to slash salaries, but you may adjust benefits or salary levels that were once higher for incoming employees. Buyers will be basing their valuation on this information, so it's better to make the necessary salary adjustments while you have time on your side than to pay the price for failing to do so later.

✔ **Reconsider bonuses.** If you're paying any unnecessary bonuses, consider suspending them to make less of a drain on total profitability.

Employees aren't stupid. Any adjustments that you make to compensation issues will hit the grapevine sooner or later. Freshen up the company before a sale with tact and intelligence so you don't push good people out the door at all levels of your operation.

✔ **Start thinking through succession.** Any buyer may waltz into a company and replace top executives with new picks, but good people are assets, too; buyers may hesitate to throw out talented managers just because they predate the new owners. However, prospective buyers may have justifiable concern that if owners — the ones who really want to take their money and run — are shouldering too much responsibility, the new owners may be stuck with a leadership vacuum. You may want to start handing off key responsibilities to talented managers who can make the transition into a new ownership situation.

✔ **Consider staying liquid.** Buyers and sellers can always agree on this fact: Cash has measurable value that anyone can see. If the fixed assets of your business may not produce that much value for you in a purchase negotiation, consider getting rid of those assets before you sell, and possibly lease what you need if it makes good financial sense for the business.

✔ **Settle up.** Various loans made by the company to its key shareholders or by shareholders to the company happen all the time, but buyers like as few potential claims on their assets as possible. Consider urging everyone to pay off those loans.

✔ **Buy some paint.** If your physical plant or office facilities are looking tired, dirty, or otherwise unattractive to visitors or customers, come up with an inexpensive way to spruce them up. Yes, in another nod to real estate sales, buyers like surroundings that are not only neat and clean but also attractive to anyone planning to spend money with the company in question. First impressions are everything — in financials as well as in furniture and window treatments. Who knows? You may even improve your current business climate by making your company more attractive to your current clients and customers.

✔ **Increase the firepower on your board.** One of the benefits of being a private company is that you can pretty much run governance how you want. But in these times, and if you're looking at a sale or merger of the company, you have to be much more sensitive to how your governance actually works and appears to an outside buyer. Consider appointing some impressive outsiders to your board who not only have marquee value but also can bring genuine value to the board discussions.

Advisory boards are big at small, growing companies. An advisory board of noncompetitive individuals who are nonetheless smart about your business can also make your business look snappy to outsiders.

✔ **Always think about estate issues.** The centerpiece of all this discussion is the personal welfare of you and your family members. In speaking with your tax or wealth-management advisors, see whether you can employ strategies to limit your exposure to estate taxes on the federal and state level, particularly if your business will be split among heirs or possibly sold or liquidated after your death.

You may not have three to five years to get your ducks in a row. You may not even have a year or two before your personal objectives change, or the shape of your industry changes, or you have an offer waiting on your doorstep. That's why most experts tell you to do whatever it takes to get your company into an upward growth pattern. Hire better management if you need it, get those new financial controls and reporting systems in place, and get some solid advice on how much you should allocate for the costs of getting all these issues up to speed. In other words, be ready for anything — that's good business strategy in any climate.

As you spend more to grow your business, costs may outrun your revenues for a time. Thus, you need to plan growth carefully as part of your overall value strategy.

Estate tax turbulence is on the way

At the time this book was in production, considerable worry was circulating about how estate taxes will affect Americans — particularly business owners who plan to sell in the next few years.

Back in 2001, the Economic Growth and Tax Relief Reconciliation Act triggered a gradual increase in the dollar threshold of estates subject to the estate tax. In tax year 2008, estates valued at more than $2 million were set to be taxed as much as 45 percent, and in tax year 2009, the threshold was scheduled to rise to $3.5 million. In 2010, the tax was scheduled to be repealed for a year.

But in 2011, unless Congress acts in the meantime, the news gets bleak for business owners or anyone considered to be a high–net worth individual: The estate tax will be reset at up to 55 percent on estates at a significantly lower threshold: $1 million. That's a potentially big wallop for privately held companies, and businesses should seek guidance if they plan to sell in the next three to five years.

If you suspect that your estate or a relative's estate from which you may inherit may fall prey to the estate tax, enlist the help of experts right now — before you sell your company. Both personal and business assets may grow over time — sometimes considerably if your efforts are successful — and your estate may turn out to be larger than you think. Keep these issues in mind during those conversations:

✔ **Expected increases in assets:** A grantor-retained annuity trust, or GRAT, is an irrevocable trust that is popular among families with assets that are expected to increase, because such appreciation can be passed on to heirs with minimal tax consequences.

✔ **A gifting strategy:** Under current law, unlimited amounts can be left to a spouse and to charity, free of federal estate tax. Other heirs can receive a total of $2 million, tax free, based on deaths that occurred in 2008. If your assets are over the estate tax limit, it may make sense to devise a gifting strategy that spends down your total taxable estate while still allowing you a comfortable lifestyle. For instance, you may consider making direct payments for someone else's medical bills or education tuition. No gift tax applies for these items, so payments can be unlimited.

Determining the Kind of Transaction You Want

Valuation isn't just about making the business look nice and making the financial statements readable. Valuation can help you sort through the best transactional options for your business when the time comes to let go. Those options include the following:

✔ An outright sale

✔ Employee stock ownership plan (ESOP)

✔ Transfer of ownership to family members

You find more on those options in the following sections.

Outright sale

A valuation professional can help you determine the best potential buyers for your business and identify the issues that will make your company most valuable. They can also acquaint you with optimal transaction data that you and your negotiators can work with.

Employee stock ownership plan (ESOP)

Valuation assistance is essential as a company develops an ESOP. Business owners use ESOPs to exit their company at fair market value while keeping ongoing management in place and providing a financial incentive to employees without paying capital gains tax. An ESOP is a popular exit strategy for many small to mid-size companies, but a valuation by an independent appraiser is one requirement for a transaction between an ESOP trust and an owner of the company that establishes the ESOP.

An ESOP is set up as a trust, and it can't pay more than fair market value for the company stock that it purchases from the selling shareholder (the owner of the company).

The ESOP fiduciary (a board of trustees, an administrative committee, or an institutional trustee) uses the independent appraisal to ensure that the ESOP trust does not pay more than fair market value for the company stock, as determined as of the date of the sale. The ESOP fiduciary must conduct the proper due diligence to make this determination in good faith.

Ownership transfer to key family members

Valuation is a particularly important issue when passing down a business directly to family members. Whereas your goal may be to get the highest possible valuation if you're selling to an outside party, you may be looking for the lowest defensible valuation if you're transferring the business to children or other family members.

Owners of family businesses tend to gift shares of the business to a son or daughter over time for particular tax advantages. Confer with a tax professional in preparation for this process.

Chapter 11

Deciding What to Do about the Family Company

In This Chapter

▶ Why parallel planning for the family and the business is crucial

▶ Facts about family-owned companies

▶ How families hurt their business's valuation without even knowing it

▶ Ways to constructively manage family conflicts

*F*amilies own or control 90 percent of U.S. businesses. According to the Family Business Forum at the University of North Carolina in Asheville, only 30 percent make it into the second generation, and only 12 percent survive into the third. Fourth generation? Only 3 percent. A family business that makes it past one generation is a success story. Past two generations, it practically becomes a headline. Past three, it's a dynasty.

If you want to see a valuation fight that's possibly uglier than a divorce, just watch kids fighting over leadership of the family business or the money they think is coming to them. Family companies that last require plenty of planning, preparation, and open communication between family members and their advisors. When businesses pass from one generation to the next, they must plan for many contingencies. For example, in a family with several siblings, brothers and sisters working in the family business may feel they have a greater right to the company's control and assets than the siblings who haven't. These types of valuation squabbles are common in families that haven't planned.

This chapter details which specific actions to take to plan for transitions in the family business and the specific valuation situations that arise. This chapter also focuses on valuing a business from the perspective of both a working and a nonworking sibling.

Planning for the Worst Possible Scenario

Suppose you've built an incredibly successful business. You have three kids — one's 16 and already working at the company after school. She's already said she wants to come back and run it after college, although you can't really hold her to it — she's a kid, after all. The other two kids are still in junior high.

Today your business has nothing but promise, and you look forward to the day you'll be able to use this wealth to fund your kids' education, secure your retirement, and then pass the business on to your kids so they can take it even higher.

The next weekend, you and your spouse are killed in a car accident.

So what does this story have to do with business value? Isn't it mainly a personal finance matter? That all depends on what you'd want to happen in your business if something this horrible were to happen. Ask yourself these questions:

✔ Does your company have a management succession plan that designates leadership within the company to take over if you and your spouse were to vanish tomorrow? Would their talents be enough to keep the company going and help fund your kids' education, and would those leaders be fine with allowing your kids into the business full time if they chose? Is this plan in writing?

✔ Does the business have a contingency plan for a sale of the company if current management didn't want to stick with it and your oldest child were nowhere close to making a decision about her future? Does the sale plan outline an orderly plan so the company you created doesn't go at fire-sale prices?

✔ Do you have both personal and financial guardianship in place for your kids? Seeing that your kids may stand to inherit sizable assets from either inside or outside the business, it may be wise to separate that guardianship by bringing in a trusted investment advisor and estate attorney to confer on such matters.

Obviously, planning ahead is best, especially where family is concerned. But what if you don't have time, or your kids are already grown and you don't have a plan in place? You can still watch out for certain things, and you can take steps to fix your situation. Keep reading.

According to the Family Business Institute, about a third of family businesses have a chief executive who's older than 60, with an average age of 54. Eleven percent are older than 71 years old.

Examining the State of the Family Business

For many small to mid-size companies, the biggest potential complication in the valuation process is family. Why? Because families always bring added baggage to the business process. Favoritism runs rampant in commerce because it's supposed to be survival of the fittest. But the family business? The fairness doctrine applied to the family dinner table doesn't always translate to the boardroom.

The business news pages — and sometimes front pages — love stories about family squabbles over money and power. Just ask the Murdochs, Redstones, and Bancrofts — recent high-profile examples of families involved in huge businesses that couldn't agree on the future of their legacy.

Are we saying that family companies have a tougher time realizing the full value of their business? Not at all. But we do believe that founders who don't have a long-term plan to work with their families on the future leadership and valuation strategies of their companies risk devaluation at the time of their death or retirement. In this section, we discuss some special issues concerning family businesses.

Specific characteristics of family companies

A 2007 study by wealth-management firm Laird Norton Tyee indicates not only how important family-owned companies are but also why their longevity can erode over time:

- ✔ More than 80 percent of the firms polled had between 20 and 499 workers, with sales ranging from $5 million to $30 million.

- ✔ Though family-owned businesses generate 64 percent of the nation's gross domestic product, nearly 60 percent of majority-share owners in family businesses are 55 or older, and 30 percent are 65 or older; however, less than 30 percent have succession plans and less than 40 percent have a successor lined up.

- ✔ Family finances are too tied to business success — 93 percent of respondents have little or no income diversification, deriving the majority of the family's income and security from the business.

- Two-thirds of family businesses don't require family members to have the qualifications or related experience necessary to be successful when entering the business. Twenty-five percent think the next generation is not competent enough to take the reins.

- Nearly half of American family businesses are operating without a written strategic plan.

- In most family-owned firms — 75 percent — strategic decisions are guided by a board of directors, an advisory board, or both. More than 54 percent of these boards consist of family members only; however, over 43 percent of the firms polled have boards with a mix of family and nonfamily members alike. Of the firms that use boards, 77 percent agree or strongly agree that they make positive contributions to the direction of the business. The remaining 25 percent of firms say they don't have a board of any kind.

What does all this mean in the context of business valuation? That many companies may not be worth as much as the owners think, simply because their companies don't follow best practices for their industry, nor are their finances or business strategy in the best of shape.

How families hurt the value of their businesses

The worst problem that family businesses have is the failure to plan for succession. Nonfamily businesses generally see plenty of woe when they haven't addressed succession. Yet in the family context, this practice gets put off mainly due to the possibility of hurt feelings among various family members in the business or an unwillingness for the current generation to step aside.

Yet the succession issue is usually linked to other critical problems that threaten the value and future of the firm:

- **No succession planning? Probably no real wealth planning, either.** Most smart financial advisors who work with independent businesspeople say that entrepreneurs should do parallel planning that addresses the needs of the family and the business at the same time. Parallel planning is based on the idea that the family comes first — which makes sense — and that those wealth priorities should largely drive business strategy.

- **Strong owners can be weak at leadership development.** Family businesses with a strong, hands-on owner may not hire the best midlevel talent because the owner is focused solely on having a particular family member take over someday. Perhaps there's been an anointed heir apparent, but what if something happens to that person or her priorities change? Sometimes a little creative tension between family members and nonfamily members in a business can be good for the overall performance of a company. Nevertheless, some owners of family businesses don't want to see outsiders jockeying for position.

✓ **No strict rules govern family members coming into the business — or back into the business.** Many owners are fine with having their kids and other family members work for other companies for a few years before they launch a career with the family business. Giving kids a choice — and a chance to succeed or fail somewhere else — is usually a good idea. But what if one of the kids chucks his job at age 40 and tells the CEO — who may be his mother, father, brother, or sister — that he wants to come back? What does that mean for the power or wealth distribution structure of the business going forward? Many families don't consider how family members moving in and out of the family business may affect the operations of its business or its wealth structure.

✓ **The next generation isn't trained to play nicely.** Just because you're related by blood doesn't mean you're natural collaborators. As with all workers in a business, family members must establish professional chemistry to get the job done. If a cousin and a son of the founder have never seen eye to eye because of some fight they had when they were teens, that shouldn't seep into the culture of the business — but often it does.

✓ **Families can be resistant to change, and so can their companies.** A big reason people start businesses is so they can do things their way. Unfortunately, that my-way-or-the-highway attitude can metastasize into "that's the way we've always done it" as founders and their children age in the business. Innovation and new product development — elements that are the primary drivers of value within any company — can face larger obstacles in family businesses when this is the case.

✓ **No formal compensation structure exists.** Asking Mom and Dad for money is a dynamic that starts early in most kids' memories. Without a formal compensation review structure, next-generation family members may feel they're going hat in hand to their folks for money, not demanding their proper compensation for the work they're doing, when asking for a raise or pay equal to one's peers in the industry at competing businesses.

Family businesses that don't review compensation on a regular basis may find that they're underpaying or overpaying family members and other employees, which is their right on an ongoing basis, but it's something that may lower a potential sale price when valuation is done later.

Add general family conflicts inside and outside the business: Maybe someone's getting divorced in the family and both spouses work in the business; the owner retires but can't stop meddling; long-term sibling rivalries reignite; the ugly secret of unequal pay surfaces; or siblings may decide to start fighting like 8-year-olds again. Can all family conflict inside and outside the business be diffused with proper planning? Certainly not. But planning involves worst-case scenarios that families may not be aware of, and considering them is important.

Facts about family-owned companies

The following statistics were collected by the Boston-based Family Firm Institute:

✔ The leadership of 39 percent of family-owned businesses changed hands by the end of 2008.

✔ Thirty-four percent of family firms expected the next CEO to be a woman; 52 percent of participants hired at least one female family member full time, and 10 percent employed two female family members of the same status.

✔ Of CEOs age 61 or older and due to retire in 2008, 55 percent had not yet chosen their replacement.

Family wealth and business: Are they inseparable?

Many owners of family businesses haven't planned for a smooth transition to the next generation. In a 2003 Raymond Institute/MassMutual survey, less than a fifth of family business participants said they hadn't completed any estate planning other than writing a will, and less than two-fifths had written a strategic plan for their companies.

Our point is this: You should work with family members from the time they're young to gauge their interest and involvement in the business, because doing so will be crucial to valuation later. Enthusiastic and talented employees who just happen to be family tend to be much more dedicated to growing the company than family members who use the business as a fallback employer.

Family members who know where they stand as participants or nonparticipants in the family business are likelier to pull together and do what's best for the business as transitions occur.

Separating family issues from business issues

Ask any loving parents who their favorite child is, and they'll likely answer, "I love them equally." And in most cases, it won't be simple diplomacy. They *do* love them equally, and they want them to inherit equal wealth.

In most families with nonbusiness assets, that kind of equal separation works as long as a proper will and supporting documents make that split clear. But when you have a family company in which all or some of the kids are employed, the story can be much different. Some parents may attempt the equal-split approach, only to find out that the kids who went on to work for Mom and Dad don't necessarily believe that their siblings who struck off on their own careers are entitled to the amount they're getting.

Consider this example: Dad created and grew a business over three decades, and he died suddenly without an estate plan or succession plan to guide the company's operations or potential distribution of assets. (This scenario happens all the time — just don't let it happen to you.) He had five adult children, but only one worked in the business. When Dad died, that sibling stepped up to the plate to keep the ship afloat and, like Dad, began to grow the company. After the funeral, this working sibling followed up with her father's verbal wish to split the ownership of the company five ways. For a while, all was fine.

Yet within a year, the new CEO began to regret her father's lack of planning. Two of her siblings were busy with their own affairs and happy with her leadership, but one — an older brother — started to involve himself more directly in the business. He said he was helping his sister as his father would have done; she thought he was second-guessing her leadership style.

As for the fourth sibling, she recently went through a divorce and was struggling financially as a single parent. To straighten out her finances, she wanted her one-fifth share of the family business. No plan covered this situation. Would the other siblings have to buy her out? Would the company have to take on debt to pay her the share of the business she was entitled to?

As you can guess, this scenario isn't an optimal situation under which to value a business. Any situation that involves time pressure — particularly the unpleasant emotional pressure among family members — leaves no opportunity to spot and correct problems that could improve its valuation later. And when such problems are spotted, that's even greater cause for conflict between family members.

Increasingly, families are looking at new ways to train their children for family business employment and diffuse the battle over family wealth creation. We get to that later in the chapter.

Does your business look like this?

Ivan Landsberg, a Yale University expert in family business, coined the term *succession conspiracy* — how business owners, their spouses, their family members, and non-family co-workers either consciously or unconsciously make damaging decisions that foil the effective succession of the business to the next generation.

He described three general types of family business management structures back in the 1980s:

✔ **Controlling owner:** A single owner is involved in every aspect of the business and makes critical decisions. Typically little or no planning occurs for this owner's departure.

✔ **Sibling partnership:** Siblings may share leadership, or a lead sibling may be designated — or designated by default — to make most of the business's key decisions.

✔ **Cousin consortium:** This structure is common among some of the biggest family fortunes in the world. When the business has been passed on to the children of prior sibling owners, eventually several branches of the family share ownership, and coalitions may be formed to create blocks of stock that represent more voting power.

Aligning with any of these ownership structures doesn't mean your family company is necessarily sliding off the rails. But if you recognize yourself in any of these structures, ask yourself whether the following also applies:

✔ The owner has created a succession plan that not only sets benchmarks for who the next-generation leadership will be but also comes with full buy-in from all family members, young and old, with a stake in the business.

✔ The owner and top family officers have spoken with family members recently either separately or in a group about their feelings about the business and whether any conflicts or issues need to be worked out. Better yet, is there a formal meeting structure?

✔ The owner has helped craft — with experienced legal and tax professionals — a quality transition plan that allows her the money and freedom to work in the family business if she's asked or to comfortably start retirement or a new phase of her career.

Why "equal" in a family business isn't always fair

A partial or minority interest is a very important concept in business valuation. By their very nature, holders of minority positions in a company don't have any say in the management of a company as those with majority positions do, and they also face an uphill battle to acquire the additional shares necessary to buy a majority stake in a company.

This is why in the valuation process, a discount for lack of control (also called a *minority discount*) is assigned when this structure is used. It's much easier to sell 100 percent of a company than it is to share a minority owner-ship position. And do very many owners of small to mid-size companies want to deal with minority owners who may not want to sell? No. It's a pain.

The value you lose through the partial interest discount can be pretty sub-stantial. Valuation professionals say that between 25 percent and 75 percent of value can be erased in a sale situation.

That's why the equal split of shares among siblings and other family mem-bers is so fraught with danger. You need to single out people for perfor-mance, whether they're your family members or not. Also, with equal stakes, you may see the dynamic of the "cousin consortium" emerge — nonpartici-pating or less-senior family members may wrest control after combining their voting power based on their shares. (See the nearby sidebar "Does your busi-ness look like this?" for more on the cousin consortium and other manage-ment structures.)

The founder who splits the family business "equally" isn't doing her family many favors; she's simply creating the battlefield for a family war. If one family member wants control — or is already working in a position senior to the rest of his family members — he essentially would have to lobby the others either to purchase their stakes or to join with them as a voting bloc to award control, depending on the company's bylaws.

Getting Your Family Down to Business

Valuable companies do more than make money. They reflect a particular stability in terms of ownership and management consistency going forward. To accomplish this stability, leadership has to be established, contingencies have to be identified and planned for, and family conflict has to be dealt with in a businesslike way.

Does that mean that family can never argue? Of course not. Even when rela-tives are angry and yelling at each other, at least they're talking. What's important for a company's long-term valuation strategy is to set a firm man-agement structure at the company and determine a means of settling griev-ances that arise — including talking openly about such issues as fairness, multigenerational issues, and unmarried partners (more about those topics later).

Bad estate planning can happen in the wealthiest of families. It's not unheard of in the richest of families for the matriarchs and patriarchs to die or become incapacitated without proper wills or directives for their heirs. Every adult family member — young or old — should commit to creating such documents and, as appropriate, have them written in a way that doesn't shipwreck the family fortune or mission, no matter how big or small it is.

So your kids are in grammar school? Plan anyway

Considering how the transfer of assets will go in a family can never start early enough. Your objective is to preserve the value of the business and personal assets you've created, no matter how old you and your kids are. As we discuss in Chapter 10, the uncertainty over the estate tax exemption in the next few years means that the best idea is to discuss strategy now rather than later.

Most financial experts advise that you revise your estate plan every five years or as lifestyle issues change.

Remember, the estate and valuation issues with your business don't exist in a vacuum. To ensure that the value of your business will benefit your kids and future generations, you need to do some very prescient planning.

Following a phased-in approach

If you're reading this book, you may be part of a mature family business that needs valuation for a specific reason. But if you're forming or buying a business and you're looking for ways to bring value-aware family members into the business as they age, consider this phased-in approach to do that:

✔ **Understand from day one that it's all about choice.** You made your own choice to go into business. Your kids must make a choice to join the family business later. You have to be prepared for them to say no — or for you to say no if they're simply not right for it.

✔ **Talk about the family business as early as possible in your kids' lives.** Share stories about your company, its purpose, and its people, and explain both the good and the bad parts of working for yourself. Mostly, communicate your passion about it. Teaching kids positive values about work and the importance of having the freedom to choose a career you love is good, and that part can't start early enough.

✔ **If your kids are interested in the business, start the kids young and increase their job responsibility as they grow older.** See whether your children want to work in the family business to earn spending money while they're young (check with your tax advisor before you attempt this approach). Then let the kids decide whether they want to move into different roles as they get into their teens and through college. This way, you get to see as the child grows whether working for the family company is just about the money or about building a lifetime career. It's probably most effective management-development program you'll run.

✔ **Start putting together plans for a series of family meetings that discuss the business before your kids are out of college.** Between you and your advisors, come up with a plan that establishes how your children will own and control your business at the time of your death. Plan to hold your first official family meeting with all your kids (assuming that the youngest one is already involved in the family business in some way) to discuss the qualifications for ownership in your company after you die or hand over the reins. We get to some scenarios shortly.

✔ **When all or a few of your children are working full time in your business, make sure they're subject to the same types of salary and performance evaluations as your nonfamily employees.** The results of those reviews should also be factors in justifying their qualifications for various jobs within the company.

Based on the discussions you've had with your tax and estate advisors, make sure you have a system set up to meet annually or semiannually with your entire family to discuss the family business. Some call these *family business councils,* and their structure should expand over time with the size of the family and the members who are involved in the business.

If you want to know more about estate planning, we suggest that you read *Estate Planning For Dummies,* by N. Brian Caverly, Esq., and Jordan S. Simon (Wiley), for a broader view on the subject.

Setting your family meeting structure

Nothing is wrong with the living room for an annual family business meeting if you're talking about your immediate family, but consider these guidelines as your business evolves:

✔ Always have a formal agenda that all participating members contribute to in advance. As in any business meeting, you should be prepared with facts and exhibits, if necessary. Distribute this agenda before the meeting so everyone can review it.

✔ Designate a facilitator for the meeting — in small groups, the responsibility can move around (it's good training for the kids), but as the group gets larger, you may want to work with a professional facilitator or someone who can manage the event without a stake in it.

✔ Appoint someone to act as the meeting secretary to keep a running history of discussion in these meetings.

✔ Make it a priority to increase the growth and value of the company, and devote at least part of the meeting to report on how that's going.

✔ Set ground rules about anger and conflict. In family businesses, emotions run high, and unchecked emotion in family meetings can derail other critical business.

✔ As more family members join the business, consider neutral territory if doing so makes the crowd more comfortable and facilitates discussion.

Addressing the fairness question head-on

Nobody knows how his or her kids are going to turn out or which one will end up being the business genius who will take the family company to a whole new level. Here are your options:

- ✔ Assuming that one of your kids turns out to be the genius and the rest are merely good water carriers, the best solution may be to name her the heir apparent early and develop a plan to give proportional amounts of nonbusiness assets to the other children at the time of the transition of leadership or at your death. If you don't have the full amount of those assets in place now, you'll probably require an investment strategy to build them — and that should also be part of the planning.

- ✔ Another option is to give the child or children working in the business the opportunity to buy out their parents' share, which would give the parents money to live on in their retirement.

- ✔ A third possibility is for the dominant child in the business to arrange a plan in concert with the parents to buy out the other siblings before or after the deaths of the parents. Again, this is a critical issue to be discussed among family members and trusted financial advisors, but one option to pay off the other siblings may involve buying a life insurance policy for one or both of the parents that would secure the payment amounts to the other siblings.

Setting up the best plan for the generations

In families with significant assets or other pressing financial issues that involve businesses or dependents, each generation's wishes for the dispersal of shared or personal assets should be documented legally and shared with all the relevant parties.

In many cases, the main topic of discussion is the multigenerational family business, perhaps one of the most complex estate issues any family will face. In others, the assets may consist mainly of cash, property, and other investments, but similar problems can occur when not all parties are on the same page about who will get what.

In the following sections, we cover some of the issues related to generational concerns and address what needs to be done to keep the family business afloat.

Preventing problems

Estate planning isn't just about splitting up money — it's also about disaster planning. If a family hasn't planned for business succession, other damaging secrets may emerge, such as problems in the business or significant debt the family may be liable for.

Also, the sudden death or lengthy incapacitation of the head of a family may turn chaotic without proper healthcare or financial directives to manage the person's illness or the money and business issues that follow.

Multigenerational estate planning may not be the easiest task in the world to accomplish, given how families communicate — or don't communicate — about money. But such dialogue may be the smartest action any family takes together.

Supporting the family legacy

Proper discussion, documentation, and review of a family's assets — with the participation of the right legal, tax, and financial planning advisors — can keep more of those assets in the family and working to the family's wishes. In the case of a family business, generations of family members have built careers there or may otherwise be depending on that income to live.

Yet a business may not even be at the heart of an issue. Families may also have foundations or other charitable activities that they've supported for years with a certain mission that the people in charge don't want changed. More than a few families have imploded in ugly legal squabbles over these situations and more. The results can be lengthy legal battles with damaging tax consequences, a potentially unfair split of assets among relatives, or simple mismanagement of those assets going forward.

Considering unmarried partners

Not everyone gets married before starting a family. Multigenerational planning should also address estate and child custody arrangements for unmarried heterosexual or gay couples who may or may not have done the appropriate legal planning necessary to secure the estates of their current or past partners and their heirs.

At the very least, all family members should understand the need for such planning to avoid conflict later. As nontraditional families become more common, families need to be open to that discussion to protect family and business assets from disputes later.

Chapter 12

Due Diligence on the Sell Side

*V*aluation is an important part of the reality check every seller should make. Think about it — examining your own company without bias is tough. That's why you need professionals to focus on that. The bottom line is that a potential seller absolutely must conduct thoughtful due diligence months — and preferably years — before the business goes on the market.

Due diligence means investigating your company with the cold eye you'd bring to any target. For anyone doing the job, it involves reading everything, asking plenty of questions inside and outside an organization, and generally leaving no stone unturned in finding out what makes a company tick and how much it's truly worth. It involves not only basic research and calculations but also the ability to forecast how a company will do years from now.

This chapter focuses on the soft and hard skills necessary to value businesses successfully before you sell.

Looking at Why a Seller Has to Do Due Diligence

Due diligence is a process in which you ask for and obtain as much timely and accurate information about an organization as you can get so you can thoroughly evaluate a transaction. When people say to "do your due diligence" about something, they're essentially telling you to do your homework before you make a decision.

In the context of business valuation, today's concept of due diligence originated during the Great Depression. The Securities Act of 1933 handed broker/dealers (people licensed to sell investments) the due diligence defense. The act essentially allowed these professionals some protection against lawsuits from investors accusing them of inadequate disclosure of information before they purchased securities. As long as brokers conducted due diligence on the investments they sold and could prove it, they'd be allowed such protection in court.

If you're selling a business, consider these primary reasons for doing due diligence with an independent valuation professional:

- ✓ **You don't want to lose out on a potential transaction.** Whether your company is planning to sell soon or at a date relatively far in the future, a thorough look at the value of your firm's assets is a starting point for a sales strategy. The process gives you the following:

  - The current value of all your company's assets, both tangible and intangible

  - An unbiased view of how well you're prepared for retirement or to pass the business on to heirs

  - A value profile that you can compare to those of similar companies in the field and plug into the profiles of potential acquirers

- ✓ **You can't produce valuation information yourself.** Although you may be well tuned into the tangible and intangible information that helps you run a business, you may not know where to look for the information that helps you do a full valuation. After a valuation by an independent professional, you'll have a better idea of how to track and store information that's key to a future valuation process from a potential buyer.

- ✓ **You need to look at your company as if you were a potential buyer.** Having a trained professional do the valuation is wise because you need someone with the skills to look at a business both impartially and critically. Even the most hard-bitten member of your management team can't accomplish this process, because it's hard to value what one creates.

- ✓ **You want to get the best advice that fits your industry.** Valuation has a way of bringing a selling company up to speed on both its strengths and weaknesses. Part of the valuation process involves gathering benchmark data that reflects the best practices in its industry — practices to emulate before a sale takes place so that the value of the company will go up, not down. After the valuation, you can clean up any problems within the business that make it less attractive to buyers (see Chapter 10 for some ways to give your company a makeover).

When valuation professionals evaluate a company, they look at plenty of information, but they don't bury their instincts. Obviously, this book is about the process and fact-gathering procedures of valuation, but due diligence is very much about what goes on with your eyes, with your ears, and inside your head through the simple act of observation.

Understanding the Three Stages of Due Diligence

We can't overemphasize the importance of people skills in valuation. So much of what valuation professionals do to build access to an organization involves building comfort and trust with the people inside. No matter what the valuation is, the process generally involves three steps, in which those people skills definitely come in handy:

1. **The meet and greet.**

   After companies have their initial discussion about a possible deal, the first stage of the process is generally an onsite meeting in which the valuation professional tours the facilities — sometimes with the client, sometimes without — and meets management and the key officers she'll be speaking with throughout the due diligence process. The purpose here is to figure out where all the key data is and which company officials will and won't be able to talk about the business.

2. **The hunting and gathering.**

   Otherwise known as the *data dump*, this stage is when company reports, financials, and other data are collected and then subjected to questioning and calculation under appropriate methods of valuation.

3. **The once-over.**

   This step involves the final fact-checking and review of any events that have taken place since valuation was done.

Beyond these basics are details that come up as a result of the type of business and people involved. For that reason, we can't devote much coverage to each of the steps, because each case is different. Just assume that you need to tailor each step to fit your particular circumstances and that you need to pay attention to any details that arise. The rest of this book can certainly help you get a handle on what to watch for.

Tricks of the Trade: Collecting and Exchanging Information

One important part of your informational game plan is setting up your rules of thumb, which we discuss at length in Chapter 9. Rules of thumb provide a good start for researching the types of other businesses that are for sale in your class. However, no company should begin and end the valuation process at rules of thumb. Without a clear look at your business, you're really just guessing.

When you plan the sale of a company, you have more data to go on — much of which you share with the potential buyer. In the following sections, we discuss confidentiality agreements and the kinds of company data you'll exchange.

Gathering your own company data

This section provides a very basic list of documents and data that companies typically exchange in the due diligence process. Most of this information comes from the company that's up for sale, but depending on the type of proposed transaction and the parties involved, some of this data may originate on both sides of the table.

In any case, if you're contracting a valuation before a sale process begins, knowing what material will change hands is a good idea. Here's the list:

✔ A summary of what's for sale, right down to the cash registers on the floor

✔ A summary of what's not for sale

✔ A history of the target company

✔ The balance sheet — or a reasonable summary — of assets and liabilities for the last three to five years (both annual and quarterly reports)

✔ The income statement — or a reasonable summary — of the company's profit-and-loss history for the last three to five years (both annual and quarterly reports)

Why use the term *reasonable summary?* Wouldn't this be automatic? Well, private companies don't have to act like public companies. Some target businesses have, shall we say, a rather informal approach to bookkeeping. If a business is looking for a buyer, a banker, or possibly public ownership someday, it should take a more formal approach to this data.

- The company's own five-year financial forecast (if it exists)

- Market share/demographic information (if it exists)

- Lists of competitors and the status of their products

- The company's ownership structure, with shareholder percentages (to explain who owns what and what voting rights they have)

- Bios of the company's directors and executives

- Tax returns for the last three to five years and information on who did them — and a record of the last year the company was audited

- A summary of all open and settled litigation for the last five to ten years

- Complete monthly payroll data, including the number of employees, their function, and their average hourly rate

- A summary of physical inventory for the past three years

- All executive and employee pension data, including information on whether various plans are fully or partially funded

- Organizational charts/résumés of top employees

- A discussion of international business (if any)

- A listing of all suppliers, domestic and international

- All customer data — invoices, payment records, order backlogs (if any)

- A listing of all sales and manufacturers representatives/commission schedules for the last three to five years

- Personnel contracts, as well as data on bonus programs, deferred compensation, stock options, and profit-sharing plans

- All data on employee insurance — health, life, disability, and so on

- All patents, copyrights, and license agreements

- A list of all legal, accounting, and consulting professionals working with the company

If you don't fully disclose your company's risk scenario to a potential buyer, it could lead to litigation down the line. Your advance due diligence efforts can pay off here. If you do a public-records data search, you can conceivably capture all the information you need on past lawsuits, liens, and even divorce and estate provisions that can delay or prevent transition of ownership. If your company's disclosure doesn't meet the results of your thorough research, buyers will see that as a red flag.

TIP

Databases to bookmark

Unless otherwise indicated, the following resources are free databases you can check in your pajamas at home, but you don't necessarily have to pay money to access the databases that aren't free — just start hanging out at the public library or, even better, visit your local college and university libraries, which generally offer access to paid databases that you can use for free. Start bookmarking these databases:

✔ **Library of Congress** (www.loc.gov): Literally the world's largest library, it's a free resource on virtually every subject out there.

✔ **LexisNexis** (www.lexisnexis.com): This is a paid service, and it can get quite pricey, so call your local library to see whether it has this one. LexisNexis has general news and publication databases that were the foundation of its business, but the company now has specialized databases for the legal, tax, corporate, and sales communities.

✔ **ChoicePoint** (www.choicepoint. com): This one is another paid service from LexisNexis, but it's a ready resource for bankruptcy and litigation records, tax liens, and commercial and incorporation filings in various states.

✔ **The Central Intelligence Agency** (www. cia.gov): Who would've thought the CIA would help the average information-hungry businessperson? No, this site won't tell you whether that strange guy down the street is really a spy (or something creepier), but it's the home of the World Factbook, which provides tons of information, including market data on virtually every country on the planet — right down to how many cellphones a nation has in use.

✔ **YouTube** (www.youtube.com): This ever-expanding video site has a surprising amount of business content. As companies large and small get more sophisticated about using video to reach people on various issues, you may find clips of annual meetings, analysts' briefings, and other specialized content. Just search for the person, company, or subject you're interested in and see what comes up.

✔ **U.S. Census/American Factfinder** (fact finder.census.gov): This database helps you gather key data on population, spending, education, and every other topic the U.S. Census covers.

✔ **ProQuest** (www.proquest.com): This is a leading database of academic, trade, and popular press publications; it's accessible mainly through colleges and universities.

Protecting your company with a confidentiality agreement

Maybe no sale is immediately in the offing, but before any financial transaction can happen, both buyer and seller have to know that sensitive information will be protected. That's universal for public and private companies — private companies may be notoriously secretive, but public companies also like to protect proprietary information from competitors and generally like to keep deal talks private until a deal is actually reached.

The due diligence process requires that both sides disclose lawsuits, debts, and other obligations that their companies face — and the most sensitive of all information: what people get paid. Thus, you typically need paperwork before due diligence can start.

Enter the confidentiality agreement. Such an agreement can be as general or as specific (mentioning exact data and documents you don't want disclosed) as you want, but above all, it should meet your specific needs and concerns for the deal at hand.

Having a template to work from is always helpful. Following is a plain-vanilla version of a confidentiality agreement signed between two parties. Attorneys or advisors may advise changes in wording and requirements, but here's the gist it should follow:

Confidentiality Agreement

By and between ABC and XYZ, nonprofit corporations incorporated in

_____ .

ABC and XYZ are engaged in merger negotiations. As this process proceeds, sensitive, confidential, and/or proprietary information may be exchanged by the parties. In order to protect the privacy and business interests of each of the parties, they agree to the following terms:

1. At the conclusion of negotiations, if a merger is not agreed to, all copies of all documents distributed to each party by the other party or its agents will be returned to the originating party.

2. Neither party will at any time during the period of merger negotiations or after merger negotiations are concluded make known to any third party any information or furnish any documents containing information pertaining to the other party.

3. In the event a merger is not agreed upon, neither party will make any use or take advantage of anything it has learned about the other party's organization, board, staff, clients, finances, legal dealings, or operations, nor will it use anything it has so learned to compete with the other party.

4. In the event a merger is not agreed upon, the parties will agree upon a joint statement to be issued to any third party requesting information about the merger negotiations. This statement will reflect positively upon both parties.

This agreement is entered into this _____ day of _____, _____.

_____   _____
Chairman of the Board, ABC   Chairman of the Board, XYZ

Chapter 13

Case Study: Valuation on the Sell Side

*M*ost valuation professionals get a call when a triggering event occurs in a business owner's life or the life of his or her family. Maybe the owner just died. Maybe the owner is just burned out or suddenly realizes for a host of reasons that it's time to retire. Maybe family members are squabbling about taking over the business. Maybe the owner is terminally ill. The designated family member calls with a familiar panic in her voice. "We don't know if anyone wants to keep running the business," she says, "and we can't afford to keep it open." And then comes the all-important question: "How much do you think we'll get?"

At this point, the best valuation professionals often have to deliver the worst news: that without a plan made while the owner was alive, family members may not see much benefit at all from selling the business. Worse, they may actually lose money preparing the business for sale or closure.

The decision to sell without analyzing the tax consequences, advantages, or disadvantages of potential deal structures or how a sale would fit your personal and financial goals can be catastrophic to you, your company, and your family. This "sign today, sell tomorrow" mentality is common, and most experienced valuation professionals see it as a decision-making process without a process. In this chapter, we provide some case studies and attempt to show you how to make sure that your decision to sell isn't met with bad news.

You can see another case study on valuation of a business in Chapter 18, dealing mainly with the investigative process buyers need to bring to bear to decipher the correct value of a company. This chapter deals with common examples that show how critical planning is to a high valuation for the company you'll sell someday.

Heading Off Common Valuation Disasters

Thinking about the sudden death of the patriarch or matriarch of the family is never pleasant. But this situation happens, and it exposes all sorts of planning deficits.

One business owner was hit by a bus and killed when he was on vacation. The family members rallied to keep the business afloat for a while. Then they made a collective decision to sell the business; they were ready to let it go. The problem was timing. The overall sale process can take anywhere from 6 to 24 months, maybe even longer. During this period, the family member who took the reins of the company began to suffer kidney failure — definitely a worst-case scenario.

This is why business founders need to link their estate, succession, and exit planning as part of a whole to make sure their families have a road map to take the business into the future. That road map should also include contingency plans for the next generation. We discuss such preventive measures in this section.

Writing down your wishes

People write wills that reveal their deepest thoughts about where they want their money to go. They also write detailed plans for everything from how they want the children to be reared to who should run the business if something happens to the owners. Such plans may not be legally binding, but as long as the family respects the business owner's written wishes, this document is a critical guidepost for protecting the value of a business.

Here's a sample letter:

> Date [*very* important]
>
> Dear Merriam, Jamie, and Bobby:
>
> Our family business has been a joy for me to build and run. I'm proud that it has provided for our family so well for the past 30 years. That said, the business was my passion. I don't expect it to be yours. You have your own dreams to pursue and your own lives to live. As a result, I have created the following plan to be used in the event that I die or become disabled. I hope that it will make the process of dealing with our family business easier.

Management:

Day-to-day executive management should be turned over to John W. Smith, the company's chief financial officer (CFO). He should assemble a management team made up of Roger Jones in operations and Bill Graham in sales. Management oversight should be provided by a board made up of Smith, Jones, and Marybeth Freeman.

Compensation:

John, Roger, and Bill are covered under the stay bonus plan that I put in place last year. Under this plan, they will continue to receive their regular salaries but also will receive a bonus equal to 100 percent of their base salaries if they stay with our company during the transition period and maintain the company's financial performance. Jane Mercer has the file on the stay bonus plan. Ken Farmer drafted the plan and can answer any questions.

Disposition of the Business:

I believe that the company should be sold upon my death or disability. Although John, Roger, and Bill are great managers, I'm not sure that they have the drive or the vision needed to continue to make the company a success. I have had preliminary conversations with Richard Ford at ABC Co., an investment banking firm, about the possibility of selling the company. In 1999, ABC thought that the business might be worth approximately $10 million. I have a great deal of confidence in Richard and his team. Please engage them to sell the company for you. They will handle everything, make the process easy for you, and do a great job. Their contact information is on the contact sheet attached.

Making sure that your records are adequate

Data has to be current any time you perform a valuation. Are the company books in shape so that three to five years' worth of financial statements can be provided easily? What about supporting schedules and data, such as equipment lists, depreciation schedules, and customer lists, or a file with all significant leases and contracts, accounts receivable and accounts payable aging, and related operational items? These documents are just a few examples of the host of documents that a valuation professional needs to do a thorough analysis, so a business owner really has to think about whether she's truly prepared to begin a valuation or sale process.

The right amount of time varies, but if an owner is thinking about selling the business, the exit planning and valuation process should start three to five years before he plans to exit the business. This time frame provides adequate time for the valuation professional to collect the data, analyze the owner's goals, and take her time throughout the process.

Taking time to plan

When a company puts its operations in order before a sale, it keeps surprises down to a minimum when the company goes on the market or if an unexpected offer emerges. It also keeps the current owner from going for the knee-jerk decision when an offer appears on the table.

Planning for a sale goes well beyond sprucing up the company's facilities and financials. It allows the entire management team to envision specific sale scenarios that are right for the company — and those that aren't. So why don't companies do more of this?

Much of the problem comes from the fact that planning for mortality or the sale of a company that's become a life's work is very hard for some people to talk about. Anticipating change is hard, but leaving fellow co-workers and family members unprepared risks a family legacy. Do everyone — including yourself — a huge favor, and get into the habit of planning.

Considering confidentiality

Many times, owners don't have anywhere to turn, so they don't complete the planning or decision-making process. Often, they don't start it until they've made a definitive decision to sell, effectively putting the cart before the horse.

Privately held businesses are sensitive to confidentiality. Some owners never want anyone else to know that they're thinking about selling. When they investigate the value of their companies, they're scared that competitors will get wind of the investigation and use it against them. They're concerned that current employees will get scared and start looking for new jobs or defecting to competitors. They're concerned about how suppliers will react. You need to consider all the parties involved before deciding whether to keep things confidential.

Setting Up Your Prevaluation Plan

Valuation isn't about waving a wand — or a paintbrush — at the time of sale and making a great result happen. It's about planning, sometimes years or decades in advance. We like to call this type of planning *prevaluation planning*.

If you think that you already have a prevaluation plan, check your preparation by answering a few critical questions:

✔ Have you met with an attorney or a financial planner to organize your personal finances? Have your spouse and other key family members who are involved in the business done the same?

✔ Do you have a will and necessary powers of attorney governing your health and finances?

✔ Do you know how much money you will need to retire?

✔ Do you know the wishes of your children and other family members regarding going into or continuing the business in case you decide to leave or something happens to you?

✔ If you were to die at 5 p.m. today, who would you want to fill your chair at 9 a.m. tomorrow?

✔ Do you have a retirement date in mind and know the kind of retirement you want to have?

✔ Do you know the current competitive landscape of your business, and do you have a plan to stay competitive for the short and long terms?

✔ Do you have qualified advisors to work with you on business, personal wealth, and tax issues, and do you communicate with those advisors on a regular basis?

✔ Do you have a plan in place to minimize the tax consequences of selling or passing on the business?

✔ Do you have three reasons in mind that would lead you to sell to or merge with another company?

✔ Are your current relationships with investors or lenders in good shape, and would they change if someone else within the company had to take over?

If the answer to any question was *no,* you don't have a thorough prevaluation plan. This result isn't a reason to panic, however; it's a reason to plan. The next subsections present a template that you can use to get started.

Finding the problems

Valuation professionals who are actively involved in prevaluation planning make sure that their clients take the time to articulate what they want to do. The summary of their responses may look something like Table 13-1, which is a report on business owner Robert's prevaluation planning. It identifies key personal and business problems that should drive the valuation planning process.

Table 13-1	Sample Prevaluation Plan
Personal goals	Robert wants to retire at age 59 and spend more time with his family. He also wants to get more involved in his church. He and his wife, Sallie, want to take at least one major cruise each year.
Personal situation analysis	Robert currently works 60 hours per week and has little time or energy left at the end of the week to enjoy his new grandchildren. He has always traveled for business and never had the time to enjoy the places he's visited.
Business goals	Robert wants to sell his company within the next few years but only if he can net enough to retire comfortably. His children aren't interested in running the business.
Business situation analysis	Robert's company currently isn't positioned to be an attractive sale candidate. Additional work needs to be done to improve its value and salability.
Financial goals	Robert believes that he needs approximately $200,000 per year after taxes to support his existing lifestyle and to retire comfortably.
Financial situation analysis	Robert hasn't done any comprehensive financial planning. As a result, he doesn't have a good idea of whether $200,000 after taxes is actually sufficient. In addition, Robert doesn't know how much he would need to net from the sale of his business to generate the annual cash flow that he needs.
Estate goals	Robert doesn't believe in leaving children a large legacy of inherited wealth. He wants to leave his children a small financial legacy and leave his grandchildren enough money to pay for their college and graduate-school educations.
Estate analysis	Robert and Sallie have done no formal estate planning other than drafting simple wills and trusts about five years ago. They have done no sophisticated planning to minimize capital gains or estate taxes.

This example reveals a lack of overall financial planning and the need to focus on two key issues:

✔ Robert doesn't know whether $200,000 a year is sufficient to provide his yearly cash-flow needs in retirement.

✔ He doesn't know how much he would net if he were to sell the business to fund a $200,000-a-year lifestyle.

The sale of the company won't fix these two problems automatically, because for now, no one knows the value of the company or what his financial needs will really be.

Are you starting to get a chicken-and-egg feeling? That feeling comes from the realization that business planning and personal finance planning really do have to be linked. Chapter 20 gives you considerably more detail on the estate planning and gifting strategies you need to consider and on the expert help you should enlist.

Analyzing the prevaluation

Prevaluation helps you find out whether a sale is a reasonable option to explore. But keep in mind that various goals change the prevaluation process. Prevaluation planning is different for each of the following objectives:

✔ Creating an estate/gifting plan for heirs

✔ Preparing for an outright sale of the company with no need for succession

✔ Creating an employee stock ownership plan (ESOP; for more information, read Chapter 24)

We can promise that if you do a valuation for each of these objectives, the conclusion is going to be different in all three cases.

In Robert's case (see the preceding section), if he finds that he can't net from the sale of the business enough to fund his retirement adequately, his timeline for selling the business gets a lot longer. He needs to improve the value of the company to sell at an optimal price.

Robert's self-analysis also uncovers conflicting goals — always a valuable discovery before any actual transaction process starts and mistakes are made. If he needs to maximize the sale price of the company to reach his retirement goals, for example, there go any plans for the kids to get the company. Younger family members typically don't have the kind of money that would solve the entrepreneur's financial problem. Ergo, the kids can't buy the company because they can't afford it, and poor Robert can't give the company to them because he needs that money to retire.

See why this planning should begin more than five years in advance?

Performing the Valuation

In Chapter 4, this book gives you an idea of the three approaches to valuation and the various methodologies used for each approach. So although performing the math for various methodologies may be nice as an academic exercise, the math is what it is.

Now's the time to manage subjectivity. Owners need to find a way to let unbiased, skilled people weigh in on their plan. They need to bring in experts to tell a well-researched, straight story that can guide their actions. A valuation professional can provide that third-party objective analysis, and the business owner needs to come to grips with this analysis before putting the company up for sale. This section runs through the valuation process using Robert as a case study.

Taking valuation from fantasy to reality

Consider Robert from Table 13-1, earlier in the chapter. If he thinks that his business is worth $10 million and the net from a $10 million sale will fund his retirement adequately, everything is peachy. But what if Robert puts his company up for sale, and the highest offer is only $7 million? The net from a $7 million sale may still get the job done — or not.

When a business owner goes through the valuation process for a sale, he needs to be prepared for a realistic range of values and make every effort to put himself in the buyer's shoes.

Tables 13-2 through 13-5 contain worksheet ideas that can help an owner evaluate various factors in detail: intangibles (see Chapter 5 for more detail), operating expenses, investments, and other financial details.

Table 13-2	Intangibles
Value Factor	*Objective Score (1 = Poor, 5 = Excellent)*
Well-defined mission and vision statement	
Owner's particular product/services knowledge	
Management's knowledge, experience, and depth	
Motivated and dependable workforce	

Value Factor	Objective Score (1 = Poor, 5 = Excellent)
Key employees bound by noncompete agreements	
Organizational structure promotes efficiency	
Management succession plan in place	
Active outside board of directors	
Long history, reputation, and name recognition	
Management focus on growth and value creation	
Industry regulations affect company profits	
Business plan is continually monitored and updated	
Owner's personal relationships (with customers, for example)	
Loyal customers	
Few competitors	
Special barriers to competition	
Strong supplier relations	
Located in a growing geographical market	
Part of a growing industry	
Reputable company advisors	
Active and visible in community and industry affairs	
Economic conditions influence product demand	

Table 13-3	Operating Expenses
Value Factor	Objective Score (1 = Poor, 5 = Excellent)
Repeat customers/customer list	
Trained and knowledgeable workforce	

(continued)

Table 13-3 *(continued)*

Value Factor	Objective Score (1 = Poor, 5 = Excellent)
Proprietary products: Patents, copyrights	
Recognizable trademark or trade name	
Large market share	
Diversified: Products, customers, geographic (size)	
Special franchise arrangement	
Favorable location to customers, suppliers, and others	
Market intelligence systems in place	
ISO 9000 registered vendor	
Brand-name distributor	
Industry specialization	
Special niche market	
Well-defined product/service differentiation	
Unique manufacturing/production process	
Special services: Delivery, repair, warranty	
Creative use of Web site to sell products or services	
Strategic partnering and alliances	
Strategic planning processes in place	
Economic order quantity (EOQ) and other inventory-control systems in place	

Table 13-4 — Investments

Value Factor	Objective Score (1 = Poor, 5 = Excellent)
State-of-the-art technology equipment	
Large inventory selection	

Value Factor	Objective Score (1 = Poor, 5 = Excellent)
Ongoing investment in information technology	
Additional capacity for growth (space, manpower, and so on)	
Well-maintained capital equipment	
Commitment to research and development	
Capital budgeting processes in place	

Table 13-5	Finances
Value Factor	**Objective Score (1 = Poor, 5 = Excellent)**
Key management have incentive compensation plans	
High margins due to efficiencies and so on	
Strong liquidity position	
Optimal financial leverage	
Optimal operating leverage	
Favorable tax structure	
Well-defined internal controls	
Properly insured against external risks	
Long-term, profitable customer contracts	
Purchasing power	
Favorable debt financing terms	
Financing plans in place to secure needed capital	
Funded buy/sell agreement	
Budgeting system controls costs and eliminates waste	
Systems in place to comply with laws and regulations	

The analysis of all these factors is where the rubber meets the road in the valuation process. Gross revenue is what gross revenue is; profitability is what profitability is. As we mention earlier in this chapter, valuation isn't just the basic math; the discount and capitalization rates are eventually used to convert the numbers to a value that become most important.

How a company performs in relationship to other companies in its industry is going to speak volumes about whether the subject company is good, average, or great. If the company is performing at the high end of the range compared with other companies in this industry, this performance will influence a potential buyer's perception of intangible factors related to the business.

Checking the structure of the deal

A major weakness of traditional valuation theory is that it doesn't take deal structure into account. The Internal Revenue Service's Revenue Ruling 59-60 (we talk more about this ruling in Chapter 18) assumes that a deal is all cash at closing. In reality, however, hardly any deals are all cash at closing, so a proper valuation needs to take deal structure into consideration. In this section, we discuss financing and tax concerns. In the next, you see how these concepts play out in a case study.

Financing

The first things to consider in the deal structure are how the transaction will be financed and how that financing will influence the timing of cash flows to the seller. If the company is engaged in manufacturing, distribution, or some other business that has significant tangible assets, a bank or some other lending institution may finance a greater portion of the transaction.

If the company for sale is a service business with few or no tangible assets, however, getting a loan for the transaction is very difficult. The buyer's ability to get third-party financing greatly influences whether the buyer can close the deal.

Businesses that don't have many tangible assets can't be sold with the majority of the proceeds coming in the form of cash at closing. These transactions typically have a lot of structure involved — that is, the money is going to come over time in the form of a seller note, consulting agreements, or *earnouts,* which are agreed-upon payments in case certain post-acquisition performance targets are reached.

Basic corporate finance relies on the time value of money: A dollar received today is worth more than a dollar received in the future. Therefore, if you agree to sell a company, the price of the company is going to be contingent on how much money is received now versus in the future.

After-tax consequences

When a transaction is executed, you have to determine the net proceeds. Uncle Sam is going to get paid, and the deal structure determines what taxes are owed and how those taxes are calculated. One needs to consider the structure of the company, such as whether it's an S corporation or a C corporation. Whether the transaction is in the form of an asset sale of a stock sale is also significant. Owners need to examine the assets being sold and what the depreciated book value of those assets is versus the fair-market value of those assets.

Looking at an example of a deal in progress

In this section, we present an example of a deal. The target company, which is an S corporation, is grossing approximately $33 million in revenue per year, with operating income of around $2.5 million. The deal is going to be structured as an asset sale. The major assets to be sold are inventory, accounts receivable, and fixed assets (office furniture, trucks, and machinery).

The company is able to negotiate a sale price of approximately $10 million, plus inventory. This deal is very attractive for a company this size, because it translates into a multiple of earnings of about five. The owners are very happy with the price and decide to move ahead with the transaction.

Financing considerations

When the sellers examined how they would receive their $10 million, they didn't pay attention to how the deal was going to be financed. Their fixed assets (equipment, trucks, and machinery) were aggressively depreciated over time in such a way that the book value of those assets was approximately $2 million.

In determining the purchase price, the buyer stepped up the value of those fixed assets to an estimated fair-market value of approximately $7 million. Therefore, when the buyer approached the banker for a loan to fund this transaction, the bank was only willing to lend an amount far below the value of the tangible assets that would be transferred in the sale.

Combined with some cash down from the seller, the bottom line of $7 million would be available between the two sources as cash at closing. How do the parties make up the gap of the $3 million?

The total purchase price is $10 million, but the buyer can get hold of only $7 million cash at closing. The $3 million has to come over the course of time in the form of a seller note, essentially borrowing from the seller to do the deal. This situation doesn't sit well with the sellers, who anticipated that they would receive the entire $10 million at closing.

Depending on how far along the negotiation process is, the sellers could renegotiate the deal and ask for more money — maybe $11 million to $12 million. If the sale process is close to closing and they want to get a deal done, their hands may be tied.

After a letter of intent is signed and both sides have spent significant time and money on due diligence, renegotiating a deal can have fatal consequences. Therefore, the seller has to be careful that the deal doesn't blow up days before a successful closing.

Tax effects

Before you get too far into the sale process, you have to analyze how the deal structure is going to influence the net proceeds.

The owners in this example didn't do any pretransaction tax analysis and assumed that any proceeds from the sale would be taxed at a capital-gains rate of 20 percent. In a $10 million transaction, the tax bill would be $2 million, so net proceeds would be $8 million. But because the company is an S corporation and the transaction is an asset sale, some or all of the proceeds (depending on the purchase price allocation of those assets) would be taxed at ordinary income rates of 40 percent instead of capital-gains rates of 20 percent, doubling the tax hit.

This situation is another reason you need tax and valuation expertise in any deal you're considering.

Tax consequences need to be in the forefront for any deal you do, and consideration needs to start early. If you wait until the eleventh hour and then try to renegotiate after you find out what the tax hit will be, then you'll most likely kill your deal.

Adding insult to injury, because of the way the deal was structured, the owners would receive only $7 million of the total purchase price at closing. Selling your company for $10 million and walking away with only $3 million at closing leaves a really, *really* bad taste.

The bottom line: In performing a valuation on the sell side, you can't just do the numbers and call it a day. You need to consider personal objectives, the buyer's ability to finance and structure the deal, and net proceeds. Make sure your expert advisors cover every detail.

Part IV
If You're Buying a Business . . .

The 5th Wave — By Rich Tennant

"All right, ready everyone! We've got some clown out here who looks interested."

In this part . . .

The flip side of the transaction is the buy side. In this part, we feature a detailed case study on the purchase of a fictional business, showing where the buyer went right and wrong. We also discuss the range of investigation that should go into a purchase, and we even introduce such intensive tactics as forensic accounting.

Buying a business is all about planning and research. It's not just about the business. How the business fits into your other business operations and, of course, your long-term financial plans is also important.

Chapter 14

How Do You Know Whether You're Ready to Buy?

*I*f you've ever watched smart business moguls in action, you may have thought they had a sixth sense about business opportunities; they pounce when others seem to be standing around aimlessly. But behind every great intuitive business mind is usually something more powerful that you don't see: preparation, which is what this chapter is all about. Proper valuation is part of the necessary preparation that goes into any successful purchase of a business.

Knowing What Typically Drives a Business Purchase

Clearly, the dream of owning the hair salon or the boutique down the street motivates people to strike out on their own. Yet like most things that look good from street level, businesses require closer scrutiny.

A business transaction is a courtship. Although friendly (or unfriendly) strangers at the start, both sides get to know each other as the process moves along. Always be on the lookout for changes in the seller's mood or the involvement of associates or family members in the discussions. (If you haven't read Chapter 11, you may want to do so just to get a broader picture of how family goals — and disagreements — can affect the value of a business.)

If you put yourself in the place of an entrepreneur, you can find many reasons for wanting to buy a business:

- ✔ **Career change:** The urge to get away from working for the Man, the Woman, or the Company from Hell can be very strong. The need for independence has pushed more than a few worker bees over the edge into entrepreneurship. Seeing employed individuals use their savings or their corporate buyouts as seed money for new companies isn't unusual.

- ✔ **Emotion:** This category is a wide one — and a sometimes-dangerous one at that. It contains some element of career change (the desire to strike out on one's own, the need to get away from a stifling organization, and so on) mixed with some other major human motivations, not all of them of the highest caliber. In some cases, people buy family companies to keep the company in the family — or away from other members of the family.

  Some people have a romantic notion about the kind of company in which they've always seen themselves. Sometimes, that notion is a very fitting reason for a person to take the leap into a particular business, but sometimes, it's just a romantic notion; the entrepreneur may not be ready for all the challenges that await him. Buying a business based on emotion can result in something great — or something regrettable.

- ✔ **Tax and estate issues:** Tax and estate issues are complicated in their own right, and no particular one-size-fits-all scenario motivates someone to buy a business. But when family businesses pass from one generation to the next, an outsider may get an opportunity usually reserved for the insiders: the purchase of that family business.

- ✔ **Continued expansion of an existing enterprise:** The opportunity to buy a business that may be complementary to your own operations may be a better way to grow a business than building it organically. Purchasing a competitor allows a company to diffuse a threat while harvesting customers, product lines, and managerial talent that can make the combined operation considerably more valuable.

Getting Ready to Buy

You're looking at a business that you think holds attractive value now and will demonstrate even greater value in the future. But how do you really know?

Sharp outsiders have ways to discover value that the current owners haven't realized on their own, for any number of reasons. The owners may not be particularly brilliant businesspeople, for example, or they may not have the will to continue in a toughening business environment.

In any event, successful buyers know the following things:

- ✔ That they have the skills to put the tangible and intangible assets of the business to work in new ways that will make the company even more successful

- ✔ That the economy is presenting favorable conditions for them to execute those plans

- ✔ That they've created the financial infrastructure in their personal and business lives to take advantage of any opportunities that surface

Smart buyers develop market intelligence about the best companies out there to buy. These buyers know a lot about the businesses they may be interested in, such as which founders are ready to retire and which well-run companies may not have the ability to expand on their own.

Value often comes from opportunities that no one else sees.

In this section, we talk about some challenges that buyers face, discuss how to determine whether a business is a good fit for you, and tell you how the sale process usually works.

Tackling challenges unique to buyers

Ongoing operations have several advantages. If you're paying attention, you can see how long a particular company has been in operation; you can investigate its activities through the news media (check the clips to see how good business has really been); and you can go online to see whether you can identify regulatory problems or court actions that the business may have suffered.

Most information about private companies is tightly guarded and must be requested only by serious parties who can guarantee that they won't spread the information to other outsiders. Finding the answers you need to make a decision is harder when you're looking at private companies. When you're considering buying a successful ongoing business or one that's in trouble, however, you can apply most principles to public and private companies alike.

Unlike people selling houses, business owners don't always announce their intentions to sell in a public way. How many times have you seen a for-sale sign in the window of a local business? Unlike a house, a business may consist of the business itself, the building it lives in, and every piece of machinery and stick of furniture in it — or it may simply consist of two guys in a dorm room designing a search engine that takes over the world. (By the way, we just told you two things: how Google was founded and how idea-based companies with no visible assets can turn into something very big indeed!)

But most people who are looking to buy a conventional business with an address and equipment have to deal with the following issues:

- ✔ **Lack of listings:** No central repository of business-for-sale information is available, save for independent listings by business brokers or independent businesspeople who advertise in newspapers or online.

    There are plenty of easy ways to find businesses for sale — companies even put themselves up for sale on Craigslist these days — but no matter where you pick up information on a company, do your due diligence (see "Step 4: Practice due diligence," later in this chapter). Never trust anything you read until you've checked it out or enlisted experienced help to investigate.

- ✔ **Competition:** For the best businesses out there, prospective buyers are usually in line before you — people who've already thought about swooping in whenever the owners get weary of the operation.

- ✔ **Lack of financial data:** Private companies don't have to make their financials public, so it's impossible to find much data until you've identified yourself as a serious prospect. You may have to put up a few thousand dollars in earnest money before you can do your due diligence.

- ✔ **Owner emotions:** Because a private company may represent a sentimental spot in the heart of its present owner (even if she's absolutely terrible at running the business), the buyer may be dealing not only with numbers and business forecasts but also with some raw emotion.

- ✔ **Lack of useful benchmarks:** Benchmarks tend to be very general if they exist at all.

Looking at whether the business is right for you

Plenty of successful entrepreneurs started their empires with a simple conversation with the proprietor of a business they frequented who just happened to mention that he was hoping to sell the business in a couple of years and retire. Such conversations are serendipitous, to be sure, but even in those situations, getting from dating to mating takes time.

Here are the key steps for getting to the finish line the right way:

1. **Before you analyze the business, analyze yourself.**

   Maybe the idea just fell into your lap. That "eureka!" idea makes running a business seem like a happy dream — and a doable one. But you need to ask yourself some pointed questions about whether you're ready for the often-draining responsibilities of running a business. (Feel free to wander back to Chapter 2 for the questionnaire for fledgling business owners.)

2. **Look past the window dressing.**

   When a company puts itself up for sale, it does a lot of the same things you do when you're trying to sell a house or car: clean it up, add a coat of paint to cover flaws, and so on, in the hope that prospective buyers will get a more favorable view of the company. This isn't wrong. Just don't let surface improvements keep you from closely examining the numbers and detailed characteristics of the business.

3. **Research the business.**

   Under your own steam or with the help of experts, find out what you can about your target company on the Internet, at the public library, or through local business organizations. Then go wider. Consult valuation databases and publications to get an idea of rule-of-thumb valuations for common businesses in that category — keeping in mind that you're looking at guidelines, not final offering prices (see Chapter 9 for more on rules of thumb). You have plenty to do yet.

   Doing initial valuation research on your own is important because even if you don't find out a lot, you'll be in a much better position to speak with experts about how they can help you. Also, if a business you thought you could afford looks as though it could be wildly beyond your means and risk tolerance, you want to know that before you start paying real money for advice.

Evaluating a failing business

If you've been doing your street-level homework, you may notice when a business you're interested in has fewer customers or keeps shorter hours. You may also see that some familiar employees aren't there anymore or that the owner isn't paying as much attention to matters as she once did.

If tough economic times seem to be affecting the company, here's some initial research you should do from a macro perspective:

✔ **Determine whether the business is failing because of the industry or the operation.** Do some research on the fortunes of the industry that the business is in; if its product is going the way of the dodo, that may be the reason the business is failing.

Example: As we write this book, many U.S. newspapers are losing circulation and cutting staff. Although some new owners are trying to make their operations work more efficiently — making more staff cuts, realigning delivery routes, and so on — many experts wonder whether print is going out of style.

✔ **Look at the economy.** If the economy is great but the business is failing, the reasons for its failure may be internal — and fixable. If the economy is wiping out an established company, you may want to understand why it's dying now instead of in earlier tough times it faced.

Example: Fuel prices are a significant factor for any business that depends on vehicles to deliver a product or service, whether it's an airline or a produce company. If energy costs are killing a company, you have a good opening to research ways to make the company operate more efficiently by outsourcing some or all of its transportation functions or to figure out ways to buy fuel more efficiently.

✔ **Evaluate the competition.** Whenever you look at a business, you need to fully view its competition to see whether newcomers are entering the market or whether the existing competition is doing something different. Also, you can't forget to evaluate how your competition operates on the Internet.

Example: If a local bookstore has a monopoly on college textbook sales but is losing money on consumer bestsellers, should it really be selling consumer books?

✔ **Consider labor costs.** If a company is wedded to local employment, that may be noble, but as a prospective owner, you should ask whether — based on current economic conditions and the labor costs of its closest competitors — the company could conceivably make more money by outsourcing or offshoring its labor costs.

Example: Many companies (your potential competitors) are outsourcing their customer service operations to domestic or overseas call centers. Could that turn things around if you owned the company?

✔ **See whether marketing and advertising failed the company.** Find out whether customers have gone elsewhere because the business failed to keep them interested.

Example: An analysis of current customer lists can reveal whether the company kept good leads in the loop or failed to reevaluate its customer list over the years.

✔ **Look at the real estate and the hard assets of this business.** Is the business a manufacturing company that hasn't updated its equipment? You need to determine whether cash needs are preventing the company from upgrading its overall technology. Ask whether a company needs to own the real estate or manufacturing equipment it has; leasing or outsourcing may be a better option.

Example: If a company has clearly not updated its manufacturing equipment in line with current industry standards, determine whether it has held off due to financial constraints or whether some manufacturing alternatives might allow a new owner to dispense with that part of the business altogether.

Understanding how the mating process (typically) works

You've found a company. You've talked to your family members, your closest friends, your banker, your financial planner, your tax professional, and your attorney; maybe you've even placed an early call to a valuation specialist. You've shown everyone your own personal research — including some initial, general valuation information — and nobody's told you that you're completely nuts.

So what are the next steps? Read on.

Always respect confidentiality when seeking to buy a business. Anyone who's ever spent time around an office water cooler knows how quickly rumors spread. When management and staff members start hearing that their employer may be putting the business on the block, regular office productivity screeches to a halt in favor of time spent trading gossip and updating résumés. Depending on how big or interesting the prospective buyer and seller are, the news media may want to get a whiff of what's going on as well. Make sure that all conversations, meetings, and correspondence are conducted with privacy and respect.

Step 1: Find the best way to approach the seller

Depending on the kind of business it is and where it stands in its life cycle, approaching the proprietor isn't always a matter of knocking on his door and saying, "Have I got a deal for you!" Your research should include details on when to make the overture and who the best first contact should be.

Stick to a simple concept: Know your audience. Buying a multigenerational family firm involves a different overture process from buying a franchised doughnut shop or the corner convenience store run by that nice old lady in the neighborhood.

Plan the meeting and the way you'll formally express your interest. Do you have to write a query letter to a home office somewhere, or can you simply ask the owner out for a cup of coffee and begin to see where she stands on the issue of selling her company? Do you need an intermediary to arrange a formal meeting on neutral turf? First impressions do matter.

Be tactful, particularly about numbers. The early stages of meet-and-greet usually aren't the time to talk price. Save that discussion for later, when you're conducting due diligence and negotiating a deal.

Step 2: Find out how the seller will be represented

Wouldn't it be great if you knew each other and the scope of the business well enough to write a deal on a napkin, shake hands, and pass the check? Yes, it would be, but that scenario is largely the stuff of Hollywood movies. Most deals aren't struck that way, largely because they shouldn't be.

You need a legally binding deal that's responsibly negotiated on both sides. Find out whether the seller is going to be aided by an attorney, a business broker, or some other intermediary and whether your representation is equal to the discussion.

When in doubt, check it out — a seller may say that she's working with a Certified Public Account, a licensed attorney, or a certified valuation professional to help do the deal, but don't take that statement at face value. Always quietly investigate the qualifications of the people who are working for the other side. Experience and professionalism on both sides don't always guarantee a smooth business transition, but they definitely increase the chance of one.

Step 3: Set up a tour

Confidentiality rules the entire process, but as you proceed, you'll want to tour the facility, perhaps with a valuation professional or other advisors in tow. This tour can be very informal or formal and may happen several times, depending on the business and on how the parties want to gather information.

If the target company creates a product that could be susceptible to corporate espionage, don't expect to wander up to the receptionist without an appointment and ask when the plant tour begins. In many situations, before a company owner even decides to let you in the lobby, he's going to want to know that you're a serious suitor. You may have to have many conversations with the owner to establish your interest, and at very least, you'll have to sign a confidentiality agreement (which your attorney should review before you sign). See Chapter 12 for a sample confidentiality agreement.

Step 4: Practice due diligence

This part of the process is where paper starts crossing the table, as each side starts to see the other's crucial financial information and other data. You're looking not just at performance numbers but also at the company's culture, its tax history (which you probably haven't seen until now), and its compensation structure. The rough outlines of pricing demands on both sides start taking shape at this stage.

Due diligence costs money, so try to estimate these costs in advance the best you can. You may be paying hourly fees to bring accountants, attorneys, or valuation professionals onsite to do the required investigation. Reviewing documents, creating reports, and gathering data mean one thing: The meter's running.

Because the formal due-diligence process clears you to start talking to landlords, bankers, suppliers, employees, and customers, the seller may require earnest money at this point to show that you're serious about the process. A separate earnest-money agreement may be necessary if real estate is included in the potential sale. Make sure that you understand not only what you're going to have to pay but also what this amount covers and what you'll be allowed to investigate during the due-diligence process. If you're paying for the right to look at a company's numbers and additional time to make a proposal, for example, make sure that you're getting your money's worth.

For most small to mid-size businesses, earnest money of $5,000 to $10,000 is typical. How long does the earnest money period last? Typically, companies have between 7 and 30 days to complete due diligence and decide whether to go ahead with the deal.

Step 5: Move on to a deal

You've popped the question, and you've forked over the ring, better known as your initial offer. Based on your due diligence and advice on valuation, you should be prepared for some negotiation, but ideally, both sides have shared enough information that they won't be far apart if they really want to do the deal (see Chapter 15 for more on negotiating). Assuming that both parties reach a final number at this stage, a bill of sale is prepared and a closing date is scheduled.

Restarting the Value Process

When you get the keys to the business, you start the process of evaluating staff and operations as an owner — a completely different ballgame from due diligence. When your head stops spinning and you get a real handle on what you have, it's time to reset the company's strategic plan to address your own valuation goals and targets. Whether you've purchased a high-quality ongoing business or a turnaround company, creating a strategic plan for the next three to five years can help you focus on growth, profitability, and your long-term plans for the value that this business will achieve.

Whether you're the mission-statement type or simply a person who likes to sit down and talk to your employees (even if you've bought a business with only one or two people working the counter), get your employees thinking about what it will mean for them if you reach your targets for increasing the value of the business. Building in affordable incentives for your people over time may not hurt either; if you grow to plan, you'll be doing more hiring, and better benefits and bonuses tend to attract the best people over time.

When you acquire your first business — or absorb the second or third in a string of transactions — you've changed the competitive landscape of a local business community and maybe even the industry in which you operate. That means a whole new round of studying and information-gathering. No matter what point you're at in your business, the valuation process never really stops. Experienced businesspeople know that business is a process of reeducation every day.

The valuation process of buying a business should give you an in-depth understanding of the business you're in or entering, and you should keep all those valuation principles in mind while you keep your mind open for the next opportunity. After a transaction is done, staying in business means learning about business practices and procedures that will improve the value of the business over time. Here are some ideas:

✔ **Join an industry networking group.** Making yourself and your business known in an industry organization allows you to learn about competitors who may become potential partners.

✔ **Keep close ties with lenders.** Always be ready to borrow even if you're not planning to borrow anytime soon. It's good to keep financials current and the condition of the business in good standing. Stay in touch with the banking community.

Chapter 15

Moving from Valuation to Negotiation

*E*veryone negotiates. People negotiate with family and friends to get things done — or done on their behalf. People negotiate with employees to get better performance from them. And people negotiate with landscapers, car dealers, pet groomers . . . you get the idea. But if you have a valuation based on dishonest or random data and operational practices, what are negotiation skills worth in a business context?

You could fill a warehouse with books on negotiation — how to do it, how not to do it, how negotiations work in various industries, how to negotiate through attorneys and other representatives, and on and on.

In this chapter, not only do we go over key points in business negotiation, but we also discuss a topic that we think is even more important: the quality of information that guides a negotiation strategy (information that you generate or that the target company generates for you). When you're valuing a company, getting quality information is the first important step that directs all your negotiations involving that business.

No absolute law says that you have to buy a business when you find an attractive company worth owning or sell it when an offer lands unannounced on your doorstep — though you should be prepared for anything. Negotiation is a frustrating, enlightening, and extremely educational part of being in business.

Knowing What Valuation Does for the Dealmaking Process

Legendary business guru Peter Drucker once said, "Erroneous assumptions can be disastrous." That statement is a fitting description of any situation in which the buyer or seller doesn't rely on a detailed valuation process before starting negotiations.

You don't have to have an offer on the table for valuation to make sense — it can educate and can guide you when a deal comes. Valuation is relevant in a pre-deal situation — when a business owner is mulling over a sale of her company, or when she's making succession or estate plans, or when she's hoping to seek venture capital financing down the line.

Identifying potential pitfalls and opportunities

Valuation allows a potential seller to discover pockets of hidden value and potholes of trouble that can sink a deal. An early, independent valuation process can unearth the following information:

- ✔ **The quality of assets inside the company:** Many owners think what their companies own and do are significantly more valuable than a buyer or a valuation professional would think. The opposite occurs in some situations, too.

- ✔ **Lackluster accounting methods:** A savvy buyer or his valuation professional won't take long to spot holes in financial logic that draw more scrutiny or a move away from the negotiating table. If numbers and processes can be clarified, the seller needs to know the situation and fix the problems before negotiation takes place.

Timing the purchase well

Valuation can help you determine the best time to move on a sale, a management succession, or an application for financing or investors.

Timing is one of the most important factors in the valuation process. If you're in control of the timing, you may also be in control of the volume of information required to reach your goal.

Using failure as a great teacher

If, in your heart, you're the engineering or design guru of your business, you'll eventually have to master the finance or sales side of the business, too; otherwise, you may miss problems day to day.

You won't be perfect at negotiation — at least, not at first. Negotiation skills evolve over time. So when do you find out how to negotiate? Every day, while you're running your business.

Remember: Everything that happens today may be valuable in a future negotiation.

People may tell you that if a particular deal doesn't work out, another will be around the corner. The economy and the state of your industry play big roles in determining whether that's true — but so do you. Use any negotiations with outsiders to build an ongoing discussion about value in your business.

Minimizing emotional shocks

One of the most beneficial aspects of presale valuation is that it allows owners to get an exact picture of their circumstances — not only so they can improve operations and results before a sale but also so they can adjust to the emotional reality that the business may not be what they thought it was.

Valuation allows sellers to wring emotions out of the process before they face buyers or other family members. It allows negotiations to focus strictly on business and not on conflict, which actually costs money.

Getting Ready to Meet the Seller

You've certainly heard the phrase "garbage in, garbage out." Whether you're conducting an internal valuation for informational purposes before you sell your company or are valuing a target company for the purpose of buying it or investing in it, quality, depth, and purity of information are everything.

What you find during the valuation process not only identifies the value of the company but also moves the negotiating process toward the conclusion of a deal — or doesn't. This fact is why we talk about setting standards for the quality of information within your organization as you approach certain milestones: a possible sale, the transfer of a business to family members or associates, a public offering, or preparation to borrow from a lender.

Everything you do in the valuation process — and we mean *everything* — either speeds or impedes your ability to negotiate for your goal.

Recognizing window dressing

We mention the concept of window dressing to describe the process that some companies go through when they prepare to sell. *Physical window dressing* is pretty much what you'd think — a fresh coat of paint on the walls and a general sprucing up of the premises to entice buyers. Home sellers do the same thing.

A company does *financial window dressing* to make numbers look better than they are, based on what a company wants to show. A company that wants to sell may engage in the following types of financial window dressing:

- Delay spending on employee training so that expenses in the current year (the year potential buyers may be looking at the books) are lower.
- Extend its terms for uncollectible accounts receivable so that it doesn't have to be as aggressive about reporting bad debt.
- Complete a sale/leaseback deal on some equipment before the end of the year, allowing the company to feature the proceeds on its balance sheet for the current year and then lease back the equipment the following year.

None of these activities is illegal, but manipulating the timing of certain spending decisions can definitely have an impact on a company's numbers. For this reason, you need someone who can spot the difference between asset levels driven by the normal course of business and those driven by accounting sleight of hand.

Remembering motives

Understanding motive isn't just for cops. Motive is critical for any negotiation, and you need to understand not just your own motivations in the process but also the motivations of the person on the other side of the table.

Here are the primary motivations in the business-sale process:

- **Financial:** If the company's wealth and the owner's wealth are intertwined, as in most small companies, the seller's personal financial goals are important motivations.
- **Personal:** How dedicated both sides are to the continuation of the business is another important motivation. The seller may finally be ready to hang it up, but you, the prospective buyer, may be new to the industry or eager to enhance the value of your operation with hers.
- **Emotional:** Emotional issues can drive the need for a valuation. The founder may have died, for example, and the kids are unprepared or unwilling to take over where Dad left off, or they're quarrelling about what to do with the business.

✔ **Timing-related:** Timing can be a big motivation. Perhaps an entrepreneur realizes she'll have to introduce massive research and development (R&D) spending if she hangs onto the business another year, and you realize that you'll lose a competitive advantage if you don't pick up her key product line.

Knowing what sellers want

When listing what sellers want, *a buyer* is a good start. But selling a business isn't just about having someone show up with a check. Sellers also want buyers who fit their specific needs. For instance

✔ They may want to make sure that certain key employees — themselves included — stay with the company for a certain period after the purchase.

✔ They may want certain product formulations and trademarks to continue after a new buyer takes over.

✔ They may want noncompete clauses and other limitations on their future ventures to be short term rather than long term.

Let's Make a Deal: Negotiating

Anyone who thinks you can keep emotion and personality issues out of the negotiation process doesn't have a clue about how business or human communication really works.

We start this chapter by mentioning the quality and transparency of information for two reasons: Getting good, transparent information is good business practice generally, and it gives you enough certainty to keep discussions rational and on point. Reliable information from both sides can speed the negotiating process and diffuse disagreements that come from too many unanswered questions.

Deciding whether to handle negotiations yourself

This book isn't about negotiation — for that topic, you can check out *Negotiating For Dummies,* 2nd Edition, by Michael C. Donaldson and David Frohnmayer (Wiley) — but negotiation is a critical aspect. Can you do it yourself?

All the time, small-business people assert that they don't have to take on a phalanx of experts to help them negotiate a price for a company. In some cases, this really may be true. Some people are born negotiators, and they have the skills to come out ahead in any deal talks. But we argue that any negotiation is as good as the information behind the negotiator — and in the case of a purchase of a business, that means having solid valuation information.

There's no one single valuation amount for a business. Although the information that goes into a valuation has to be accurate, so much of the process is analytical and subjective. That's why you may see five different valuation professionals come up with five different prices for the same asset or the same business.

But in general terms, all buyers should realize that the final price ultimately depends on how quickly the seller wants to sell and how badly the buyer wants to purchase the business. The greater the incentive the owner has to sell, the further below the asking price she's likely go. By the same logic, however, the more you want to buy the business, the faster you'll want to get the deal done (and you'll probably pay a higher price as a result).

Getting ready to negotiate

Even though sellers may have a longer time than buyers to prepare for a deal, it makes sense for buyers to set their parameters well before they find a target. Here are some thoughts on how to be ready for the negotiation process:

1. **Think about the best-case scenario of the way you want a negotiation to end.**

   Develop a profile of the kind of business you want to buy, the way you'd want a deal structured, and the financial terms that would make the best sense for your business and personal life. Start talking to estate planners, your family, and your business and tax attorneys about scenarios that make sense for you.

2. **Start networking.**

   Good relationships can lead to efficient deal making, so get to know officials of target companies casually. Based on your particular objective in a deal — finding a business inside your industry or outside — you may want to get involved in local or national business organizations to meet executives from other companies to boost your knowledge of what possibilities may be out there.

3. If there's interest, meet.

Meetings between potential business partners can be as formal or informal as necessary. Never pass up a chance to make a useful contact. You may be buying that person's company someday, and good, long-term relationships can make that process easier.

4. Be prepared to sign a confidentiality agreement.

In most business negotiations large and small, the step before kicking the tires is signing the piece of paper that says, "I shall not tell anyone that I kicked your tires." Confidentiality agreements are a necessary step before a company will open its books to you, or for that matter, its data or facilities to your inspection.

How you write the confidentiality agreement is up to you and your lawyers, but generally, if talks break off or the deal doesn't go through in the final moments for any reason, that agreement is your insurance. (See Chapter 12 for a sample confidentiality agreement.)

5. Prepare the list of everything you want to see.

You should present the target company with an organized, comprehensive list of all the information you'll need to make a purchase decision (which is one reason to talk to your team of experts before the due diligence process begins). Asking questions in dribs and drabs makes you look like an amateur — follow-ups to major issues are okay, but make sure you make all major requests together.

You'll ask for comprehensive (and hopefully audited) financials, of course, but you'll also want the target company's recent tax returns, contracts from top revenue-producing clients, and any records from current or past legal proceedings. Be very aware of any hesitation in sharing information.

Tempers may flare during the negotiating process over matters large and small. Your executives may feel that they're being asked questions that go beyond the bounds of what should be disclosed about the company. An accountant who rubs everyone the wrong way may come onsite. And when so much money is at stake, there's stress. When things get heated, remember not to take too much personally.

6. Get to know the facility.

Either you or your representatives — and particularly your valuation professionals — need to spend quality time at your target's facility. How do you really get an idea of valuation without actually looking at the facility, its offices, its machinery, its buildings, and heck, even the way people work together?

7. **Do the valuation.**

   You, your valuation expert, or both of you together should execute the valuation based on all your data and arrive at a price range for the business. Before you present your offer, put in place the elements to pay for it — cash, debt, or a note that you'll offer to the seller.

8. **Start negotiating.**

   Negotiations get more intense as you offer contract language for the seller's review. Unless the buyer has offered you everything you had in mind in Step 1, you come back with your response and request changes based on your conclusions and those of your advisors.

9. **Do a final walk-through.**

   Before you sign the final papers, the buyer and seller usually do a final walk-through of the business with a final inventory count of assets agreed to in the sale. Settle any remaining problems in the deal then, or the deal may go sour at the last minute.

Understanding what you should do in negotiation

You can load your arms with varying titles on negotiation the next time you go to the bookstore, but for now, here are general guidelines for keeping a negotiation calm, informative, and efficient:

✔ **Don't talk; listen.** You're going to have to talk at some point, of course; we're not suggesting a vow of silence. But the real discovery experience in a business negotiation comes from what you hear, not from what you say. You should take the time to listen to

- A target company's key employees, particularly the chief financial officer if the company has one

- Your family, because your goals for your business affect them directly

- Your advisors — your business and tax attorneys as well as any financial-planning experts you work with on a regular basis

✔ **Respect confidentiality.** If you've been successful in business, you ideally know how to guard information as well as use it. As you gather information, make sure that everyone you speak with understands your need for discretion. Don't be a blabbermouth about what's going on, and tell the members of your inner circle to be responsible about any information you discuss with them.

✔ **Keep an open mind.** Potential sellers come to the table with agendas that may seem at the outset to be very different from your own. If these agendas seem as different on Day 30 as on Day 1, you may have a problem, but you should always try to understand what a potential target is thinking and what her immediate concerns may be (refer to "Remembering motives," earlier in this chapter).

Even if talks don't lead to a deal, negotiation puts you in a considerably stronger position to understand your business and the competitive environment it lives in. No matter how firmly you believe that your way of running a business is the best way, an open mind is far more valuable than a take-it-or-leave-it mindset.

✔ **Watch behavior as closely as words.** The essence of negotiation is in understanding how a customer, employee, supplier, or potential business partner behaves and how that behavior leads to specific actions. Buyers and sellers each want things that the other side has, and manipulation is part of the game. But is this manipulation the kind that goes on in the normal course of everyday business or a dangerous kind that may lead you to give up more than you'd choose to?

You may be dealing with a complete stranger or with someone you've known for 30 years, but if you've never negotiated with this person before, you need to watch whether he behaves with openness or with stealth. Problems with integrity can kill not only a deal but also a relationship.

Working with someone who's negotiating for you

The size of the business, the complexity of the potential deal, and your personal preferences affect who you bring in to advocate for you in the purchase of the business. Here are some of the experts who may help you negotiate:

✔ **Attorneys:** Consult the lawyers you deal with in the regular course of your business and personal life about their thoughts on the best way for you to approach a business purchase. The best sudden-offer scenario is one you get after you've already consulted trusted advisors who give you a battle plan.

Even the simplest business acquisitions have complicated contracts. The average business-purchase agreement has dozens of clauses to be negotiated beyond price, down payment, and ongoing terms. Other topics of discussion include noncompete clauses (which may last for several years after a deal is closed), lease assignments (the transfer of payment details on all leases from the seller to the buyer), inspections, adjustments, employee matters, and anything else that crops up as a feature of this individual deal. Tax, estate, and business attorneys you work with form an ad hoc team of advisors you may see based on need.

✔ **Your officers:** If you run a company large enough to have a dedicated chief financial officer and other executives in legal and operating posts, you hopefully brought trust into the picture when you hired them. Keep them in the loop on your plans for purchasing a new company and use them as conduits to ferret out information on potential targets.

✔ **Your valuation professional/professional intermediary:** An attorney may be a valuable negotiator for the right company, but attorneys don't always have significant training and experience in business valuation. The good ones will tell you when they don't, and often, they'll have such valuation experts in their Rolodex.

Here are two reasons to use an intermediary:

- Intermediaries can be the good cop or the bad cop in a valuation assignment, which may allow the buyer and seller to maintain a more cordial relationship. For example, if a deal-breaking situation comes up in the valuation, instead of your saying, "No way," your intermediary can say something more diplomatic: "I know this issue here isn't in the best interest of my client, and I'd be violating my duty to her if I suggested it."

- Just having someone who does deals for a living can pay off because based on his financial knowledge, the intermediary can spot different ways to do a deal before attorneys or accountants step in. Intermediaries can do drafts of letters of intent that the company attorney can review prior to closing date. If you're paying the cost of an intermediary already, having him do these intermediary steps before other hourly professionals come into the process can save significant dollars and time.

See Chapter 7 for more on all the professionals who can help you with the valuation process.

You can't abdicate all responsibility for negotiating the deal to your experts. Their job is to advise and protect you — nothing more. You should viscerally understand every aspect of the deal before you sign. You have to know whether a change in Clause 15 or Clause 45 would turn out to sour the deal. Nobody knows your goals better than you do, and nobody is in a better position to decide whether the business you're examining is right for you.

Chapter 16

Due Diligence on the Buy Side

*I*n this chapter, we cover the preparation and study that buyers should do in advance of a deal — the flipside of Chapter 12, which discusses due diligence for sellers. In truth, both sides should do about the same preparation. However, this chapter focuses on the skills and tasks you need to make a complete valuation of a business as a buyer.

Seeing What Due Diligence Means in Practice

Due diligence is the process of thoroughly investigating a business, from the quality of its facilities to the quality of its customers, its brand identity, and most importantly, its numbers. Due diligence happens when you approach a seller and ask for permission to view the company's operations before you make an offer for the company. The process almost certainly involves signing a confidentiality agreement.

For a prospective buyer, the process determines the following things:

▶ **The quality of the company's overall financial reporting:** When you're actually allowed to see numbers, it pays to have expert help ensure that the data is in order. In some cases, you may want to involve a forensic accountant in the search for errant financial information. (For a look at what forensic accountants do, turn to Chapter 17.)

- ✔ **The current value of all the company's assets, both tangible and intangible:** Valuation professionals who are familiar with your industry will have a good idea of how to price the target company's assets.

- ✔ **The existence of any ugly secrets:** Lawsuits waiting to happen, employee problems, regulatory hang-ups, and similar issues need to be investigated both inside and outside the company. Sometimes you get wind of legal hassles through news stories. At other times, it's worth wearing out shoe leather and cellphone batteries to talk with area regulators and licensing agents, just to make sure that the business's operations are in proper shape.

- ✔ **How the company's physical operations are maintained:** Plenty of companies spruce up before a sale, and that's great. But you need to look past the new coat of paint to find out whether the expensive equipment and machinery that you're acquiring in a deal are in good operation or ready for the junkyard.

- ✔ **The quality of the workforce:** When you buy a business, you may be buying its human capital. Due diligence should give you an idea of the quality of the top management at a firm; this information should help you decide whether to create incentives to keep these people in place or incentives to get them to go.

- ✔ **The investment required to maintain and grow the business over time:** You'll always find operational surprises after you take over any company, but the due-diligence process should give you a good idea of what investment and cash-flow standards you'll need going into the business on Day 1 of ownership.

- ✔ **The best time to act:** Good timing comes from an intimate knowledge of how a business works, and that involves continuing education. When you're buying a company, you have to weigh whether now is the time to enter the marketplace with your kind of mousetrap. You need to see what capital you have to invest or may need to borrow. You also may need to start thinking about additional investors to come in with you at the start. Furthermore, you have to look at the quality of competing products in the marketplace, the overall economy, and the economy of the specific industry you're considering. Then you have to decide whether to jump in at this point in the business cycle or wait a little while.

Looking at the Unofficial First Stages of Due Diligence

Due diligence commonly refers to the process whereby a target company lets you see its financial data and allows you to come inside to kick the tires, so to speak. But if more buyers were to make this process broader by looking at valuation from the start, we believe fewer businesses would fail.

Asking for info: Due diligence production

Due diligence production (also known as a *due diligence request)* is the formal name for what you're doing: asking for information.

Standard due diligence production includes requests for incorporation documents, corporate bylaws, minutes of board and shareholder meetings, employee organizational charts, capitalization tables, shareholder lists, option-holder lists, litigation information, regulatory compliance documents, security filings, employee contracts and information, nondisclosure and noncompetition agreements, property and equipment leases, asset lists, intellectual property information, financing information, tax filings and returns, and all other material contracts. Whew!

The list of documents varies by the kind of company, but if you get permission to come inside, the company should give you what you request pretty much immediately. If it can't, raise an eyebrow. Either the business isn't very well organized (a sign of poor management), or the owner is trying to hide something (a sign that you may want to walk away).

In this section, we talk about the unofficial but necessary first stage of due diligence in a purchase situation: researching a company before you approach the owner to make a deal. We also talk about getting some assistance, because bringing in help confidentially at this stage may be a good idea.

Researching the company

For potential buyers, the due diligence process should start with fully researching the business, its industry, and the economic outlook for the business. As a potential buyer, you owe it to yourself not only to study the target company but also to do the following:

- ✔ Read everything possible about the company and the industry in which it operates.
- ✔ Look over rule-of-thumb valuation data (see Chapter 9) as a starting point for pricing data.
- ✔ Check the success of the company's product mix.
- ✔ Assess your capability to finance and manage the company.
- ✔ Consider the cost of replacing management and staff members, if necessary, after the purchase.
- ✔ Get a better idea of the company's competition and customer response through outside intelligence.
- ✔ Review the quality of the business's marketing and advertising.
- ✔ Interview valuation professionals who may be able to assist you in the purchase process (see the next section).

The financing environment for businesses is a critical factor in planning the purchase of a company. Even if you're able to self-finance the purchase, you may need credit to acquire operating capital later. Establishing financing relationships is an important preparatory step in buying any business.

Consulting your family and the pros

In big and small businesses alike, you need to know your capacity for handling the management and financial responsibilities of business ownership. Finding out how prepared you are for this big lifestyle and career change isn't something you should do in a vacuum.

Here are some of the people you may want to consult before you start the process of buying a company:

- ✔ **Your family:** You need to consult your spouse and your kids about how this major decision will affect the family's lifestyle and finances. Business really is personal when you're starting or buying a company. Family finances almost always change when one spouse or another (sometimes both!) decides to go into business.

- ✔ **A certified financial planner:** Anyone who considers purchasing an existing business without examining his personal debt, savings, and investment situation is courting trouble. A visit to a certified financial planner who works with independent businesspeople may be a good first step in this process.

- ✔ **Your tax professional:** Few people realize the impact of entrepreneurship on their personal tax situations. Make time to discuss your plans with your Certified Public Accountant (CPA), and consider the advice you're given as part of the business-planning process. Your personal tax situation may influence the ownership structure you choose for your business.

- ✔ **Business and estate attorneys:** A good business attorney can educate you on the basic legal requirements of operating a business in your community. An estate attorney can work with you, your tax professional, and your financial planner to plan how you'll grow the business to build your personal fortune — and protect yourself from various risks along the way.

- ✔ **Business valuation professionals:** Whether you plan to use a business broker, a business appraiser, or an accountant or attorney who's certified as a valuation professional (see Chapter 7), it's a good idea to contact and review candidates well ahead of any purchase. Interviewing these professionals may give you a broader view of your ideas for owning and operating a company.

Thinking cash, not debt

In the rush to own a business, many people focus on the selling price and not on the ongoing costs of staying in business or the risks inherent in being new to a business. Likewise, people who start companies also fail to examine how much cash they'll need to keep operating before profits start trickling in.

An ongoing business with a solid customer base, staff, and operating system in place is in a much better position to keep generating the cash that's the lifeblood of any business. (Are you as tired of that cliché as we are? Oh, well, it's probably still the best description of cash flow.)

So we'll go out on a limb and say it: Your plan to buy a business should include projections for the worst-case scenario for the company's cash needs. Based on that scenario, you should go into the purchasing process with a surplus of cash to handle contingencies that can arise when a business changes hands. These contingencies can include the following:

✔ **Employee turnover:** Some high-producing employees may be lured away to competitors during the ownership transition, and your sales may go down until you bring in suitable replacements for these people. (Alternatively, you may want to install an incentive system to keep the best employees right where they are.)

✔ **Promotional costs:** You may have to incur promotional costs to assure existing customers that they'll still be well taken care of

and to assure prospective customers that now is a good time to come onboard. You also may offer discounts or other savings to loyal customers to keep them in the fold.

✔ **Repairs:** Computers, machinery, and anything else with a plug or a fuel tank may break during the first year you're in business. Yes, you may have inspected all the assets with a fine-toothed comb, but breakdowns happen.

If you're making a purchase decision during flush times, you may be tempted to go to lenders to finance the purchase. But when times get tough, banks want their money back. It may be a better idea to invest your own money or to get people who are close to you and who understand your skills and your company involved in your business as investors. This arrangement is called *equity financing.* Talk about it with experts you trust. Equity is better than debt because investors have decided to take the ride with you, and you get to set the terms under which they'll be able to pull their money out of the business. Banks don't have the same alliance with the owners of the company; when times get tough, banks are seldom as understanding as shareholders will be.

A balance sheet loaded with debt will devalue your business over time. Therefore, if you find that you have to take on debt, treat it as a short-term expense to be extinguished quickly. (That's not a bad idea for your personal finances, too.)

The Informational Game Plan: Cracking the Books (and the Internet)

Prospective buyers need to be planners, and no matter how many experts are helping you in your quest for a business, building your own independent knowledge of your target company and industry makes good sense.

The nation's bankruptcy courts are filled with men and women who put everything they had into owning a business but failed because they never took the wide or the detailed view. A valuation professional can help you with the detailed view — the best ones are trained to spot valuation challenges specific to the industry you've chosen. But the wide view? That's where you need to start.

Without a full understanding of the kind of business you want to buy, the industry it's part of, and the economic and operational challenges affecting it now and expected in the future, you literally have no business being in that business.

Remember that readers are leaders. (Yes, we're suckers for corny old slogans.) But a big part of due diligence is good old-fashioned book-cracking — or in today's parlance, Web surfing. Granted, you can't believe everything you read in newspapers or in magazines, and certainly not on the Internet. But even if you're bringing in experts to help you value a business, the ultimate decision to buy rests with you, so you have to be smart enough to know whether the people you hire to evaluate a deal are representing you properly.

What should you be reading? Here are a few ideas:

- ✔ **Trade publications:** Virtually every industry has a trade publication following it. At one time, many trade publications were excessively friendly to the industries they covered, but today, the best of these publications are more objective and journalistically written. They're great resources for up-to-the-minute industry news, trends, and gossip. If you come across a major business-news story in the paper, on television, or on the radio, chances are that the first rumblings came from the trade journalists who regularly speak with companies, suppliers, and customers every day. In many cases, trade publications are simply closer to business news than general publications are.

Do an Internet search on your industry name and the phrase "trade publication" or "trade journal," and see what comes up. You may have to try several combinations of words, but soon you start finding titles to work with. Find and bookmark the journals that have the largest circulation; generally, those publications are the leaders in their industries. Many trade publications have their circulation listed with the Audit Bureau of Circulations (www.accessabc.com), and you can check the largest ones in their category there. But the Internet has made it easy to spot major publications by the way they turn up in searches.

When you find your selection of trades, go to their Web sites and search their archives. You also may want to subscribe to print versions of the publications, but first see whether you can score a free subscription offer and consolidate your research during the free-subscription period.

✔ **Online databases:** Major online databases can help you find news stories, Wall Street analysts' reports, and company-issued news releases in most industries. Because many of these are paid databases, check with your local public and college libraries to see whether you can access them there for free. For a great list of databases you should bookmark, check Chapter 12.

✔ **City business publications:** Most major and mid-size cities have some form of business weekly that focuses on the activities of local companies. Search for stories about competitors of the target company and about the local economy.

✔ **Trade-association data:** Manufacturing, technology, and other industry groups in a particular region may compile annual guides that list all their members — your potential competitors or target companies. Depending on how many years such a guide has been published, checking it is a good way to identify current and past executives, as well as critical reported numbers, products, and other data over a company's history.

Join a professional organization in your community, the chamber of commerce, or even a civic or nonprofit board that can put you in touch with people who are connected to the industry in which you want to buy.

Gathering the Company's Data

When you're touring a facility or speaking with executives at a company that you're considering buying, always do the following things:

✔ **Look at how a company keeps house.** Cluttered or messy offices don't necessarily mean that disorganized or untalented people work there. Facilities that are literally falling down, filthy, or otherwise neglected, however, may indicate that the company is facing financial difficulties or, at the very least, a loss of vision or purpose.

On the other hand, does the place look as though it's been sanitized to cover up deeper problems? That happens, too. Don't be afraid to judge the surroundings privately. Keep your questions to the owner polite, but don't be afraid to ask her why things are the way they are. If you consider such problems to be fixable, housekeeping problems may not be bad, because they may give you a better negotiating position on price.

✔ **Check the work environment.** Ideally, you know what a healthy work environment looks like. Employees will have disagreements, but in the right environment, they communicate well and even have fun at their jobs. No workplace is perfect, but if you sense that people have a bunker mentality, or if you see fields of empty desks at various times during the day, by all means, ask *why*.

You may think it'd be fun to clean house and start over with your own team, but hiring and firing people are extremely costly in terms of time and money. If you buy a company and choose to replace someone who's been there for 20 years, you may lose a crabby, unproductive employee in a layoff, which is good, but you may need to pay his replacement a lot more, which is a sizable expense that you have to figure into the valuation. Every whim in business has a potential cost.

✔ **Observe body language.** Any potential transaction always involves a bit of nervousness, with the parties dancing around each other in the early stages of information sharing. But if you sense fear, evasiveness, or uncertainty about giving you what you need, the situation isn't too tough to read.

If you've been an employee before, just put yourself in the other person's shoes. Figure out whether she's just nervous about talking to the potential new boss or whether bigger problems are afoot.

✔ **Decide whether you like the seller.** You may be looking to buy a company whose owner you've known for years, and the purchase process is like two friends' working together to make something great happen. That scenario is the kind of feel-good situation that everyone loves. In most cases, however, you deal with a stranger. The owner may have mixed feelings about the sale; after all, he made this baby. He may be looking to dump a lemon on you. Or in his heart of hearts, he may not think that you've got the right stuff to buy the company. Talk about a complex dynamic!

Most people don't wake up in the morning and say, "Hey, I'm going down to Smitty's to buy his business!" Smart business deals aren't born in a day; it may take years to know what you really want and possibly longer to get it. Thanks to the Internet, any storefront or business started in someone's attic has the potential to become a global company, so you need to do due diligence to figure out the true potential of any company.

In the next few sections, we suggest some questions to ask about the target company.

Knowing which questions to ask about the target company

Ask more than one source to answer the following questions. Due diligence begins with basic queries of prospective sellers, such as the following:

✔ What's your impression of how the company is viewed by outsiders — competitors, the press, the industry, and the community at large? (If you know that the company has problems with its public image, you need to know whether it's in denial about these problems.)

✔ What kind of gifts and incentives does the company give customers? (See whether these rewards skirt ethical boundaries.)

✔ If the company isn't doing overseas production now, did it plan to do so in the future?

✔ Does the company pay in dollars or use a system to hedge against currency risk? If so, how does that system work?

✔ What are the company's most valuable intellectual property assets?

✔ Does the company have any copyrights, licenses, or patents that are ready to expire?

✔ What quality-control systems are in place in various departments of the target company?

✔ What proprietary technology or systems are most valuable to the business?

✔ What are the company's largest vendors and suppliers? What percentage of the overall purchasing budget do they represent, and how long has the company been working with them?

✔ Who are the company's biggest customers? What percentage of total revenue do they represent, and how long has the company been working with them?

Checking with the company's departments

Not only do you want to tour the business you're thinking about buying, but you also want permission to talk to its employees. Make sure you're cleared to talk with employees so you can find out what they're like; if you're thinking about buying this company, its people may become your people. Would you want them? Here are key departments on which you should focus.

Legal/audit

The company's legal and auditing counselors depend on the target company for fees or paychecks, so they're unlikely to say anything controversial. But if they want to keep the company as a client or as an employer, being straight with you is to their advantage.

You need to understand their processes and how they work with the firm; you also need to sound them out for clues about problems and added complexities in the business that you may not have heard from management. Consider asking the following questions:

✔ How open is the company in working with you on legal and audit issues?

✔ What's your relationship with the chief counsel or chief financial officer?

✔ Is top management involved in managing legal, tax, and accounting issues?

✔ How would you describe the recordkeeping and support technology for legal and financial matters?

Information technology

Technology is a tremendous driver of business as well as an enormous source of risk. You need to question both top management and the company's information technology (IT) chieftain (if any) about the state of the company's technology, how the technology is used in each department, and how secure it is. Here are some questions to ask:

✔ Is the Internet a big part of the company's operations? If so, how is it used?

✔ What computer hardware does the company own, and how old is it? Does the company have any plans to upgrade its system?

✔ What software is used in the various departments of the company, and how often is it upgraded? Should I be aware of any major software revisions?

✔ May I see a summary of the company's proprietary data and security procedures?

✔ How do customers interact with the company's technology? (You want to know whether the technology is doing all it can to support, improve, and speed the customer experience.)

✔ How do suppliers and vendors interact with the company's technology? (You want to know whether the technology is doing all it can to improve the supply chain.)

✔ Has the company's IT department ever had a crisis situation, such as a hacker attack or the loss of important data? If so, how did the crisis affect the company's operation and its relationship with customers?

✔ Does the company use outside consultants to service its information systems?

Sales and marketing

Sales and marketing personnel are important sources because you need to understand who's pushing the gas pedal on revenue. Here are some questions to ask:

✔ Who does the sales forecasting in the company, and how is that information shared?

✔ Does the company have an internal sales and marketing staff, or does it work with independent reps or contractors?

✔ What are the seasonal sales patterns in the business?

✔ What were the company's sales trends during the past three years by product or business line?

✔ How did success align with the company's advertising and marketing spending?

✔ What are the most successful marketing and advertising approaches that the company has taken in recent years?

✔ Does each division have standard payment terms, and if so, are there exceptions to those terms (such as different arrangements for certain types of customers)?

✔ What's your marketing focus for the next one to three years? Are there specific new territories you plan to enter, and are new products that will lead you there in the pipeline?

✔ How does the Internet figure into the company's sales and marketing plan?

✔ How does the company measure the performance of its sales and marketing expenditures?

✔ What are the forecasts for goals and spending for the coming year, and how often are forecasts reviewed and tweaked?

✔ Does the company have a relationship with an advertising or marketing agency? If so, how long has the relationship existed, and what do you regard as the agency's best work?

✔ Have you always had the same advertising or marketing agencies? Why or why not?

✔ What are the three best sales and marketing initiatives that the company is executing right now?

Collecting Outside Data about Your Industry and the Economy

Information about the economy and the particular industry in which the target company operates is critical to the due diligence process for any business. A prospective buyer needs to understand how the general course of the economy will affect the company he's targeting.

If you took a course in economics, you've heard of the *business cycle:* the periodic, irregular, up-and-down movements in economic activity, measured by fluctuations in gross domestic product (GDP) and macroeconomic variables. Overall growth and contraction of the domestic and international economy tend to lift and lower all boats, yet each industry has its own peaks and valleys based on where the economy as a whole stands. You need to know what those peaks and valleys are.

Breaking confidentiality can get you into trouble

If either party to a deal breaks a confidentiality or nondisclosure agreement, she leaves herself open to legal action and potentially more publicity than either party is going to be comfortable with. Here are some of the laws people may risk breaking in the due diligence process:

- ✔ **Economic Espionage Act of 1996:** This law makes the theft or misappropriation of a trade secret a federal crime. The law contains two sections criminalizing two sorts of activity. The first section criminalizes the misappropriation of trade secrets (including conspiracy to misappropriate trade secrets and the subsequent acquisition of such misappropriated trade secrets) with the knowledge or intent that the theft will benefit a foreign power. Penalties for violation are fines of up to $500,000 per offense and imprisonment of up to 15 years for individuals and fines of up to $10 million for organizations.

  The second section criminalizes the misappropriation of trade secrets related to or included in a product that is produced for or placed in interstate (including international) commerce, with the knowledge or intent that the misappropriation will injure the owner of the trade secret.

- ✔ **Uniform Trade Secrets Act:** UTSA is a model law that defines the rights and remedies of a common-law trade secret. The law imposes civil rather than criminal liability for misappropriation of trade secrets and creates a private cause of action for the victim. Remedies for misappropriation of trade secrets under the act are injunctions; damages, including exemplary (punitive) damages; and in cases of bad faith or willful and malicious misappropriation, reasonable attorney's fees.

Nondisclosure agreements may protect you from careless or unscrupulous companies and contractors, but they won't protect you from the law. These agreements can be overruled legally if a legitimate reason to do so exists (as part of a court case, for example). Also, they can be rendered invalid if they're worded incorrectly, so make sure you get proper legal documents that clearly define the terms and conditions of the agreement.

Confidentiality is meant to work for you, too. A prospective seller definitely wants his financials and other key data to be kept secret from competitors, but he also wants data on your qualifications to buy the business. Just make sure that the confidentiality agreement doesn't shield you from getting any information that you'll need in due diligence production. In this situation, working with a good valuation professional or lawyer makes sense.

Make sure that the target company has three years' worth of financial data for you to examine, and check carefully to see whether those numbers were audited by a good accounting firm. If not, you've spotted another potential trouble sign. Go to Chapter 12 to see what a seller should do in preparation for a sale and for a sample confidentiality agreement.

Many people buy businesses outside their range of expertise, only to find that they've bought into a down business cycle in that industry. Have you ever tried to sail a boat in a dry creek bed? It doesn't work so well.

When you study economic activity, you need to understand how your chosen industry responds to the economy as a whole, and you need to understand what key economic indicators are. Here are some of the most common examples:

- ✔ **Gross domestic product:** As the measuring stick for the nation's total output of goods and services, GDP is the broadest economic measure.

- ✔ **Job growth:** Businesses and consumers feel more at ease when the job market is expanding, and they also feel more comfortable opening their wallets. When job growth evens out or starts to shrink over a period of months, it's a signal that the economy is heading for a slowdown.

- ✔ **Consumer confidence:** The Conference Board (www.conference-board.org) and the University of Michigan (www.sca.isr.umich.edu) maintain separate indexes of consumer sentiment based on interviews with heads of households and other resources. Even if you're not in a purely consumer-oriented business, virtually every economic trend filters up from individual spending.

- ✔ **Institute for Supply Management (ISM) index:** The ISM index (www.ism.ws) is viewed as being a solid measurement of whether the manufacturing economy is contracting or expanding. Each month, more than 400 companies provide the ISM with data on changes in production, new orders, new export orders, imports, employment, inventories, prices, lead times, and the timeliness of supplier deliveries. By compiling the responses, the ISM can piece together a national economic picture. An index reading above 50 percent indicates that the manufacturing economy is generally expanding; a reading below 50 percent means that the economy is contracting.

The preceding list represents only a fraction of the national data that's available. You also need to dig around in your own state and municipality for data that can directly inform your decision making. Your assignment is to study the economic indicators and metrics that affect the company you plan to buy. A good way to find industry metrics and measurement tools is to conduct an online search for the phrase "industry metrics" and the name of the particular industry.

Chapter 17

Forensic Accounting and the Due Diligence Process

*T*hanks to the growing number of police shows on TV that focus on the science of blood and guts, the word *forensic* has worked its way into the mainstream. It's worked its way into mainstream accounting, too. But unlike the fictional character Gil Grissom of *CSI*, though, forensic accountants tend to work in clean surroundings. Only the numbers are dirty.

Wait, though — aren't forensic accountants hired only for big-company situations? Not anymore. Where numbers are withheld, incomplete, questionable, or possibly fabricated, professionals with backgrounds in forensic accounting can be useful to businesses of all sizes. Even law enforcement officials involved in counterterrorism measures use forensic accounting techniques to detect the tiny amounts of money funneled through cash-based shell businesses, such as convenience stores and tobacco shops.

This chapter focuses on what forensic accounting means, what practitioners do, and what benefits accrue to buyers and sellers who engage forensic accountants in the due diligence process of a business purchase or sale.

Understanding Forensic Accountants

Thanks to prime-time TV, most people know what the *forensic* part of forensic accounting means — an examination after something undesirable has happened. But forensic accounting definitely involves more. Forensic accounting mixes accounting, auditing, and investigative skills to determine fraud or other hidden or mistaken activities in an organization's or person's finances. The Forensic Accounting Academy, part of the National Association of Certified Valuation Analysts, offers a definition that's quite clear and succinct: "the art and science of investigating people and money."

Forensic accountants often work in tandem with attorneys (estate, bankruptcy, divorce, and corporate) and federal, state, and local law enforcement officials to uncover mistaken or illegal activities within organizations. In a business-valuation context, they frequently work to find evidence of value — or lack of value — that others may prefer to conceal.

Characterizing a qualified forensic accountant

If you're hiring a forensic accountant, don't automatically assume that he has training in valuation. Check to see which certifications he holds on the valuation side. Certified Valuation Analyst (CVA), for example, is a leading certification that requires specific training and testing in valuation. (For more information on certification and training, turn to Chapter 7.)

What should any forensic accountant you hire know? Some of the items in the following list may be somewhat familiar, because they're the same qualifications you require of a valuation professional:

✔ Expert knowledge of accounting and control systems

✔ Solid investigative skills

✔ Good instincts and training in legal and illegal human behavior

✔ Knowledge of the industry in which an investigation subject operates, including knowledge of key stakeholders such as customers, suppliers, regulators, shareholders, and lenders

✔ Knowledge of technology that criminals use to steal money and goods

✔ Understanding of banking practices and issues related to the flow of money into and out of an organization

✔ Understanding of commercial, civil, and criminal laws in the pertinent jurisdiction that could affect a particular organization's valuation

✔ Awareness of differences in business practices and restrictions in various countries

✔ Creativity, speed, and accuracy

The forensic accountant who caught Capone

Frank J. Wilson, a U.S. Treasury Department accountant, was the guy who put Al Capone away for evading taxes on income. The true story isn't quite like the movie *The Untouchables,* but it's close enough. Capone got away with dozens or perhaps hundreds of murders, but an aggressive bean counter brought him to heel through Capone's own financial records.

Wilson and his team worked 18-hour days, reviewing more than 2 million documents and other key evidence seized in various raids on Capone's operations over a 6-year period starting in 1929. They analyzed phone records and investigated banks and credit agencies. They developed a network of snitches, tapped phones, and seized various sets of financial documents related to Capone. Eventually, they found evidence linking Capone to gambling proceeds through a dog-track operation in Florida.

Capone unsuccessfully ordered a hit on Wilson and his wife, who moved from hotel to hotel while the investigation went on. Undeterred, Wilson gathered evidence to prove that Capone had a total of $116,000 in nondeductible expenses after claiming no income. Capone was found guilty and sent to prison in 1931.

Forensic accountants may work in concert with investigators and other covert players in the investigative process, but they need to know the legal restrictions on certain investigative tactics. Therefore, you need to confirm that your forensic accounting professional understands the laws that are likely to apply. If you're hiring a forensic accountant, ask what her investigative limits would be for your situation, and ask what things she would and wouldn't do. If she indicates that she operates without limits or is unable to answer your question specifically, go with a candidate who can.

What training is involved

Forensic accountants begin as trained Certified Public Accountants (CPAs), but most have something extra: a taste for the discovery and presentation of evidence to fill in the blanks in valuations, divorce proceedings, corporate investigations, and dozens of other kinds of cases and projects. They may spend plenty of time in court testifying on their findings, so they have to think faster than the lawyers who are peppering them with questions. (Forensic accountants may never have to defend their results in court, but their responsibility is to prepare their results as if they will.)

Forensic accountants are often asked to investigate cases that involve fraud, shareholder lawsuits, insurance claims, personal injury, business valuations, and other proceedings involving money transactions. Since 2001, counterterrorism has also been a fast-growing segment of most skilled practices.

Combat CPAs

Darrell Dorrell is a CPA, CVA, and ASA (American Society of Appraisers business analyst) with financial forensics in Lake Oswego, Oregon. He has trained employees of the Justice Department and the Federal Bureau of Investigation in forensic accounting. Dorrell, who grew up in a military family, only half-jokingly calls accountants like himself "combat CPAs" because they have to work fast, quietly, and thoroughly to get results — sometimes before the object of the investigation knows that forensic accountants are onto him.

Dorrell says the "combat" part applies only partially to the process of investigation. The other part has to do with the tough courtroom grilling many accountants get over valuation assignments and other financial data they uncover. He maintains that typical CPAs trained in valuation alone are not always prepared for tough, detailed questioning on the stand in a particularly nasty divorce proceeding or corporate fraud case.

"Our job is to look behind and beyond the numbers," Dorrell explains. "Classic ratio analysis used in business valuation is predicated on comparing one set of numbers to another and reaching conclusions based solely on those figures. The observations really don't tell you about the veracity of the numbers.

"Our job is to drill down into the composition of the numbers and tell you whether something's wrong or purely structural. Forensic tests such as indices can assess whether financial statements have been manipulated and where the manipulation has likely occurred."

Most forensic accountants may have experience in auditing: reviewing the accuracy of a company's or person's figures along accounting guidelines. Beyond basic accounting training that leads to CPA certification, the forensic accounting field (like most industries) is exploding with certifications in a variety of forensic accounting–related skills. Here are a few:

- ✔ **Certified Fraud Examiner (CFE):** This designation comes from the Association of Certified Fraud Examiners, a 25,000-member organization in Austin, Texas. Though many CPAs have this designation, you don't have to be a CPA to earn it; indeed, the CFE was designed for members of the law enforcement and security communities who lacked CPA certificates.

- ✔ **Certified Forensic Financial Analyst (CFFA):** This designation is provided by the National Association of Certified Valuation Analysts (nacva.com).

- ✔ **American College of Forensic Examiners:** This organization (www.acfei.com) offers a cornucopia of certification courses in a variety of areas, including consulting, accounting, nursing, medical investigation, homeland security, information security, and disaster preparation.

Expect forensic training to grow in the future.

Where forensic accountants work

Many accounting firms are dedicated to the practice of forensic accounting or have forensic accounting divisions. Some of the biggest employers of forensic accountants are the U.S. government and corporate America.

The Internal Revenue Service, Federal Bureau of Investigation, and many state and local police departments have forensic accountants on staff to address local law enforcement needs, whereas corporations may have forensic accountants on their own payrolls to stem internal fraud.

Some major accounting firms may say that they have forensic departments, but you still need to check an accountant's experience. Checking a forensic accountant's qualifications and training is critical.

Recognizing situations that link forensic accounting and valuation

The chief job of many forensic accountants in valuation assignments is to reconstruct income and/or identify the ownership of various assets — most often, its illegal path into the wrong hands inside or outside an organization. In some cases, forensic accountants, such as Darrell Dorrell, CPA, CVA, and ASA, use existing information, such as public-company data or industry benchmarks, but often, they need a subpoena to access needed information.

Following are some typical situations that unite forensic accountants with valuation assignments:

✔ **Mergers and acquisitions:** Forensic accountants may make appearances on due diligence teams in a host of deals. Forensic accountant Darrell Dorrell says involving a forensic accountant is a good thing to consider in most due diligence situations. Investment banks and other lenders also bring in forensic accountants to safeguard their interests.

Besides scrutinizing numbers, forensic accountants question human beings in the process and do onsite inspections of the facilities being sold to verify the pricing in the deal. Fake or inadequate assets listed as being a major part of a deal may be found by any valuation professional, but forensic accountants specifically look for them.

✔ **Purchase of troubled assets:** In a tough economy, the last guy standing with cash in his pocket is in a position to make some great deals on business assets or whole businesses. But troubled companies — ones that are barely keeping the lights on, that have idled property and machinery, or that have padlocks on the door — got that way for a reason. Forensic accountants can check to see whether mistakes or malfeasance devalued those assets.

✔ **Investigation of company theft:** Some of the worst financial crimes happen right under the nose of the boss. *Ghost payrollers* — fake employees getting real checks — are common in companies and governments alike. Crooked employees can create such scams very easily, based on resources close to them. They can funnel cashable paychecks through currency exchanges that are in on the scam, for example. Forensic accountants are trained to spot irregularities in accounts that can reveal such mischief.

✔ **Divorce investigations:** Never underestimate the loss potential of love gone wrong. We talk about valuation issues in divorce in Chapter 19, and forensic accountants may play a big part in that process. In family law, a lot of the friction occurs over the lack of information sharing and suspicions that shared numbers are far below — or sometimes far above — where they should be.

✔ **Global terrorism:** Increasingly, companies have to meet legal standards to make sure that employees in the United States and abroad are not involved in illegal activities that could affect local, state, or national security. Terrorists gather their funding through many disparate sources, delivering small amounts that largely go undetected, says Dorrell.

The USA Patriot Act, signed after the terrorist attacks of September 11, 2001, requires financial institutions to establish and maintain anti-money-laundering programs. In addition, all U.S. companies are required to comply with the Foreign Corrupt Practices Act, which establishes acceptable business practices. Many states have laws governing private investigation practices that apply to CPAs.

From a valuation professional's perspective

Most of the time, a valuation professional does "amateur" forensic account-ing work on her own, but her work doesn't replace the formal procedures and tests done by a trained and certified forensic accountant. Valuation professionals get close to the forensic process when they begin to normalize the financials of the business. Most of the time, they're just adding back the owner's perks or making adjustments for fair market rent, fair market wages, and various other financial activities inside the company. If a valuation professional sees something that doesn't look quite right, she simply notes it in the valuation report.

Here's an example that should raise the eyebrows of a valuation professional but could be found more easily by a forensic accountant doing some closer snooping: A medical-device company takes an order, delivers the equipment to the patient's home, and charges the customer (or his insurance company) for the items. So far, things seem perfectly normal. But suppose that the customer no longer needs that oxygen tank or hospital bed in his home, and he returns it to the company.

The transaction was originally structured to declare the patient the owner of that equipment. Here's the problem: When the material is returned, the company illegally takes the equipment back into its inventory without recording it and then uses the returned equipment to fulfill new orders as they come in. This process works to understate the company's actual inventory and its overall cost of goods, making the company appear to be more profitable than it actually is. Higher profit means higher valuation — which may be based on fraud.

Because this operation is likely being done off the books (with no formal records being kept), a valuation professional may not catch the fraud. But if she were to smell something funny — such as margins wildly higher than those of competitors in the industry — she'd either try to investigate it herself or recommend an audit. The forensic exercise would take place as part of the audit.

In essence, the forensic accountant would perform an investigation to uncover the truth behind the numbers; then the valuation professional would use the results of the forensic exercise to renormalize the numbers. The two professionals would combine their efforts to establish and reinsert the true normal inventory costs, thus realigning gross margins to what they should've been.

Many appraisers working on small-company deals don't catch this sort of operation unless they're very talented and experienced. They simply don't have records to tip them off and have to rely on other signals, such as erratic margins or other swings in financial performance that can't be explained through traditional business evidence. But if a forensic accountant is brought in during due diligence, this situation is exactly what he should be looking for.

An audit can be the very thing that keeps a new owner from overpaying for a business, so if you're a potential buyer, budget for audits that include the services of a forensic accountant.

From a forensic accountant's perspective

The relationship between a valuation professional and a forensic accountant should be close. A valuation professional is something like an emergency medical technician, whereas a forensic accountant is like a pathologist. Both parties need to be talking. The same relationship rules go for attorneys and other professionals brought into the process.

Like valuation professionals who are CPAs, however, forensic accountants have only one allegiance: to their certificate, meaning the set of professional standards to which they're required to adhere. "We have to honor those standards ahead of our client's preferences because we are often called on to testify to those findings under oath," says forensic accountant and CPA Darrell Dorrell. "We are the only credential holders in the United States with the word *public* in our title. The public expects us to be independent and objective above all else."

Comparing Basic and Forensic Accounting

Most people think that forensic accounting is part of the basic accounting process. In most cases, the processes are very separate and distinct. According to Darrell Dorrell, the following holds true:

- ✔ An *audit* is a CPA's commentary on the representation of financial statements produced by management. Typically, virtually no forensic accounting is applied.

- ✔ Basic accounting, such as the day-to-day assembly and reporting of a company's financial transactions, requires virtually no forensic accounting.

- ✔ Forensic accounting typically assesses basic accounting reports and compares them with reality, identifying departures, undisclosed items, and related matters.

"Traditional accounting is scorekeeping according to a set of rules such professionals must follow. Forensic accounting is about investigation," Dorrell explains. Yet he points out that forensic accounting isn't just about fraud; it's also an essential component of accurate business valuation based on facts and circumstances.

"It's not just people outside the accounting profession; people inside the accounting profession often confuse forensic accounting with fraud. The two are related, but fraud is a subset of the forensic accounting discipline," says Dorrell, whose company provides valuation services in addition to the more common activities associated with forensic accounting. Dorrell continues:

"Business valuation must consist of forensic tests because by exercising forensic tests, you resolve valuation-related questions. For example, with forensic tests, you can determine the actual pattern of cash flows — the ultimate measure of value, what kind of normalization (adjustment of financial statements) needs to occur, the optimal capital structure of the business — measure the similarity of guideline transactions, assess the fit of a discount rate, and so on."

Can small companies afford forensic accounting?

For many companies, professional bookkeeping and accounting services can be a significant expense. Here are some appropriate questions to ask yourself about affordability:

✔ Do you have a concern about the financials of a target company or a company you already own and think that an investigation is necessary? Assess the reasons you think a forensic investor would be appropriate in this situation.

✔ If the first point is relevant, what are the potential costs of *not* doing an investigation? The company may face possible civil or criminal charges, or cash may be disappearing at a rate that threatens the viability of the business.

✔ What are the costs in your area for forensic accountants with the correct training and

certification, and do they work for companies of your size?

The more complicated the investigation — and whatever chores are tied to the investigation, such as valuation — the more the investigation will cost. Professionals typically don't charge fixed fees in such complex matters, but fees are worth asking about.

An effective way to manage fees is to instruct the forensic accountant to conduct the work in phases. In other words, consider writing into the work agreement a statement like this: "When you have reached $5,000, let me know your findings and where else it might be beneficial to investigate." A legitimate specialist will advise you to stop when there appears to be no reason to continue.

Recognizing Business Situations That Trigger Forensic Accounting

Forensic accounting is not all about illegal activity, though questionable financial behavior certainly is a major catalyst for many such investigations. Here are some of the kinds of situations that forensic accountants may be hired to investigate in organizations:

✔ **Ownership:** Evidence of improper or illegal manipulation of ownership within a company or hidden assets relevant to heirs, shareholders, or soon-to-be ex-spouses

✔ **Succession planning:** When there's doubt that a new management team was formed with proper diligence and planning

✔ **Bankruptcy:** When there's suspicion of illegal or incompetent financial manipulations that led to companies' going into bankruptcy or liquidation

✔ **A need for added oversight:** When an owner or shareholder needs someone to assess a business valuation done at the request of the controlling shareholder

✔ **Skimming and embezzlement:** Anything from petty theft to scams that create massive financial losses within an organization

✔ **Top-level corporate fraud:** Companies such as Enron and WorldCom — two major firms that failed in the early 2000s — owed much of their demise to illegal and questionable acts by top management

✔ **Mergers and acquisitions:** Errors, either intentional or unintentional, may surface in the valuation of assets when companies are getting together

✔ **Tax evasion:** Evidence of hidden tax liability and possible illegal tax avoidance that can become a major liability for future management

✔ **Money laundering:** Suspicion that a company may be filtering ill-gotten money through a series of financial transactions so that the money looks as though it came from legitimate sources

✔ **Contradictory financial reporting:** When a company has reporting inconsistencies in its financial data, it may not be illegal, but it's exceptionally important for a prospective buyer or seller to determine what the inconsistencies are and see that they're fixed before a purchase or a sale

Doing a Forensic Accounting Test

This book can't give you in-depth knowledge about forensic accounting processes, but here's the basic definition of a *forensic test:* a financial formula or process that puts a company's numbers through different paces to test or determine the accuracy and completeness of its figures. "By doing forensic tests, you can determine what kind of normalization needs to occur on a balance sheet," Darrell Dorrell says.

Valuation involves few specific formulas, specific tests that apply within forensic evaluation. A well-known test, TATA (total accruals to total assets), looks something like this:

$$\text{Total Accruals to Total Assets} = (\text{Working Capital} - \text{Cash} - \text{Current Taxes Payable} - \text{Depreciation/Amortization}) \div \text{Total Assets}$$

A TATA test compares the consistency of results period to period. You'd do a TATA computation for, say, two consecutive quarters. Your index should remain about 0.7 throughout all the comparison periods. If you start to see material increases or decreases, digging a little more is appropriate.

Looking at Forensic Accounting Case Studies

Forensic accountant Darrell Dorrell won't cite actual situations, to ensure the privacy of clients, but he tells a few stories about small companies that could've used outside forensic accounting and valuation help:

✔ **Case 1:** "Two companies were competitors within a geographic region," he says. "One was large and had been operating more than 70 years; the other, much smaller and had been operating about 5 years. The two companies agreed to merge, and each company had its own very high-profile accountants and attorneys conducting due diligence over an 18-month period. After closing the transaction the following May, the combined operation was out of business within 90 days."

Dorrell's firm was called in to diagnose what had happened. They found that the firms' due diligence had failed to identify the extreme seasonality of the businesses, and both firms went ahead with a leveraged buyout that happened at the precise time when each business historically began losing cash due to the seasonality. "They simply ran out of money. This is an example of how traditional tools and techniques are simply inadequate," Dorrell says.

✔ **Case 2:** "A company hired a national business valuation firm to determine the value of its shareholdings in anticipation of a sale. One of the shareholders believed that the results made no sense in comparison to his understanding of the company," Dorrell says.

Dorrell's firm was called in to assess the results and found that that the national firm had used an earnings before interest, taxes, depreciation, and amortization (EBITDA) multiple but failed to account for the post-transaction capital structure. Consequently, the private financing firm backed out of the transaction because it was doomed to fail. (For more on EBITDA, go to Chapter 4.)

✔ **Case 3:** The founder of a company that was more than 40 years old wanted to retire. "The longtime CFO, a supposed friend of the family (he had completed the entire family's tax returns for many years), structured a deal that was portrayed as beneficial to owners, employees, customers, and lenders," Dorrell explains.

The trusted chief financial officer had two national valuation firms determine value, and based on that result, he secured additional debt and equity financing to buy most of the owner's stock. The nature of the accounting treatment enabled the CFO to redeem all the old stock and issue new stock with a private benefit to himself. He gave himself an ownership position of nearly one-third without paying even a penny for his stock.

Within two years, the company was struggling under the new capitalization plan, and it became clear to the remaining family members that the deal had been made for the CFO's benefit.

Dorrell's firm was called in to assess the problem, diagnose a remedy, and implement changes. It found that the valuation firms had overvalued the company to trigger the CFO's accounting treatment. The overvalued company resulted in a debt load that nearly strangled the company. The firm was revalued at its correct value, and the capital was restructured, and the CFO no longer works for the company.

Says Dorrell, "This was to have been a simple sale of a company where the owner had been around for 40 years. He relied on his CFO to arrange the buyout and wasn't as closely involved in the process as he should have been, but indeed, the CFO structured a deal that ended up giving two-thirds of the company's stock to the owner's son and the other third to himself."

Dorrell has seen many situations in which attorneys, valuation professionals, and corporate accountants and CFOs didn't make a thorough evaluation of what the deal would cost the company post-closing. He maintains that the preceding examples are only a few of the reasons it's important to bring in a forensic accountant before any major financial transaction takes place at a company to make sure that its numbers are in order.

Chapter 18

Case Study: Valuation on the Buy Side

*I*n this chapter, we give you the step-by-step valuation process for a potential purchase of a company, putting into practice the concepts and steps we outline in the other chapters in Part IV. We start with full disclosure. If you're planning to use this chapter as a one-size-fits-all template to value a company you're planning to buy, forget it. No two companies are alike, and no two buyers are alike; therefore, no two valuation assignments are the same, either.

The purpose of this chapter is to tell you a story about one owner's ups, downs, and in-betweens in the valuation process. The story isn't a true story; the names and details have been changed to protect real clients. But to say the least, the road to value doesn't always run smoothly, which is the main point you should take from this chapter.

Use this chapter as a way to prepare for the unpredictability of the valuation process and a way to better prepare yourself before you attempt to buy a company.

Being Frank: Selecting an Industry

The story we're about to tell you involves an entrepreneur named Frank. Frank was a 50/50 partner in a prosperous consulting firm that placed consultants for information technology projects. When Frank and his partner were unable to come to terms on the future of their business, Frank's partner agreed to buy him out, which has left Frank sitting on a considerable pile of cash.

Frank decides that he's going to play golf; he even gets a job at the local golf course. Six to nine months later, Frank's wife realizes that when he isn't at the club, he's spending a lot of time at home and underfoot. It's not that Frank's wife is unhappy with her husband's success, and she's glad he's had a chance to relax a bit, but now he's disrupting her world, and she's starting to lobby Frank on his next move.

Frank realizes that he's getting a bit bored and that it's time to start looking for the next business to invest in. Whether he realizes it or not, he's already begun the valuation process. He started to consider what kind of business he wants to start and what business may be recession-proof, or at least relatively so. In other words, he's echoing the first baby steps of valuation outlined in the Internal Revenue Service's Revenue Ruling 59-60 (www.irs.gov), which requires potential business owners to consider the following:

- ✔ The nature of the business
- ✔ The history of the enterprise from its inception
- ✔ The earning capacity of the company
- ✔ The dividend-paying capacity of the company
- ✔ The economic outlook in general
- ✔ The condition and outlook of the specific industry in particular

Frank has zeroed in on the medical equipment and supply industry. His logic: Medical equipment is a relatively recession-proof business because no matter what else happens, people have illnesses. At the same time, people are living longer. Frank takes special note of his generation of Baby Boomers, the largest chunk of the nation's population. As that group ages, he thinks, the demand for medical equipment and supplies is only going to grow as people are discharged from hospitals and require more therapy and care at home. Therefore, the companies that supply hospital beds, walkers, oxygen tanks, and the like are going to be in a very nice position.

Doing Research in Advance

Frank, like most experienced entrepreneurs, isn't afraid to hit the books. He starts with Internet research to determine the best resources on the medical equipment industry and then heads off to the local university library to gather the data he needs. (For information on basic company research and preparing for the valuation process, go to Chapters 12 and 16.)

When he pulls those resources together, he's off to see his business attorney, his tax attorney, and his personal finance advisor to talk the idea through. They seem to think that the idea makes sense. Frank's ready to start looking for companies to buy. *Tip:* If you think that valuation is all about spreading the numbers, consider Frank's story to this point. He hasn't begun analyzing the figures in depth, but he's developing a general knowledge of the business and visualizing his participation in it. The numbers are next.

Frank's first steps are to contact a broker, do some Internet research, and visit the various Web sites that list businesses for sale.

To get an overview of which businesses are available, go to the Internet. Three good Web sites are FirstList (www.firstlist.com), BizBuySell (www.bizbuysell.com), and MergerNetwork (www.mergernetwork.com).

Frank finds one business located in Florida that looks very interesting. He contacts the broker who listed this business for sale.

Contacting the Target

Through the broker, Frank contacts the target company. He's required to sign a confidentiality agreement to see the introductory data on the company for sale. Within a few days, Frank receives a small marketing package describing the company.

Frank's marketing package is fairly standard. It provides details on how and when the business began, how the business has performed over the years, and how it has grown, as well as details on the owners and members of management. The package also includes what ideally are audited financial statements of the target company, signed by the auditor. Most potential buyers go straight to the financials to perform their own version of a quick-and-dirty valuation, which we cover in the following section.

Negotiating the quick-and-dirty valuation stage

Frank starts with rule-of-thumb guides (refer to Chapter 9), which are only one part of the initial quick-and-dirty valuation stage. In addition to using rules of thumb, he applies certain market multiples and performs a basic capitalization-of-earnings calculation.

A *market multiple* is a formula tailored to the specific attributes of an industry to measure its performance. A *capitalization-of-earnings calculation* allows you to calculate the present value of future cash flow, which is a way to predict future earnings. If you determine that future earnings won't be greater than the ones the business is making now, why buy the company?

These standard computations can give a prospective owner his first ballpark idea of a company's current and future value. If the future looks good, the buyer can move forward.

Knowing when to talk . . . and when to hang up

The Florida company's numbers look good, so Frank organizes a conference call to find out more about the company's operations. Over the course of a couple of weeks and a few more phone conversations, he finds out even more about what's going on with the company, its management, and its employees. He even gets a couple of customers to talk on the quiet.

If you've read Chapter 16 — the chapter on buyer due diligence — this process is familiar. If not, stick a bookmark in this page, and start reading Chapter 16 now, because Frank dodges a land mine by doing due diligence.

Frank hears from a customer that the company shipped a bunch of recalled oxygen dispensers to a client by mistake. No deaths or injuries were reported as a result of this mistake, but because Frank did his homework, he realizes that such liabilities can surface months or years later. Figuring this risk into his calculations, he decides to terminate the talks, which is good, because this company may have brought him significant headaches.

Frank is one month older and back to square one, and his wife isn't happy.

This example shows you two important things: Finding the best company to buy takes time, and if a company is up for sale, you need to know exactly why.

Moving on to Company Number Two

Frank sets his sights on a similar company that's based in Atlanta. He does his initial due diligence and finds that the firm is doing about $1 million a year in gross revenue, with a profit of about $300,000 a year — a very nice set of numbers. Instantly, Frank wants to know more, so he gets out his calculator again.

Frank's initial figuring puts the company's value at between $600,000 and $900,000, which sounds good so far and should make his impatient wife happy. He decides to bid at the high end, so he lets the broker know that he's interested in putting down $600,000 in cash down at closing and the remaining $300,000 in the form of a seller note payable in quarterly payments over four years at 8 percent interest to make it really worthwhile for the sellers.

Seeing How Failing to Consult an Advisor Can Cost You

At any point during the scenario we explain in the preceding section, do we mention that Frank talked to any advisor before making that tentative offer? Nope, we don't — and nope, he didn't, which is a potentially big mistake. Certainly, Frank is an intelligent guy, and he knows that it's in his best interest to get a professional advisor involved at some point, but he doesn't want his costs to escalate out of control.

Doing the quick-and-dirty analysis to educate yourself in the early stages of the valuation process is fine, but it's not fine to move ahead without the analysis and approval of a professional advisor who has experience in these types of transactions. Failing to consult with a professional advisor can create a very bad situation for you.

Knowing when to involve advisors

Should an advisor have been involved from the beginning, even though Frank was just trying to find out about the opportunity? Maybe someone should have asked him these questions:

- ✔ Do you have enough capital that you can afford to lose a little in case of a mistake?

- ✔ Do you have such a thorough knowledge of the company's business and its competitors that you won't leave any stone unturned?

- ✔ Are you truly your best advocate, or can you find a better one?

Frank has never worked in this industry before. He's made a cursory investigation and worked the numbers to his satisfaction. The gods may be with him, and the deal could work out beautifully. But if he hasn't vetted the decision and his knowledge turns out to be inadequate late in the transaction period — or worse, after the transaction is done — he can't do much about the mistakes of poor investigation and valuation.

We maintain that you should get a valuation professional involved earlier in the process rather than later, based on the experience you have with the business and industry you're targeting. Getting backup can help you make better use of your money and time by uncovering fatal flaws in the business.

Failing to work with an advisor early can cost you a lot more time and money than engaging a valuation professional from the start, and it more than likely determines your ability to succeed. This was Frank's mistake.

Too many times in privately held businesses, you find a story behind the numbers, and this story can be dangerous. Owners can bury extraordinary personal expenses in line items or under-the-table transactions deep within financial statements. In particularly egregious cases, even a professional advisor may not uncover some fatal flaws. But in our experience, it's generally better to have an expert on the team early, because later, those problems can end up in court.

Encountering problems

Frank leaps in with both feet and completes the deal.

Any acquisition involves a transition period in which the new owner gets both feet wet. That transition period can be bumpy if the new owner has never worked in the industry, as in Frank's case. Frank is busy for the first few months finding out about the customers, the operations, the employees, and dozens of other aspects of the business. A typical business learning curve can last anywhere from three months (for someone who's operated in the business) to nearly a year (for inexperienced individuals like Frank).

At the six-month point, Frank starts to see things that don't look quite right. His cost-of-goods reports and inventory numbers, which are supposed to be complementary, are way off.

This situation affects his bottom-line cash flow, because he seems to be spending a lot more money on inventory than the previous owner did, which drives up his cost of goods and slashes his profitability.

The buyer's due diligence and the owner's cover-up

After Frank valued the company, he made an offer based on the financial statements provided by the previous owner during the sale process. Right after he got the nod, he went to his local banker to finance a portion of that deal. He decided that the company's profits would more than pay down that loan and supply him a nice weekly paycheck. Now, staring down at his uncertain operating figures, he finds himself wondering whether he can pay the bank, much less his own salary. So much for due diligence.

Frank is determined to get to the bottom of the problem. The first mistake he uncovers is incorrect inventory numbers supplied during due diligence. He finds that the company sometimes refurbished used equipment and turned it back into inventory without a record of having done so. The next time a patient needed equipment from the company, a used, refurbished, and possibly broken piece of equipment went out into the marketplace.

Aside from the potential liability of product failure, this situation constituted fraud. Accounting rules prohibit companies from charging a customer for an item and then taking it back into inventory without recording it or paying for it. Technically, the company no longer owned that piece of equipment, because the cost of the equipment had already been charged to someone else. Also, a potential buyer had no real way of knowing about this practice just by taking a cursory look at the company's financial statements.

The company's fraudulent practice made the due diligence numbers that Frank evaluated look a lot better. Some orders or fulfillments didn't have a cost of goods attached or a corresponding purchase of a new inventory item to fulfill each order. This illegal activity overinflated the numbers and made the company look more profitable than it actually was.

Yes, owners sometimes lie

Frank finds more adventures in the accounts receivable department. In the medical equipment and supply industry, equipment is used to fulfill orders. Then someone or something is billed: the patient, a hospital, an insurance company, or state or federal government through the Medicare and Medicaid programs. Each of these entities has a different schedule for paying its bills. Some of these entities pay in 30 days; others, in 60 days; others, in 90 days. Therefore, working-capital requirements are a critical factor in this business.

Frank heard something about this sort of behavior in the industry during his due diligence and asked the previous owner of the company about it point-blank. The problem was that the owner lied, saying that everything was fine.

Frank's mad now. His inventory and working capital are in shambles. He refuses to make any payments on the seller-note portion of the deal (the $300,000 piece of the $900,000 deal we mention earlier in this chapter). Harsh words ensue, and Frank moves the whole mess into court, where he claims that the previous owner misrepresented the profitability of the company and that as a result, he was duped into paying far more for it than it was worth.

Seeing what could've been done

Over the next two years, Frank shells out thousands of dollars and considerable time to bring the previous owners to heel. In the end, he straightens out and runs the company, and he's forgiven payment on the $300,000 seller note, but his win comes with considerable personal and financial cost.

Suppose that Frank had hired a trained, experienced valuation professional at the start of the transaction. The problems with the business were essentially a result of the previous owner's practice of running the business off the books. With no clues in the financial records to go by, what could that valuation professional have done?

In a full valuation scenario, trained professionals should do a ratio comparison of the financials with those of similar companies in the same industry, including current ratio, quick ratio, accounts receivable turns, and inventory turns (see Chapter 8 for some of the ratio formulas). Then they turn to a host of industry-specific metrics that measure comparable industries in a closer way. Checking these computations against those that are common in an industry can bring certain abnormalities to light.

An *inventory turn* is the inventory turnover, the ratio of a company's annual sales to its inventory, or how long average items remain in that inventory. Every industry that has inventory has a common healthy inventory turnover period. If a company is ahead of its industry turnover period, typically, this news is good. If the company is behind its industry turnover period, this news usually is bad.

In Frank's case, the inventory and accounts receivable numbers were seriously out of whack, but he didn't dig deeply enough to discover this.

Checking Benchmarking Data

The Risk Management Association (RMA) keeps data on more than 700 industries and tracks all aspects of their operations. Granted, Frank could've checked that resource and many others in his search, but he chose not to.

Benchmarking data helps you understand performance and operational targets that are typical for the best-performing companies in an industry so that when you do an in-depth evaluation of a particular firm, you can see whether it's on par with the best performers. The RMA (www.rmahq.org) provides this data to subscribers, but some libraries carry it.

Had Frank made this analysis early in the process, he would never have made an offer or certainly would've made a far smaller offer.

Understanding Deal Structure

We give you a thorough overview on rules of thumb in Chapter 9 and tell you where this guidance may be useful. Keep in mind, though, that you can go very wrong with these rules of thumb, as Frank discovered.

If you're trying to follow up on the hundreds of details involved in buying a business, you probably don't have adequate time to do a thorough valuation, even if you're properly trained to do one. If you get an industry rule of thumb or find out that businesses in this industry are trading for a certain multiple, you still won't know exactly what the structure of that payment will be, which is known as the *deal structure*. Deal structure affects value.

Every one of the deals listed in the RMA benchmarking tables has a different structure. A certain amount of money comes in at closing in the form of cash; another portion of the overall price takes some other form, such as a seller note or stock. Sometimes, the form is contingent on future performance.

Just looking at a few transactions, the overall purchase price, and the resulting multiples on price to revenue or price to earnings doesn't always give you an accurate picture. Valuation professionals who understand your industry can do a better job of zeroing in on the elements you need to build a deal.

The moral of the story is that a very deep analysis of any target company is necessary. Buyers must be willing to take the time to do research; they must have patience and the financial strength to place significant amounts of money upfront. Often, hiring an expert to take an unbiased, tough look at a proposed transaction can save you considerable money in the long run.

Part V

Don't Try This at Home! Turning Things Over to the Valuation Experts

The 5th Wave   By Rich Tennant

"I read about investing in a company called Unihandle Ohio, but I'm uneasy about a stock that's listed on the NASDAQ as UhOh."

In this part . . .

We haven't been shy at all about telling you to get help when you feel that you're out of your depth in any part of the valuation process. Because we think this point is so important, we decided to drive it home in this part by providing examples of three situations that call for professional assistance with the various tasks needed to arrive at business valuation: getting a divorce, estate planning and gifting, and attracting investors and lenders to a business. We say, "Don't try this at home," because we find that unbiased advice is exactly what people need in these situations.

Chapter 19

Divorce

. . . .

. . . .

Divorce can be one of the biggest threats to the future of any closely held business, as well as to the people who depend on it.

When married business owners begin a divorce action, whether one party or both parties were involved in the day-to-day business, they set a series of financially threatening events into motion. Children, stepchildren, in-laws, business partners, and employees are affected by these events on both a short-term basis (the split of assets in divorce) and a long-term basis (the distribution of assets among multiple families at the time of a former spouse's death).

In this chapter, we talk about prenuptial and postnuptial agreements, and we also discuss the role of business valuation during divorce proceedings.

Doing Estate Planning Regardless of Marital Status

In estate matters (see Chapter 20), it's a good rule of thumb to review your plans every three years or whenever a material change in your family's lifestyle occurs, such as a marriage, a divorce, a remarriage, the birth of children, the loss of an immediate family member, or a major rise or fall in assets.

Planning for the future of a business isn't just about the possibility of divorce. Proper discussion, documentation, and review of a family's assets — with the participation of the right legal, tax, and financial planning advisors — can keep more of those assets in the family according to the family's wishes.

In the case of a family business, generations of family members may have built careers there or otherwise depend on that income. Yet the business may not even be at the heart of an issue; families may have supported foundations or other charitable activities for years with a certain mission that the people in charge don't want changed.

More than a few families have imploded in ugly legal squabbles over these situations and more. The results can be lengthy legal battles with damaging tax consequences, a potentially unfair split of assets among relatives, or simple mismanagement of those assets going forward.

One should consider all these issues with respect to valuation of the business. As you can see, divorce complicates everything, but it's just one piece of a crowded puzzle of issues involving business valuation, family legacies, and money. In good times and bad, you need to think about all those issues together.

Planning Prenuptial and Postnuptial Agreements

If you watch any TV show with a lawyer in the lead role, or if you're addicted to the divorce blotter in any gossip magazine, you probably know what a prenuptial agreement is. But in case you don't, a *prenuptial agreement* — casually known as a *prenup* — is an agreement made and signed by two people before the wedding to establish financial ground rules during the marriage and to set clear courses of action for marital assets in case of death or divorce.

This chapter is about business valuation in case of a divorce, so why are we talking about prenuptial agreements? Because anyone who's considering marriage while operating or planning to open a business should work with a future spouse to develop a prenuptial agreement. This agreement should set ground rules on the use and distribution of financial assets not only during the marriage but also at the end, either through divorce or death.

A prenup is not about when you'll be sending the kids to bed or who will do the chores. Rather, a prenup ensures a financial balance of power in a relationship. Yes, the agreement is literally about the money, but it also may be about saving pain, heartache — and yes, money — if a relationship ends.

Courts have a long history of looking closely at prenups, because in the past, they were often written in a way that clearly supported the wealthier spouse. Courts can invalidate a prenup, so make sure that both sides get the advice of talented matrimonial law, estate, and business valuation professionals beforehand so that the document will be durable.

A *postnuptial agreement* sets out the same issues and conditions, with one critical difference: It's made after the parties say "I do." A couple without a prenup may consider a postnuptial agreement for a variety of reasons, but determining the future of a family business started either before or after the marriage is just as good a reason as any.

Doing a business valuation before the wedding is a good idea. If the marriage is preceded by a recent divorce, a business valuation from the divorce may be applicable. In any event, if the valuation is more than a year old, it should be updated. The new valuation should be attached to the balance sheet of the business and footnoted as part of the prenuptial record.

Breaking down a prenuptial agreement

Getting a spouse to sign off on a prenup isn't much of a picnic, but creating a breakup agreement years after the honeymoon is an even greater challenge. The prenup process may not be easy to go through — creating a prenup agreement requires both sides to be very honest about how they feel about money — but it represents, at minimum, smart business planning and prescient thinking in case a divorce actually happens.

Here's the full range of financial issues that a prenuptial agreement typically addresses:

✔ **Which finances you'll commingle and which ones you'll keep separate:** Depending on your state's law governing assets accumulated during marriage — often called *community property* — a prenup can state exactly how you'll split assets at the end. See the later section "State laws on splitting property" for details on how states regard ownership.

✔ **How you'll handle debt coming into the marriage:** If one of you has (or both of you have) sizable personal or business debt coming into the marriage, you want to lay your cards on the table and address how that debt will be allotted in case of divorce.

A good way to start the disclosure process before you start hammering out a prenup is to exchange credit reports — the reports issued by the main credit bureaus, Experian (www.experian.com), TransUnion (www.transunion.com), and Equifax (www.equifax.com). Looking at each other's credit history may be the least romantic thing you ever do, but it's a first, honest step toward a lifetime of transparency in all your financial dealings.

✔ **How you'll provide for kids from previous marriages:** The agreement isn't just about the money or business assets you keep for yourselves; it's also about making sure that your heirs keep what's theirs.

✔ **How you'll keep family property in the family:** This part of the agreement is particularly important for family businesses intended for children from previous marriages, but it also applies to homes and other forms of property. If property is important, you can and should designate its intended ownership in this legal document.

✔ **How your estate goals will align with your other asset goals:** A prenup is both a defensive document against divorce and an important support for the spouses' respective estate plans. A prenup's language should dovetail with both parties' wills, trusts, and health directives.

No important financial agreement is an island. Whether you're talking about a prenup, a will, a trust, or a business ownership agreement, the agreement needs to complement your overall financial plans and goals. In other words, a prenup should address estate and business issues and vice versa.

✔ **What both sides will get to keep at the time of divorce:** A prenup can specify what each partner will get — and won't get — in the event of divorce. Depending on the type of business assets and the spouses' willingness to set a baseline value on business assets going into the marriage, a valuation may be done at that time.

Prenups are all about the money — nothing else. If a prenup specifies when and where your spouse can go without you or how you'll discipline the kids, these issues can't be enforced in a court of law. Stick to the dollars.

✔ **How money will be handled throughout the marriage:** Are you going to file joint tax returns or separate returns that allocate particular income and deductions? What kind of bank accounts will you have, and who will pay the bills? Is there a plan for buying a house or a business together? A prenup can be as general or as specific about your financial affairs as you need it to be.

✔ **What standard of value you'll agree to use when you divorce:** As we say throughout the book, the valuation method you choose is affected by many factors that are unique to you and your business. In general, family-law courts accept fair-market, intrinsic, or investment valuations (see Chapter 3). It makes sense to agree on value methodology at the start of a relationship to prevent an endless debate over methodology at the end.

✔ **Full disclosure of all debts and assets as of the marriage date:** Again, it's wise to pull credit reports and other financial data at the beginning.

✔ **The status of any gifts or bequests you receive, either before or after marriage:** A good example is a gift by one spouse's parents of a down payment on a house. Is the gift to the couple or just to the donors' child?

✔ **The beneficiaries of all retirement plans, such as 401(k)s, pensions, and individual retirement accounts (IRAs), in the event of your death or divorce:** This is particularly important if each individual in the marriage has children by the current relationship as well as children from former relationships.

✔ **How you'll handle the day-to-day living, college, and healthcare expenses of your kids:** This can dictate behavior during the marriage as well as intended behavior after a divorce.

Events that void a prenup can depend on state law. In some situations, adultery can void a prenuptial agreement.

Creating a postnuptial agreement

A postnuptial agreement may not be a bad idea for a married couple who is starting a business together but has never addressed the subject of separating assets. To do these agreements well, you need two things:

✔ Truthfulness

✔ An experienced lawyer to represent your interests

Most states recognize postnups via statutes that allow married people to form contracts with each other. Keep in mind, however, that courts examine postnups as carefully as prenups (which we cover in the preceding section), because some judges believe that certain spouses have less bargaining power after they're married and may be forced into signing such an agreement.

Seeking the Correct Professionals

Divorce is one of the most intense examples of when you need to blend the skills of a number of qualified experts. Remember, personal and business objectives are always linked, and in a highly emotional process like divorce, you need skilled professionals who have the ability to work with others. If your marriage is breaking up, you may need to consult some or all of the following experts and put them in touch with one another:

✔ **Valuation professional:** This trained expert values the business based on the parameters you set, and your soon-to-be-ex-spouse may hire his or her own for the same purpose.

✔ **Tax attorney:** This legal expert may be among the first experts you consult about the potential tax ramifications of selling or splitting certain assets held jointly, or believed to have been held jointly, in the marriage.

✔ **Divorce attorney:** The best divorce attorneys act as ringmasters of all these professionals, blending the results of their work into a successful negotiation for a divorce settlement.

✔ **Estate attorney:** Divorce may be the endpoint of a marriage, but it can redirect your financial life and certainly the financial life of your heirs. An estate attorney has a distinct perspective on the valuation and tax questions inherent based on the interests of his or her client.

Looking at What Happens to a Family Business in Divorce

Deep emotional stress and clear thinking about money don't mix. Divorce can spark some pretty colorful valuation scenarios based on what each spouse believes the business is worth. And after emotions spill over, arguments once confined at home can move into the office. For this reason, divorce may rank highest among the don't-try-this-at-home scenarios.

Also, no clear standard of value exists in a divorce situation. (For a review of standards of value, see Chapter 3.) When couples split up and try to determine the value of shared assets in a company, one spouse may try to get the number as high as possible to boost his or her takeaway, whereas the other does everything possible to keep the valuation low so as not to lose too much of what he or she feels entitled to.

This situation can get to be very nasty, depending on the planning (or lack of planning) both spouses brought to the business during their marriage. But make no mistake: Divorce is just as big a triggering event in the life of a business as a natural disaster, an unwanted takeover, or the loss of a major customer.

In terms of valuation, divorce actions can spark a sudden need to do the following:

✔ Determine the continuing share of ownership in a company for one or both spouses who want to continue working in the family business.

✔ Set a breakup value for a company if the spouses end up liquidating and taking their splits with them.

✔ Find ways to protect the estate of the founding family of the business against actions threatened by the in-law family.

✔ Take immediate action to calm customers, employees, and suppliers who fear that the divorce action will decimate the company.

Without an enforceable pre- or postnuptial agreement (see the pertinent sections earlier in this chapter), a family business is simply another asset in the marital estate that's subject to distribution after a divorce, so we can't overemphasize the importance of divorce planning before starting a business.

Business valuation gets tough during a divorce for the following reasons:

✔ **Conflicting goals:** Each company has complexity in terms of tangible assets such as cash, inventory, tools, fixtures, furniture, and machinery. But intangible issues — ranging from customer lists and patents to various forms of intellectual capital that one or both spouses contributed — may complicate matters even more. Even if a spouse didn't get a weekly paycheck from the business, he or she may consider his or her non-monetary support of the other spouse in building the business as entitlement to a significant portion of the value of the business.

✔ **Questions about control:** Depending on where the business is in its life cycle at the time of a divorce, the spouses may have young children who aren't involved in the family business or adult children who have an ownership stake and already have careers in the business. Also, both spouses may be working in the business, though at different levels of seniority. If all adult family members have a stake in the company, they have a stake in the outcome of negotiations for its control.

✔ **Inadequate basis for evaluation:** Buy/sell agreements may be adequate to settle partnership issues, but courts tend not to look at those agreements as the final word on the worth of a business, because they tend to serve the interests of the active owner of the business, not the divorcing spouse outside the business.

If you're interviewing divorce attorneys and tax professionals before a divorce proceeding, ask them whether they work with a certified business valuation professional who specializes in divorce. Though no one wants to end up in court, the best valuation experts in the divorce field not only know how to value assets in this situation but also understand state statutes with respect to both valuation and matrimonial law.

✔ **Inadequate access to information:** One of the most difficult aspects of valuing a private company involved in divorce is access to critical information that would help the nonactive or less-senior spouse in the business get a better idea of the health of the business. Although not all spouses hide information illegally, many wouldn't choose to make it easy to find.

State laws on splitting property

Keep in mind that where you live matters in determining how property is divided in the event of divorce. Pay particular attention to your state law when developing pre- and postnuptial agreements. You need to work with qualified attorneys and valuation professionals who understand how the law will affect your assets and develop a negotiating strategy from there.

Community-property states

Do you live in Arizona, California, Idaho, Louisiana, Nevada, New Mexico, Texas, Washington, Wisconsin, or Puerto Rico? These areas of the country are known as community-property states. (Puerto Rico isn't a state, of course, but it has the same law.) In a *community-property* state, each spouse owns an undivided one-half interest in most property acquired by a husband or wife *during the course of a marriage.*

For a business started before a marriage, community-property law isn't necessarily a protection. Businesses tend to grow during a marriage, and unless the inactive spouse legally refuses a right to those assets through a prenuptial agreement or some other document, she or he is unlikely to be shut out.

If the spouse who wants to continue working in the business is challenged by the spouse who wants his or her share, the result can be the sale, shutdown, or dangerous leveraging of the company. Without planning and with significant acrimony, family legacies go down the drain all the time.

Here's one more wrinkle: With women now earning the majority of college degrees and taking time out to rear families, more couples are starting businesses together. In 2002, MassMutual Financial Group and the Raymond Institute reported that husband-and-wife chief executive officers (CEOs) of family businesses increased from 8 percent in 1997 to 14 percent in 2002. Both spouses need to think seriously about property while the relationship is healthy.

Equitable-distribution states

No matter how much you plan and no matter how much you do to protect what you believe to be yours, state legislatures have put their own spin on what your settlement will eventually be. In certain cases, judges apply their own interpretation of what a fair distribution of assets should be.

In most states, property is classified as being either separate property or marital property. *Separate property* includes property owned before the marriage, inherited during the marriage, received as a gift during the marriage, or otherwise excluded from marital property by a prenuptial agreement. *Marital property* is all other property acquired during the marriage, no matter which spouse owns it.

Nine U.S. states and one U.S. territory follow community-property law (see the preceding section), which essentially means that property or assets acquired by the husband or wife during the marriage (with the exception of certain inheritances and gifts) are owned 50/50 by the husband and wife.

In *equitable-distribution* states, all property, whenever or however it was acquired and regardless of its legal title, is subject to equal or unequal division. The definition is a bit of a wild card. In some states, if your spouse got a big inheritance before you walked down the aisle and he never touched those assets for family use or investment, a judge may have the right to divide those funds between the two of you. If you're talking about a marriage that lasted only a year or two, you could be looking at a pretty unequal settlement — at least from the standpoint of the person giving up the money!

Wherever you live, your state's divorce laws indicate specific factors that judges need to follow to make an equitable division of property or award of alimony. Some states also allow discretionary factors that allow judges more leeway in their decision-making. Following are some of these factors:

- ✔ The length of the marriage
- ✔ The ages, health, and occupations of both parties
- ✔ Lifestyle issues, including issues related to children
- ✔ Each party's contribution to the marriage in terms of money issues (wages, investments, and so on) versus domestic contributions (homemaking, child rearing, and so on)
- ✔ The behavior of the parties during the marriage
- ✔ The employable skills of both parties

As you can see, judges do have a lot of power in the divorce-settlement process, so both parties in a divorce need to be aware of how state law will affect what they're likely to keep in a divorce. That knowledge may influence valuation efforts during the divorce.

The marital balance of power

Justin L. Cherfoli, managing director of the Dispute Advisory and Forensic Services Group at Stout Risius Ross, a Chicago-based law firm, regularly works with both sides in a divorce — business owners and their spouses who aren't active in the business. "If there's one thing I've learned, it's that whoever controls the finances of a business holds all 52 cards in the deck, and they don't give out more than they feel they have to," Cherfoli says.

Those who aren't on the side with the cards definitely need valuation expertise to counter any valuation estimate offered by the spouse who is active in the business. Cherfoli says that many valuation clients don't always like the results because valuation professionals are supposed to value the business independently and without bias — even if that means upsetting the person who's paying the bill. "A valuation professional's job is to provide an honest investigation and appraisal of the business. Sometimes a client may or may not be happy with the results," Cherfoli says.

Valuation professionals have another excellent reason to focus on the valuation assignment and not the client's wishes: They may have to defend their opinions in court. Many valuation professionals spend significant time in court defending valuations that clients hired them to do, and in some cases, the courts themselves hire valuation professionals to review situations independently before a judge or jury makes a decision.

Information — and the availability of it — separates a divorce business valuation from any other business valuation, according to Cherfoli. In a typical business valuation that's aimed at a strategic purchase or sale, both sides are generally willing participants in the process, because they want a deal to happen — or at the moment, think they do.

In a divorce, however, the conflicts inherent in the breakup of the marriage tend to seep over into the business-valuation process. If the parties have an absence of trust, a possible corresponding absence of information will force the valuation professional to do more digging and investigation than she would have to do in a friendly situation.

Divorce valuations can be such a challenge that spouses outside the business may consider hiring a forensic accountant to determine whether information is legitimate or even available. (We discuss forensic accounting in detail in Chapter 17.)

If the business paid the nonactive spouse a salary, the court may want to know whether that spouse was paid fairly for his or her work, so it's important to have an idea of what ordinary employees would be paid for such work. If the parties agree, or if a court rules that a spouse is due extensive back pay, that ruling is going to affect the overall settlement — and in some cases, the overall value of the business.

Determining the Business Value in a Divorce

People devote their lives to building companies, so they're bound to have an attachment to the business that goes beyond simple numbers. As we say earlier in this chapter, valuing a business in divorce isn't just about the present value of that business; it's also about the growth prospects for that business and how the family will — or won't — continue to be involved after the divorce.

The following factors can establish the value of a business in a divorce situation:

- **Loyalty to the business:** Even if the spouses are no longer loyal to each other, one or both may still want to operate the business. Some people can go from being soul mates to being strictly business partners, but that transition requires serious planning and ground rules — financially, operationally, and personally.

- **A desire to cash out and go:** One spouse may just want to sell the business or negotiate a buyout so the departing spouse can use the cash to fund living expenses or possibly to start a new company.

- **The need to take care of the kids:** Whether the children in a divorce are toddlers or young adults, both parties in a divorce may seek valuation advice not only to address their immediate goals but also to make sure, if the business is going to continue, that it can support the children. If the business is *not* going to continue, proceeds from the sale of the company need to be invested for the kids' education or other goals.

- **Retirement issues:** If one spouse has (or both spouses have) money tied up in the company's pension plan, both parties must discuss what will happen to the plan if one spouse decides to remove his or her money or transfer it to another retirement vehicle.

Keeping Valuation Dates in Mind

One of the most critical considerations in divorce-related business valuations is the date on the calendar — not so much the date today but the date on which you and your soon-to-be-ex agree that you're going to set the valuation for the business.

What's the best date? Good question. Only you and your attorneys, tax advisors, and other experts can select good candidates. Ultimately, however, it's your job to pick the valuation date, not a valuation professional's.

Generally, your choices, which may be combined or averaged, are as follow:

- The date of your marriage
- The date of your legal separation
- The date you filed for divorce
- The date your divorce trial started (if you're unfortunate enough to have to go to trial)

The date you agree on for the valuation of the business can lead to a tremendous advantage for one party and a disadvantage for the other. The right choice depends on both parties' cash needs, tax situations, and nonmonetary issues that shaped the decision to divorce in the first place. If your spouse is getting a house — and the expenses of running that house while losing his or her job at the family company — you have a new set of financial circumstances to address.

If you're working with a valuation expert, divorce attorneys need to advise that expert of the valuation date early in the game so she can work with the clearest information possible.

In a divorce scenario, the same methods are used to value a company. The only twist is that given the jurisdiction, the valuation professional may be directed to use a certain standard of value and/or valuation date, which would lead to a different conclusion of value than if the valuation were being done for some other purpose. In essence, however, the goal is the same as in most any other valuation: to determine what the value of the company would be if it were sold on the open market.

You often hear the phrase *intrinsic valuation* applied in a divorce largely because of the contributions that the spouses made to the business. The spouse who wants to retain control of the company may downplay certain aspects of intrinsic value — intellectual property that could yield huge product advancements later or a brand identity that's just taking off, for example — because he or she doesn't want to hand off too much value in the negotiation. That strategy isn't illegal unless that spouse is deliberately hiding documents or other proof that this potentially large center of value exists. *Intrinsic value* implies having more proprietary knowledge of a company and its operations than an ordinary investor may possess. Good negotiators never want to give too much away.

By the way, it's possible to oversell a company's intrinsic value. This fact is what makes business valuation an art as well as a science (a topic that we discuss in Chapter 3).

Chapter 20

Estate Planning and Gifting

In This Chapter
- ▶ Planning for unexpected family problems
- ▶ Creating succession and estate plans
- ▶ Getting expert help when you need it
- ▶ Working with buy/sell agreements
- ▶ Setting up a gifting strategy

*W*hen a company plans for any kind of ownership transition, business valuation needs to be part of the process. If the company is changing hands between strangers or nonfamily members, both sides have a certain idea of value that they want to confirm before the negotiation starts. Settling on a price only after a thoughtful and thorough analysis of what the company is actually worth makes sense.

Surprisingly often, however, valuation is neglected when a business asset is passed down within a family. Often, a patriarch builds a company from scratch, runs it his way, and expects family members to take the operation blithely into its second and third generations without giving any thought to the real value — or possible lack of value — of what he's built. The owner's perception of value may not match his children's perceptions or the perception of the marketplace. This lack of objectivity — or at least reluctance to bring in an objective expert to value the business — causes many businesses to shut down or go up for sale before they make it to the next generation.

If a founder is passing down his company to his kids, both sides — the founder and the heirs — are wise if they insist on an independent and early valuation process to get an idea not only of what the business is worth but also of the tax implications of the transfer.

Proper estate planning requires the entire family to do something that most families find quite difficult: leaving egos, history, and emotions at the door as they determine what their business assets are really worth. In this chapter, we discuss succession and estate planning, gifting, and valuation as it relates to buy/sell agreements.

Succession Planning: A Critical Part of Business Planning

We talk about exit plans in many valuation situations for a reason: Exits are common facts of life, whether or not business founders want to admit their existence and certainly whether or not the founders want them to happen. Founders die in the prime of life, business partners get sick of working together, and kids decide they don't want the family business. Economic and industrial realities change, and suddenly, founders are forced to survive in ways that they hadn't planned.

Exits can — and should — be planned, and business valuation is a critical part of exit planning (for more on exit planning, turn to Chapter 2). But exit planning is tough to do. Most business founders are too tied up in the day-to-day activities of running the business to spend a lot of time thinking about how to pass on the business to children or employees.

Think about the ending in the most positive way possible: in terms of the startup and continuation of the business.

Considering Family Matters

Family businesses typically are small businesses — companies with annual revenue well under $1 million. The business revenue may feed and clothe a houseful of immediate family members and relatives, as well as educate them and provide them with summer jobs and full-time careers.

Family businesses, however, aren't forever. Only 30 percent of family businesses are passed down to the next generation. These closely held businesses often fail to outlive their founders. Add that fact to the threat of estate taxes and the job of finding competent managers and employees inside and outside the family to keep the business going, and you can see why business survival is such a challenge.

Anticipating problems

Challenges in passing the family business to the next generation can involve anything from tax issues and founder reluctance to family conflicts and drama. Succession planning and valuation are necessary parts of estate planning if the founder wants the business to continue.

Thorough planning can help owners anticipate and avert problems that can threaten the business over time, such as the following:

- ✔ **Personal conflicts:** Siblings or other family members who always had a role in the business may resent the people who haven't but who still believe they're entitled to an ownership stake. Estate planning and valuation can provide a basis for open discussion within the family and allow the founder to outline an equitable division that won't be a surprise to the parties involved.

  Also, relationships forged in childhood don't always translate into effective working relationships in a shared business concern.

- ✔ **Marriage:** A marriage may occur after the business is launched. Estate planning becomes an ever-widening activity after this event, because new spouses or children may — or may not — be considered to be heirs to the estate.

- ✔ **Divorce:** Divorce breaks up more than a few family businesses (see Chapter 19 for info). After a divorce, a new estate plan needs to address which family members — or former family members — will inherit the estate. Both parties in a divorce frequently do valuation if a family business is involved as a prime asset.

- ✔ **Death:** When a founder dies, a family can go to war for reasons far more emotional than economical.

No estate or succession plan should be made without a commitment to reevaluation when major life or business events happen. Death, incapacitation, marriage, divorce, mergers, sales of divisions, and departures of key executives are good triggers for revisiting an estate plan to make sure that it properly represents the wishes of the business owner.

Considering blended and nontraditional families

Fifty years ago, planning for the future of a *multigenerational business* — businesses in which several generations of a family participated at all levels — was a complicated task in its own right. Usually, though, all the people involved were blood relatives.

The U.S. Census Bureau reports that blended families and stepfamilies are common in America today. Roughly 50 percent of all first marriages end in divorce, but the breakup rate for second marriages is even higher: more than 60 percent. At the same time, the number of stepfamilies is growing. Between 1980 and 1990, the number of stepfamilies increased 36 percent, according to the National Center for Health Statistics.

In addition, more families are being built by same-sex couples, through adoption, and by extended-family members living under the same roof and often working together in the same business. All these constituencies have an interest in valuation, and owners need to prepare for it.

Failure to plan may mean that family members who made recent and meaningful contributions to the business may not be recognized in terms of ownership or responsibility. It's not uncommon for successive spouses to resist sharing assets with the minor or adult children of a deceased spouse's previous marriage or marriages.

Same-sex couples need to do extensive planning for the safety and continuance of a family business. It's particularly important to select an estate attorney who can not only craft conventional wills and health power-of-attorney documents but also create designation-of-agent documents for issues such as hospital visitation rights, funeral arrangements, and possession of personal property.

Multigenerational planning should also address estate and child-custody arrangements for unmarried heterosexual or gay couples who may not have done the appropriate legal planning necessary to secure the estates of their current or past partners and heirs. At the very least, all family members should understand the need for such planning to prevent conflict later. As nontraditional families become more common, business owners need to be open to estate discussions that consider all these family members.

Creating contingency plans for relatives who renege

"Mom, I don't want the business" is a phrase that has been uttered in more than a few family-owned companies, sometimes years after the person who says it made that business his career. If a founder is lucky, she's alive to hear it and can rethink her succession, transfer, or sale plans.

But for any number of reasons, such decisions may be made after the business owner's funeral, when children, siblings, and in-laws finally settle into the reality that the responsibility for the future of the company is theirs and theirs alone. People can and do change their minds about whether they want a family legacy to continue. Business owners always need to have a Plan B for other owners and family members to put in place if next-generation leadership decides not to lead.

Valuation isn't just about bricks and mortar and the machinery on the shop floor; it's also about management talent and vision. People *do* matter in the valuation of a business. A prodigal son may finally be put in charge and realize that he really doesn't want the job. Smart owners need to consider that possibility in their estate plans if they want to ensure a financial future for other family members and employees.

In Chapter 24, we talk about employee stock ownership plans (ESOPs), which are among the options founders may build into their estate-planning strategies. Business founders create an ESOP as a way to pull assets out of a business while securing the business's future into the next generation.

Creating a Succession Plan

You often hear that a solid succession plan needs to go into effect three to five years before a founder leaves. But any time an estate plan is written or updated, it makes sense to think through — and put in writing, if possible — an updated succession plan.

In the best scenario for a small business, succession planning should be one of the most important activities under the business-planning umbrella. This planning should start as early as possible, but later-stage planning comes closer to the founder's retirement, when she has a better picture of the company's management and financial health and can decide whether the company should continue with the next generation or be sold.

Here are the key steps involved in creating a succession plan:

1. **Spend some time thinking about family dynamics.**

   As an owner, you need to consider the family before you consider the business. At a certain point, it's important to consider whether personality conflicts at home can spill over into the work environment.

2. **Bring in a valuation professional early.**

   Develop a baseline valuation for the business to get a preview of whether you can do anything to minimize the tax impact of transferring assets to your heirs.

3. **Consider possible successors.**

   You have to decide which members of the family to put in charge. You need to know whether multiple members of the next generation can work together and what provisions you can make for those who don't want to be involved but deserve a slice of the family assets.

4. **Train the possible successors.**

   You may want to start a formal training program for the relatives you want to put in positions of leadership. This program may involve giving these relatives apprenticeships in the company or possibly paying for them to get undergraduate or graduate training in business or a field specific to a strength needed inside the firm.

5. **Make the choice.**

   This step is about making the tough final decision about which family member (or nonfamily member) will succeed you in your job and which contenders will take lesser roles.

6. **Make the ownership transfer.**

   This step is where the legal and tax considerations come in. You may be able to blunt the tax impact by selling or gifting shares of the business to children during times when share values are low. (For more information on gifting, see the "Taking Gifting into Consideration" section, later in this chapter.)

Creating an Estate Plan

Estate planning is a combination of personal wealth planning and strategic planning for the business. It anticipates and answers questions such as the following:

- If the founder dies or becomes incapacitated, who will run the business, and under what circumstances?
- If no family member wants to run the business, how will it be disposed of?
- Are wills and choices of executor and trustees in place for personal assets?
- What plans are in place to gift or dispose of certain assets to family members to reduce the estate-tax hit?

Founders shouldn't address these issues in a vacuum. In addition to enlisting the help of experts (see the section titled "Finding the Experts You Need for Estate Planning," later in this chapter), business founders need to talk with their spouses and other key members of the family who are employed in the business (such as children, siblings, cousins, nieces, and nephews) to get an idea of how they feel about the following issues:

- How to continue the business after the founder retires or dies
- Which family member should be elevated to replace the founder of the business after he leaves that post

✔ What kind of estate and succession plans would be good for the next generation

✔ Which designated events in the life of the founder or the business call for a valuation to take place

✔ How in-laws who are involved in the business should share in the assets

✔ How minor children should share in the assets

✔ How spouses and former spouses (depending on divorce agreements) should be treated at the time of the owner's death

✔ How to continue or change any philanthropic activities set in place by the owner

Founders have to realize that an estate plan isn't an attempt to control a company or a family from beyond the grave. When a powerful person dies, the death creates a vacuum that eventually has to be filled. With the right outlook, planning, and communication in building that estate plan, however, the founder communicates a vision for the firm that the next generation will want to embrace while adding their own ideas to improve what the founder created.

Finding the Experts You Need for Estate Planning

One key reason to bring in valuation professionals for business estate matters is to get a measure of potential tax consequences for those who will inherit the family business. Here are the experts that business owners should consider bringing in as a team to ensure proper estate planning as well as proper valuation:

✔ **Accountants/auditors:** These professionals help ensure that thorough, professionally prepared tax records exist over a period of years for the business. Income and spending need to be documented and verified. Annual tax data is critical for pointing out estate-planning issues that owners need to watch, and it sets the stage for accurate, in-depth valuation.

✔ **Valuation professionals:** As long as you ensure confidentiality, you should keep in touch with trusted, skilled appraisers and other valuation experts during the life of a business. They can keep you abreast of ways to maximize the value of your firm.

✔ **Estate attorneys:** Attorneys are the primary legal experts involved in creating a combined personal/business estate plan. They know the laws and procedures related to estate matters, and if they aren't also Certified Public Accountants (as some estate attorneys are), they work closely with CPAs who specialize in estate matters.

- ✔ **Financial planners/advisors:** A trained and certified financial planner can be the quarterback in a long-term estate-planning strategy.

- ✔ **Divorce/family-law attorneys:** Involving a divorce or family-law attorney is critical if the founder has children or other heirs from a previous marriage.

See Chapter 7 for tips on finding and hiring the correct professionals in the valuation process.

Fitting Buy/Sell Agreements into Estate Planning and Valuation

Creating a buy/sell agreement isn't estate planning per se, but it should be coordinated with an estate plan to make sure that transactional issues in a business coordinate with the intentions set forth in a partner or owner's estate plan.

A *buy/sell agreement* creates an infrastructure for setting the value of a business for estate-tax purposes and improves your estate's liquidity by ensuring a ready market for your business upon your death. Such an agreement also protects your business partners from having to share ownership with a deceased stockholder's family.

Buy/sell agreements come in two flavors:

- ✔ **Cross-purchase:** In an insurance-funded cross-purchase arrangement, each business owner buys an insurance policy on the other, naming the other as the beneficiary. At the death of one of the owners, the surviving owner receives tax-free insurance proceeds to use to purchase the deceased owner's stock from her estate.

- ✔ **Stock-redemption:** In an insurance-funded stock-redemption arrangement, the corporation purchases the stock of a deceased shareholder. In this situation, the business is the owner and beneficiary of life insurance policies on each shareholder. A partnership looking for a business continuation plan may use a similar arrangement, called an *entity purchase.*

You can find more information on buy/sell agreements in Chapter 23.

Taking Gifting into Consideration

As business assets are passed down from one generation to the next, the tax hit can be huge. For this reason, some estate planners urge you to consider various gifting strategies as part of a comprehensive estate plan.

Gifting is exactly what it sounds like: You make a gift of your assets to friends and relatives over the course of time to bring down the level of your assets so that your heirs won't be clobbered as badly by estate taxes when you die.

Gifting shouldn't be an automatic decision. It requires the help of a trained tax advisor.

Gifting strategies

People can choose from a variety of options to give away money and assets in a way that will serve the company and family:

- **Using life insurance trusts:** An irrevocable life insurance trust can keep the proceeds of the insurance out of your taxable estate. An added benefit is that such trusts may permit spousal access to the cash value of the policy. Note, however, that the trust is irrevocable — the decision can't be changed.

- **Planning for increasing assets:** A grantor-retained annuity trust (GRAT) is an irrevocable trust that's popular among families with assets that are expected to increase, because such appreciation can be passed on to heirs with minimal tax consequences.

- **Gifting to grandkids:** The federal generation-skipping transfer tax (GSTT) taxes transfers of property that you make, either during life or after death, to someone who is more than one generation below you, such as a grandchild. The GSTT is imposed in addition to — not rather than — federal gift or estate taxes. You need to be aware of the GSTT if you make cumulative generation-skipping transfers in excess of the GSTT exemption, which was $2 million in 2008. A flat tax equal to the highest estate-tax bracket in effect in the year in which you make the transfer is imposed on every transfer you make after your exemption has been exhausted. Note that some states also impose their own GSTT.

Successful business owners need to think about a lifetime gifting strategy. The generation-skipping transfer tax is one approach to this idea, but depending on what happens with the estate-tax forecast in 2009 and beyond, a low-rate environment may make it a good idea to take full advantage of these strategies.

Gifting techniques

You should consider — and in appropriate situations, implement — gifting techniques that leverage the lifetime exemption. We discuss some of these techniques in the following sections.

Intrafamily loans

With an *intrafamily loan,* the business owner can lend money to the transferee (a person, trust, or business entity), with the loan being documented by a promissory note bearing interest at the applicable federal rate (AFR). The borrower can use this loan to pay down higher-rate debt or make investments that are expected to achieve a rate of return higher than the AFR. Any returns in excess of the AFR are retained by the borrower free of gift or estate tax.

GRATs

In a *grantor-retained annuity trust* (GRAT), the business owner transfers assets to a trust for a certain period. During the term of the trust, the grantor receives an annuity payment, at least annually, of either a fixed dollar amount or a fixed percentage of the fair-market value of the property placed in the trust. The interest rate used to calculate the annuity payment is the applicable federal rate (AFR). At the end of the trust term, any remaining principal is distributed to the trust beneficiaries.

Installment sales to IDGTs

Intentionally defective grantor trusts (IDGTs) are similar to GRATs. IDGT assets are sold by the owner to a trust in return for an installment note that bears interest at the AFR. The note may provide for installment payments over a specified period, or it may provide for annual interest-only payments with a balloon payment of principal payable at the end of the term. Any income and appreciation on the trust assets exceeding the payments required to satisfy the note belong to the trust beneficiaries free of estate or gift tax at the end of the trust term. The owner pays no tax on his gain from the sale of assets to the trust and is responsible for paying income tax on the future income earned by the trust — a benefit to the trust beneficiaries that is not treated as an additional gift by the grantor.

How the estate tax was born

According to the Washington, D.C.–based Heritage Foundation, the tradition of taxing assets at the time of death began with the Stamp Act of 1797, which required a federal stamp on wills in probate. The revenue was used to pay off debt during the undeclared naval war with France in 1794. The Stamp Act was repealed in 1802.

For the next hundred years, estate taxes were used on a sporadic basis to finance wars, and when peacetime came, such taxes were repealed. But after the turn of the 20th century, the modern sales tax emerged, along with another tax we note with fondness: federal income tax.

The Revenue Act of 1916 contained an estate tax with many features of today's system. After an exemption of $50,000 — equal today to roughly $11 million — tax rates started at 1 percent and climbed to 10 percent on estates of more than $5 million (more than $1 billion in terms of today's wealth).

Estate taxes were increased in 1917 as the United States entered World War I. This time, when the war ended, the tax stayed. Even though the country had a budget surplus, Congress increased rates and introduced a gift tax in 1924. Like the estate tax, the *gift tax* is a levy on the transfer of property from one person to another.

From the 1920s through the 1940s — the Depression years — estate taxes were used as a way to redistribute income. Tax rates of up to 77 percent on the largest estates were supposed to prevent wealth from becoming increasingly concentrated in the hands of a few.

Lawmakers went back to work on the estate tax during the 1960s and 1970s. By 1976, the previously separate exemptions for estate and gift taxes were transformed into a single unified estate and gift tax credit.

By 1981, the top rate went from 70 percent to 50 percent, and an increase in the unified credit took a lot of smaller estates — those under $600,000 — off the tax rolls.

In 1997, Congress made the first increase in the unified credit since 1987. Gradual increases, which began in 1999, raised the unified credit to $1 million by 2006.

The Economic Growth and Tax Relief Reconciliation Act of 2001 was the first step toward eliminating the death tax. It provided for a scheduled phase-out of rates and an increase in the unified credit, finally repealing the tax for calendar year 2010. Those provisions sunset in 2011 with a return to the 1997 levels of a top rate of 55 percent and a unified credit of $1 million.

Under current law, the federal estate tax is scheduled to change as follows:

- **2009:** $3.5 million exemption, 45 percent tax rate
- **2010:** No estate tax
- **2011 and beyond:** $1 million exemption, 55 percent tax rate

CLATs

A *charitable lead annuity trust* (CLAT) provides for the payment of a fixed dollar amount to one or more charitable beneficiaries for a specified period, at least annually, regardless of the income generated by the CLAT. At the end of the term, the remaining assets of the trust pass to individual beneficiaries. The trust may be established for a term of years or based on the lives of the people living at the time of the trust's creation. Gift leverage is obtained because the reportable value of the gift at the creation of the CLAT is the fair-market value of the assets placed in the trust less the present value of the annuity.

Chapter 21

Attracting Outside Investors to Your Startup

*E*very owner of a young company needs good advice to prepare him for the many stages of investment that will eventually take his business to the desired size as a private company or all the way to public ownership.

Particularly in the technology arena, many business owners work hard to solicit financing to help their companies grow at very fast rates. But because proving value in new companies that may not yet be producing much in revenue and profit is difficult, you need outside expertise.

In many ways, the process of attracting outside investors is not much different from the process of bringing in a conventional buyer or banker. Even if you started your company in a garage or a basement, you have to present it as an organized company, with transparent operations and finances, to any potential buyers, investors, or lenders; otherwise, they just won't care.

This chapter outlines the importance of getting valuation expertise when starting a business and the areas in which you should use outside help.

Exploring Your Startup Resources

We emphasize throughout this book that no two valuation professionals analyze the value of a business in exactly the same way. When you're talking about a startup, you're talking about a particular valuation challenge because startups may not produce revenues, much less profits, for months and possibly years.

For this reason, you should network with experienced investors in startup companies similar to yours to get an idea of what they look for in fledgling companies. If some of these investors are successful at sniffing out values in new business ideas, you should find these people, listen to their advice, and then start building your company to produce the most value you can.

You can take several steps before you start chasing investors. The Ewing Marion Kauffman Foundation's Angel Capital Education Foundation (www.kauffman.org) publishes a host of startup resources. One of these resources is the Valuation Worksheet, which follows. It serves as a general guide to the startup valuation process.

The worksheet asks you to evaluate three aspects of a company — the strength of the management team, the size of the opportunity, and the competitive landscape — and it lists percentages to help you assign a weight to each question. The questions represent the factors and issues impacting the valuation of a pre-revenue startup company (a company that hasn't yet begun to bring in revenue).

Valuation Worksheet

Strength of Management Team (Weighted Ranking: 0–30%)

Impact	*What is the founder's experience?*
– –	Straight out of school
–	Experience only as a salesperson or technologist
+	Many years business experience
+	Experience as a product manager
+ +	Experience in this business sector
+ +	Experience as a COO, CTO, CFO
+ + +	Experience as a CEO

Impact	**Is the founder willing to step aside, if necessary, for a new CEO?**
Deal killer	Unwilling
–	Difficult to convince
0	Neutral
+	Willing
+ +	Key part of the plan

Impact	**Is the founder coachable?**
Deal killer	No
0	Yes

Impact	**How complete is the management team?**
– –	Very incomplete (none identified)
–	Somewhat incomplete
0	Good start
+	Rather complete team
+ +	A complete and experienced management team

Size of the Opportunity (Weighted Ranking: 0–25%)

Impact	**What size is the specific market for the company's product/service?**
Deal killer	< $50,000,000
0	$100,000,000
+ +	> $500,000,000

Impact	**What is the potential for revenue in five years?**
Deal killer	< $30,000,000
0	$50,000,000
+ +	> $100,000,000

Competitive Landscape (Weighted Ranking: 0–15%)

Impact	**What is the status of the intellectual property (IP)?**
0	Trade secrets only
+	Core patents pending
+ +	Core patents issued
+ + +	Complete patent estate

Source: Ewing Marion Kauffman Foundation

Seeing How Valuation Professionals Work with Startups

When a valuation professional gets involved in valuing a startup, the analysis centers on a discounted cash-flow methodology under the income approach to valuation. (For a review of all the professionals who may get involved in the valuation process, see Chapter 7.)

In essence, the valuation professional is trying to determine a future valuation of the company so that the entrepreneurs, angel investors, venture capitalists, and so on have some idea how much equity they should have in the startup, given their investment and the corresponding return on investment (ROI). (For definitions of investor types, see the section "Working with Investors," later in this chapter.)

Valuation terms you hear in a startup

The world of startup investing has its own valuation language. Here are some of the terms you may hear:

✔ **Pre-revenue startup:** A business that's burning through cash in its accounts because it hasn't yet begun to bring in revenue for the product that it plans to sell; it may have an office in place and a prototype but nothing that's bringing in cash; some investors see this type of company as a problem, whereas others see it as an opportunity

✔ **Pre-money value:** A company's value before it receives outside financing or the latest round of financing

✔ **Post-money value:** A company's value after outside financing or the latest round or injection of equity funding

✔ **Divergence:** The difference between the growth rate of the company's valuation and the valuation of the shares investors receive because of dilution by subsequent investors and other factors

✔ **Full dilution:** This counts not only the shares that have been issued but also all shares that would be issued if all options and warrants were exercised and other promises or contingent agreements to issue shares were given effect

✔ **Terminal value:** The valuation of the company at exit — that is, the proceeds of the sale of the company via a merger, acquisition, or an IPO, at which time the investors' ownership can be liquidated

✔ **ROI:** The return expected for such an investment when the investors expect to get their money out

---

The process is very similar to the discounted cash-flow technique used to value a mature business. The major difference lies in the discount and capitalization rates. A company that isn't producing substantial revenue and/ or profit, that lacks the necessary infrastructure to take the company to the next level, and that doesn't have the next generation of technology in development is inherently more risky for angel investors or venture capitalists. After all, if it weren't more risky, the entrepreneur could simply go to a bank for financing.

Creating the Starting Point: The Business Plan

This book is about business valuation, not starting a business. For information on that topic, you can check out *Small Business For Dummies*, 3rd Edition, by Eric Tyson, MBA, and Jim Schell (Wiley); *Accounting For Dummies*, 4th Edition, by John A. Tracy, CPA (Wiley); or *Franchising For Dummies*, 2nd Edition, by Michael Seid and Dave Thomas (Wiley). Even so, an appreciation for business valuation starts with a business plan.

If you want people to invest in your business, or if you need bank loans, you need a business plan. Consider a business plan to be a calling card for your new business, and keep the emphasis on the issue of value at every stage.

The standard business plan runs anywhere from 10 to 30 pages and contains the following elements:

- ✔ **Executive summary:** An executive summary should be no longer than one page. It sums up the business, its products and services, and its risks, opportunities, target strategies, competition, finances, and projected ROI.

  The summary includes the first words anyone will read, but write it *after* you create the rest of the document. Doing so ensures that you're clear on the full thrust of the document so you can better summarize it in front.

- ✔ **Mission statement:** This one- or two-sentence statement describes the culture of your business and its goals.

- ✔ **Business concept:** Here, you explain the business that you want to finance and the technology, concept, or strategy on which it's based.

- **Management team:** List the chief executive officer (CEO) and key members of management by name, experience, and — very importantly — past successes.

- **Industry analysis:** This section provides an informed overview of market share, leadership, players in the market, market shifts, costs, pricing, or competition that provides the opportunity for the new company's success.

- **Competition:** In this section, you outline the competitive challenges you face and how you plan to defeat them.

- **Goals and objectives:** This section — essentially, a three- to five-year plan — requires you to outline measurable objectives for market share, revenue, profitability, and value.

- **Day-to-day operations:** Here, you describe staffing plans, training, and other personnel-related issues. This section also talks about business-support activities, such as advertising and marketing.

- **Financing:** This detailed section explains what you have to invest and what you need from lenders. Most importantly, it explains how long you expect to take to pay back those lenders.

- **Appendix:** This section contains tax returns and any other third-party information that tells prospective investors more about the business.

You're not writing a business plan for insiders; you're writing it for outsiders. You're writing it to sell the concept of the company to people who are willing to sink money into it — lenders, investors, customers, and suppliers. They're your audience, and you have to sell your value proposition to them.

Working with Investors

Valuation is a contentious subject in any business transaction, but startups are particularly controversial because assets are either undeveloped or nonexistent. Some companies are in operation for a year or more and never bring in a dime of revenue because they're too engaged in product development and early work to build clientele.

The search for money to fuel a new operation can be almost as big of a job as getting the company operating on a day-to-day basis. Therefore, in the art-versus-science discussion of valuation, the startup world presents some rather massive challenges.

In this section, we discuss the three primary types of investors who typically deal with startup and young companies:

✔ Angel investors

✔ Venture capitalists

✔ Investors in an initial public offering (IPO)

How do you find these sources of capital? If you're truly familiar with the industry in which you're planning to start a business, you'll have done your homework trying to determine how companies like yours are best funded. If not, you need to focus on research. Here are some primary ways to find out where to start researching such investors:

✔ **Industry associations:** These organizations bring together people working in the same industry. Read their publications, visit their Web sites, and talk with their members not only to find out more about the industry you plan to work in but also to discover about how other business owners financed their startups.

✔ **Angel investor directories:** These directories provide you with names of angel investors all over the country. *Inc.* magazine publishes an online directory (`www.inc.com/articles/2001/09/23461.html`) through which you can find out the kind of companies these investors are interested in supporting. We talk more about angel investors in the next section.

✔ **Local business groups:** Industry associations are typically national groups, but if you live in an area that contains a number of businesses in your chosen industry, you may be able to use local business groups as a way to find the right kind of investor for you.

Pre-money valuation refers to the valuation of a company prior to investment or other form of financing. Angel investors and venture capitalists use pre-money valuation to determine how much ownership or equity they'll demand from the company in exchange for their investments.

Angel investors

An *angel investor* provides capital to one or more startup companies. Usually, she's a wealthy person who likes to dabble in young businesses with great potential.

Most new businesses tap friends and family members for early seed money. This early money — and your handling of it — can make your business more attractive to angel investors if you have a hot idea and the talent to bring it forward. *Angels,* as they're often called, tend to be the first rung of outside financing for companies that hope to go to the next stage: expanding product distribution, starting advertising and promotion campaigns, or expanding staff.

Sometimes, you can find angels by word of mouth in your industry. Some angels pool their resources with other angels and make their funding decisions in a group. Like venture capitalists (see the following section), who are much bigger fish, angels like to see not only good road shows but also solid presentations and figures by the eager entrepreneurs they meet.

Angels focus on the youngest companies because these investors usually aren't in the game for big money; they come in with thousands of dollars, not millions. Most individual angels invest no more than $100,000 (most often, less than $30,000). According to the Ewing Marion Kauffman Foundation, the typical combined angel contribution is around $1 million to $3 million.

On average, angels buy 20 to 40 percent of a company's equity and seek a return of 20 to 30 times their investment over five years.

The best angels don't just hand over a check; they're also good sounding boards and teachers. Make sure you pick a good angel investor who has much to teach you about building a company.

Venture capitalists

A *venture capitalist* (VC) is similar to an angel investor in that he (or a firm created to make venture capital investments) wants to put his money in promising companies for big returns. Generally, a VC comes after angel financing and may be the final stage of private investment. The minimum investment by VCs is $1 million, and these investors are more hands-on than angel investors in their relationships with new firms. VCs typically want a formal advisory role with new companies, usually as board members.

Getting VC financing brings you one step closer to the big leagues: public ownership. These investors finance companies that haven't had the value of their stock tested in the public markets.

VCs look at companies that have made it through the self-investment or angel stage with considerable promise but many unknowns. These companies may have a great business concept, but they also may have untested management, unknown customer response, and other aspects that make valuation tougher — not the least of which is lack of profit.

As you create your business plan (refer to the "Creating the Starting Point: The Business Plan" section earlier in this chapter), your job is to work with experts in finance to value your potential business and markets properly. Venture capitalists want to know that you're paying proper attention to valuing your company reliably. After all, to invest in your company, they need to understand its value, and most importantly, they need to know that you understand its value.

IPO investors

For entrepreneurs, angel investors, venture capitalists, and ordinary investors, an *initial public offering* (IPO) is a fancier phrase for something that tantalizes everyone: a big payday. The IPO is the first sale of stock to the public. You've probably read business stories that contain phrases such as "highly anticipated IPO."

Google was one such IPO that had investors licking their lips in 2004, even at a relatively high offering price of $85 a share. Was the Google IPO worthwhile? Despite a market turndown, during the writing of this book, Google stock was trading above $300 a share.

Business valuation continues into the pricing process for companies that go into the public markets after early angel financing and one or more rounds of VC financing.

Traditional valuation procedures don't always work for an IPO, because virtually all valuation is based on the future of the business — not on the present. You can't value an IPO based on its book or liquidation value, except for the purpose of establishing a floor price for the business.

Obviously, if you're talking about a startup, it's going to be a while before you're ready for that IPO. Still, an IPO may well be in your future. At each stage of investment, you need experts who understand valuation at that stage.

Part VI
The Part of Tens

The 5th Wave   By Rich Tennant

"I don't take 'no' for an answer. Nor do I take 'whatever,' 'as if,' or 'duh.'"

In this part . . .

This part is called The Part of Tens because each of these chapters offers ten points of interest on critical topics we introduce throughout the book. This part gives you a chance to get a little more familiar with these issues. In this part, we spell out reasons to consider a prenuptial agreement, things to build into a partnership agreement, and things to consider before transforming a conventional business into an employee stock ownership plan (ESOP).

Chapter 22

Ten Reasons to Consider a Prenup

In This Chapter
- Defusing money fights during a marriage
- Using a solid agreement to protect family members' jobs in case of a divorce
- Preserving a family's financial and business legacy
- Linking today's prenup to tomorrow's business valuation if there's a divorce
- Keeping all the money from going to the accountants and lawyers

Ah, love and marriage — they go together like a horse and carriage, as the old song goes. But love, marriage, and money? You just never hear much about dollars and cents in a love song, unless it's in some twangy old country song about love gone wrong.

But what if a worldwide law forced new-spouses-to-be to sit down at a table for a few days with smart legal and tax advisors who'd force them to share credit reports, bank and brokerage accounts, and most importantly, their feelings about money and what they want to do with it for the rest of their lives?

That doesn't sound like a bad idea, does it? How many couples do you know who talked extensively about money before they got hitched? If you answered, "the divorced ones!" that's just what we wanted to hear.

Prenuptial agreements are a way to sort out financial issues before a marriage starts so that a couple knows what they have and where they're going with it. Even if one spouse doesn't own a business before the wedding, this subject is important to consider if one of them wants to start one later.

Why does a book about business valuation even mention this subject? Have you ever read a news story about a celebrity divorce and murmured to yourself, "There goes her money down the drain"? Prenuptial planning is good business planning — when done correctly, both sides have an exit plan that may not minimize pain but does go a long way toward fighting uncertainty. So without further ado, here are ten reasons to consider a prenup.

It Gets You to Talk Honestly about Money at the Start of a Marriage

First, we take a minute to define our terms. A *prenuptial agreement* is a legal and binding agreement between two potential spouses indicating how their finances will be handled in the case of a divorce. It's not about how you're going to raise the kids or whether one plans to convert to the other's religion — it begins and ends at money, period. A *postnuptial agreement* is the same, but it's hammered out after the couple is married, usually because some significant assets or other money issues have changed since the marriage.

The word *prenup* tends to set people's teeth a bit on edge. For most people, it conjures up an image of you and your future spouse in an adversarial role even before you walk down the aisle. Who wants to talk about divorce before the honeymoon, anyway?

But believe it or not, in the right hands — meaning family law and tax attorneys who really know their stuff — this process doesn't have to be an adversarial one. Think of it as a way to discover not only what money and assets the two of you have but also all the fears, hopes, and dreams about the use of that money.

A lot of couples don't talk about these issues before they get married, and this oversight costs them down the line. A prenup forces two individuals to come clean about their credit, what they have at the bank and in their retirement accounts, and finally, what they want to do with an existing business or a business they hope to build someday either together or separately.

Your Life's Work Shouldn't Go down the Drain

Say you're the spouse who's going into a marriage with a successful business with excellent prospects. No, you'd never expect your future wife or husband to someday try to take over the business to force you out and liquidate it, but read the papers — it happens every day.

Roughly 40 percent of all marriages fail. No, that doesn't mean that yours will be one of them, but if you've created a company, you need to think seriously about how both you and your company would survive a divorce.

For this reason, involving a valuation expert in the prenuptial process is helpful because it gives you an idea of what your company is worth in terms of not only brick and mortar but also all the intangibles that may well exceed the value of whatever hard assets you own. Your ideas, your employees, and your branding are part of the valuation process, so doing two valuations may be wise: one for peacetime, one for wartime. The first would value your business as if you were going to sell your company in a friendly deal on your terms, and the second would help you defend yourself and your company if a spouse petitioned for those assets.

In essence, a prenuptial valuation may become a way to support a defensive strategy for a company when it's threatened in divorce court. Obviously, if you have extensive fears that this situation may happen, you may want to rethink your relationship with your intended spouse. Running the numbers and being honest about those fears with your potential partner right now may save considerable time, expense, and agony later.

If Both Spouses Have Sacrificed to Build the Business, They Need to Share

You've heard the scenario before. The wife or husband works hard to put the other one through medical or dental school and then settles down to raise the kids (forgoing any salary) after the practice takes off. Life is good, but a few years down the line, the marriage screeches to a halt and suddenly the spouse with the lucrative partnership doesn't want to share so much with the nonworking spouse. The nonworking spouse faces years of catch-up on building a career, as well as affording retirement and huge expenses for the kids if they're not properly taken care of in the divorce settlement.

We didn't identify the losing spouse by gender, but today, women still face the greatest financial risk in a divorce by virtue of the following:

- ✔ As of 2008, women still aren't at an even pay level with men. Most estimates say women earn only 76 to 80 cents on every dollar a man earns, so they typically bring fewer assets into a marriage and they never really catch up when working.

- ✔ Women frequently bear the child-care responsibilities, and many still give up or take breaks from full-time paid work to address that need.

- ✔ On average, women live five to six years longer than men. Thus, they need at least that number of years' worth of savings to see them through their retirement years and end-of-life expenses.

When an entrepreneurial effort is underway or planned, a prenuptial agreement forces a discussion on what both spouses think they're entitled to if the marriage fails. Again, this conversation can force a shocking reality on the relationship — or an agreement that makes the marriage seem even stronger.

The Working Spouse Shouldn't Lose the Business Entirely

Often, you see an argument made in a divorce that one spouse may have contributed the business idea and the financial knowledge to start a business, but the other spouse provided the occasional office support and kept the home fires burning during its early days. For this reason, some states take the upper hand and decide that all community property will be divided 50/50. But in some cases, a legal agreement amends or supersedes such arrangements — which is why prenups were created.

For this reason, it's critical for both sides to seek respective legal counsel in deciding how business assets should be split. A prenuptial agreement can not only protect ownership and a control interest in a closely held business but also declare a set formula that the married couple can use to value and split stock in the event of a divorce.

More is involved in this process than having both spouses come to an agreement on assets. Also important is structuring this agreement in a way that preserves the business if it's expected to be passed on to the kids or sold someday as an asset that will benefit all members of the family.

Kids from Earlier Marriages Need Protection

Families with considerable wealth may have businesses that have lasted several generations, which means that many more people than just the current CEO depend on that business. In a private company, stakeholders may include children and other family members from previous marriages.

And we're not talking about family members who sit on their butts and wait for checks to show up in their mailboxes. We're talking about generations of family who are active workers in the business — and those who may join in the future.

It's not so easy for the mega-rich, either

In the annals of great American family wealth, many people may not know the name Pritzker, but they probably know the name Hyatt Hotels. The Chicago family's $20-billion empire was thrown into disarray after the death of the family patriarch, Jay Pritzker, in 1999. Various cousins began to fight for what they thought was their fair share of the family assets after the new head of the empire, Jay's son Tom, took over.

The dispute within this intensely private family exploded after Liesel Pritzker, the daughter of Jay's brother Robert from an earlier marriage and, at that time, a young actress in Hollywood, challenged the distribution of family assets among all the cousins. Liesel, whose parents divorced when she was a young child (Robert had other children as well) charged that she and her brother Matthew were being cheated out of their $1-billion inheritance; they eventually settled for a reported $500 million, making them two of the richest people in America younger than 30.

This lesson shows that, within even the most private of families, separation of assets requires a long-term plan and a fair amount of transparency.

Now consider for a moment the family situation of Rupert Murdoch, global media baron. At press time, the 76-year-old Murdoch was on his third marriage, with six kids total: one daughter from his first marriage, three kids from his second, and two kids from his latest. Granted, his company's stock trades publicly, but family members control the company.

Murdoch is just one more captain of industry who has shown no desire to retire, but during the writing of this book, he was already positioning one of his two sons from his second marriage — James — as the heir apparent. Will James keep that advantageous position within the family business by the time Rupert gives up the reins? Who knows? But it's an interesting scenario that applies to virtually any couple with previous families to think through before they marry. Consider why:

- When you're talking about involving kids in the family business, it's great if you have one kid who's a clear, recognized choice to take over. But when half-brothers and half-sisters (and maybe *their* kids) abound in a company, you have to set a structure that nurtures both talent and the family relationship. Today's black sheep can be the company's savior a decade from now. This subject certainly goes beyond what legal documents can solve, and that's why prospective spouses need to talk about it.

- Depending on how you've allocated the stock for the business over the years, it's possible that a former mother-in-law (who may have written a check to start the business in friendlier times) may want a say in who gets put in charge now that you're on your third wife or husband. Prenuptial discussions need to address how all the individuals who are part of a power structure in an existing business may affect the value of the company's assets going forward.

Oh, one more thing about the Murdoch example: Rupert and his third wife have two kids who are currently under age 10. Couples with previous families who are going into a new marriage need to think not only about the kids who have come before but also about those who may arrive in the future.

Kids from Your Next Marriage Need Protection, Too

The emotional competition between siblings from a single marriage can be cutthroat enough in a business setting; that competitive fever escalates with the kids from Dad's second or third wife or Mom's new husband.

Understandably, a child from someone's first marriage may feel both happy and uneasy about the arrival of a new sibling, even if the little one is a full generation younger. If a clear succession and ownership structure isn't laid out for the business before the founder retires or dies, warring factions of siblings and other family members can deplete the value of a business by fighting for their share of the pie.

Granted, no parent can anticipate everything their kids may do in the future, but as you prepare to marry, this topic deserves plenty of exploration.

Planning for Worst-Case Scenarios Is a Good Habit

In Chapter 24, you see the benefits of doing an exit plan for a business; the thought process that goes into a prenup is similar. Business owners must think of worst-case scenarios within every new initiative they try.

If a business already exists at the time of a marriage or becomes a reality afterward, optimally, both parties will take the time to think through the role a marital breakup would have in the overall course of the business.

Also important is realizing that business problems and marital problems don't occur in separate vacuums. Any number of entrepreneurs can tell you that industry downturns or sudden shifts in a company's fortunes have a real impact at home.

Your Business and Personal Finances Really Are Connected

Particularly for small, closely held companies, business assets can really be marital assets, and it makes sense for any business owner to take a tough look at anything that can go wrong in a marriage and in a business concurrently.

Toward the beginning of this chapter, we mention a couple in which the husband or wife paid the educational bills for the other to start a professional practice. Many spouses have surrendered their paychecks or personal investments as startup funds for all kinds of businesses.

When doing a prenup, you need to talk about the possibility of these sacrifices going forward and how they're connected to marital assets based on state and local laws governing such subjects.

Family Legacies Need Protection

Whether it's the gas station on the corner or the regional bank your great-grandpa started back in the 1800s, a family business is more than a cash register. It's an important source of history to people who share blood, skills, and experiences, regardless of whether they get along.

A business may also be a critical asset to the community. In an age of globalization and sameness across all industries, closely held companies that keep family members as employees and managers have a unique way of touching everyone around them. After generations of tough economic times, daunting competitors, and other business threats, a marriage going bad shouldn't be what finally kills a family legacy.

When spouses begin talking about a prenuptial agreement, if the family legacy is critical, it should be one of the first issues to come up in conversation.

When a Marriage Ends, a Prenup (Or Postnup) Can Save You Both Money

One of the reasons couples resist the idea of a prenup is that it's such an unpleasant idea. What couple in love and with all hope of staying together a lifetime wants to talk about a breakup?

But if a business exists before marriage or is created after marriage, it's best to talk about how that business will live — and for what reasons — if a divorce happens. And it's absolutely best to discuss those possibilities while both sides are friendly and have the benefit of independent counsel to take them through a valuation process and the creation of an ownership structure that ensures the future of the company for one or both spouses or their children.

It's not unthinkable that everything you've worked to build will go to the government, lawyers, and tax experts. Is that what you want? This concern may also create the need to review your prenuptial agreement whenever business conditions change.

Chapter 23

Ten Questions to Answer Before Considering a Partnership Agreement

*P*artnerships are unincorporated businesses in which two or more individuals manage the business and are equally liable for its debts (see Part IV for details). You can find variations on the level of liability based on the legal definition of the partnership. Partnerships are a particularly interesting valuation challenge because they typically don't have many hard assets to value. In fact, a lot of partnership value is intrinsic — it's tied up in the skills of the individuals who form the partnership. Individuals may change their legal business status from a partnership to another designation over time — becoming a corporation or a limited liability company (LLC), for instance — when the purpose or sheer size of the business changes.

But even in the earliest stages, partnerships shouldn't be informal arrangements between individuals, even if they're siblings, spouses, or close friends. As with any business contract, partnership agreements aren't written for the good times; they're written for the bad times — or at least, for times of big change for the business, which can be positive or negative.

Why put a chapter on partnership agreements in a book on valuation? Because partnerships have their own valuation challenges. In many cases, the main asset value of a partnership isn't something you can physically touch. Many law firms and medical offices start off as partnerships, and aside from a few hard assets such as office furniture and computers, you don't actually see the real value of these businesses. The real value resides inside the heads of the partners. Partnerships are almost always about intellectual capital.

Both intellectual capital and financial capital are required to run a partnership. So take a look at the ten critical elements that a partnership agreement should cover.

Who Will Be in the Partnership?

The partnership agreement must spell out the name of the business, its location, the names of both partners, and their places of residence. It also must state the starting date of the partnership to define the start of the legal connection between the partners.

This point may seem rather obvious, but in case of the breakup of the partnership or a legal challenge from outside, having this information recorded in a legal document is important.

How Much Capital Does Each Partner Have to Kick In at the Start?

Particularly important is stating the exact amount of money or other assets each partner brings to the enterprise on the first day of business. Yet it's not so important that partners do an even split of the business — in fact, doing so may be a bad idea from a management standpoint. Here's why: The business needs a dominant partner (or partners) who can break a tie over strategic key decisions (we get to this issue in more detail shortly).

In most partnerships, money isn't the only form of capital. In various professional practices, and particularly in medical practices, professionals with great reputations (or great potential) may be wooed into joining a new practice. They may be asked to join up with a certain contribution of consultation hours or a commitment to certain services that benefit the overall partnership. They may even be responsible for developing a whole new division of that partnership. And here's where intrinsic value comes in: A partner who comes in without a major cash or hard asset infusion may have his part of the partnership agreement drawn with certain performance targets to meet.

If partners can't agree on which partners will be responsible for key functions of the business, maybe they have no business being partners after all. Creating a partnership agreement may unearth power-sharing problems that can sink a business, and knowing this information in advance can save time, money, and most importantly, professional and personal relationships.

How Will Decisions Be Made?

Some professionals are born managers; others are born innovators. Some are born salespeople; others are born bean counters. A business needs all these personalities and skills, in addition to the basic professional skill (medicine, law, consulting, and so on) the practice is built around.

The partnership agreement should spell out, in as much detail as necessary, how much authority each partner has and over which specific issues and areas of the business each partner has that authority.

For instance, do all partners have the right to solicit and sign contracts with specific vendors or investors? Isn't that a little like having a joint checking account in which both spouses write checks like crazy and don't figure it out until the overdraft notice arrives? Also, will one partner have 1 percent more ownership in the partnership than the other partners to break tight votes over particular decisions?

Do You Have a Plan for Resolving Disputes?

This particularly important point is the exact reason you need to write such agreements for the bad times, not the good ones. Planning how you'll handle disputes within the partnership involves not only exploring the various deal-breaking issues between partners but also looking at all the potential outside conflicts and occurrences that could sink the partnership.

Many partnership agreements specify arbitration for most disputes simply because that process is generally less expensive to pursue than disputes in open court. A trained mediator or arbitrator usually handles arbitration.

Addressing how the immediate family of a deceased or incapacitated partner may fit into the dispute-resolution process is also wise. Depending on how the total partnership agreement is written, spouses and children may have leverage to endanger the partnership by making a claim on the departed partner's assets.

How Will the Firm Admit New Partners?

Recruiting new partners is necessary for some partnerships but not for others. Valuation may be an important consideration in this issue because in the case of partnerships intended to continue beyond the founding partners' retirement (such as medical or dental practices), recruiting new, talented partners over time is critical to the overall value of the practice.

Requirements may change over time, but founding or managing partners must decide before recruiting new partners exactly what will be required of these new partners to enter the practice. Will they have to cough up considerable capital to join? Will some in-kind arrangement with experienced or younger professionals allow them to earn their way into the practice? Will new partners have to promise a certain number of hours to the practice or start up a lucrative division that the original partnership did not have?

Bringing in new partners is often more complex than bringing in new salaried employees because you're giving them an ownership stake that affords them whatever power you grant them. Founding or senior partners should confer with an attorney who is experienced in partnership agreements about related growth and power issues.

How and When Will Profits — or Losses — Be Shared?

The issue of sharing profits and losses speaks to the operating and ownership structure of the partnership. Depending on the kind of partnership you create, you and your partner may share profits or losses in certain conventional ways, but think through these key considerations:

- Will all the partners — junior as well as senior — share profits and losses equally? (The answer generally is *no.*)
- How often will profits be paid out, and in what form?
- What are the tax implications of the way this money is paid out?
- What safeguards are in place to make sure that individual partners can cover losses?

What Happens If a Partner Leaves or Dies?

Welcome to the world of buy/sell agreements, which are perhaps the most important segment of a partnership agreement. Why? Because these agreements can save a partnership when a partner dies, becomes incapacitated, or leaves the practice (under a variety of circumstances) or when the deceased's family members come knocking on the door for what they believe is their share.

Buy/sell agreements have two primary structures: *cross-purchase agreements*, in which the remaining partnership owners buy the departing partner's stock or partnership interest, and *stock-redemption agreements*, in which the company buys the stock of the departing owner.

Get advice from tax experts and experienced business attorneys about which model works best for your situation. Cross-purchase agreements may have certain tax advantages that stem from the way the market value of that business is calculated at the time the agreement is triggered. Shareholder models can get complicated based on the number of shareholders the partnership has and based on any valuation issues that come into play.

The partnership agreement that you and your two or three founding partners write in year one of the business may not fit you or the firm in years 15 or 20. Make a plan to revisit the efficacy of the agreement throughout the life of the partnership.

How Will the Partnership Be Sold or Dissolved?

We spend plenty of time in this book discussing exit plans, which are particularly important in partnerships. Succession takes on a slightly different tone in a partnership because of the multiple-owner structure.

An owner of a corporation designates the successor, who may or may not have an ownership stake in the corporation. In a partnership, all partners are owners (possibly to varying degrees, but they're still owners). Addressing retirement, departure, and succession issues is in their best interest, to ensure the highest ongoing valuation for the firm.

The buy/sell agreement may address some of these issues, but if the partnership is terminal — meaning that it ends when the current set of partners leaves, dies, becomes incapacitated, or retires — that ending must be planned and spelled out for designated parties to execute.

How Will Legal Disputes inside and outside the Partnership Be Handled?

We've already talked about internal disputes being subject to arbitration or mediation. Depending on the industry the partnership is in, you may be able to blunt the impact of lawsuits or other complaints against the business from clients, suppliers, or other constituencies in certain ways.

No one-size-fits-all solution applies to this issue, and because such threats may affect the valuation of the firm, it's extremely important to get legal advice on such protections.

Will Noncompete Issues Be Covered?

If a partner leaves the firm or practice, do you want her to hang out her new shingle right across the street? Probably not. Most conventional partnership agreements include noncompete clauses to keep departing partners from immediately setting up a competing business that would be detrimental to the former practice or partnership.

Many of these agreements force the departing partner out of their market for a certain length of time, meaning that they may be forced to practice in another state before coming back home. After all, it's all about saving the originating practice.

Chapter 24

Ten Things to Consider Before Transforming Your Company Into an ESOP

*A*n *employee stock ownership plan* (ESOP) is a trust established by a company for the allocation of shares to employees. It sounds almost altruistic: A business owner works hard; builds a profitable, successful company; and then, out of the goodness of her heart, creates shares that she allocates to all her wonderful workers.

Okay, we're being a bit snide here. In truth, ESOPs can work out very well for a business's founder and her workers, and some owners really do want their employees to share in their success. But make no mistake: In nearly every case, ESOPs are created in the best interests of those who create them. In most cases, the creator is the business owner or the company's top management, but sometimes the workers propose ESOPs.

Why are ESOPs a valuation issue? Getting an ESOP off the ground means establishing that the company is a valuable asset in its own right, which requires expertise and planning. This chapter names ten things to do before creating an ESOP.

Research How ESOPs Are Created

In the conventional model for creating an ESOP, a business owner sets up a trust to which he makes annual contributions of stock, and that stock goes into individual employee accounts within the trust. Workers own stock based on their salary levels or years of service.

Printing stock certificates on your computer doesn't make your company an ESOP. You need to fund the stock offering. Some companies use their own resources, get employees to contribute, or borrow money from banks, insurance companies, or private parties.

ESOP shares must vest before employees are entitled to receive them. Under rules set in 2006, vesting must be completed after three years (for *cliff vesting* — employees remain unvested during an initial period of service but become fully vested after that) or six years (for *graded vesting* — employees become vested in 20 percent of their accrued benefits after an initial period of service; they become vested in an additional 20 percent in each subsequent year, with full vesting four years later).

We're not going to get into the minutiae of the ESOP creation process because this book isn't about ESOPs. But it's safe to say that you're going to need a variety of experts — attorneys who have specific knowledge of ESOP creation, as well as your private attorneys, accountants, and financial planners.

ESOPs, like most major business transitions, aren't born in a day. At least, they shouldn't be. In a family business, you may need months or years to sell this idea to other family members, because the idea is all about sharing the wealth.

Understand Why ESOPs Are Attractive in Certain Situations

According to the ESOP Association (www.esopassociation.org), the two most common uses of an ESOP are to buy the stock of a retiring owner of a closely held company (probably a big issue for people reading this book) and to create an additional employee benefit or incentive plan to ensure the company's growth. But ESOPs have other purposes as well, such as to finance a company's expansion, spin off an operation into a separate company, or take a public company private.

In very few cases (about 2 percent), the ESOP Association says, ESOPs are formed as a last-ditch effort to bail out a company that's dying — you see both employees and owners attempting to save companies in this way. This process isn't for the squeamish.

You also hear about companies that create ESOPs to prevent unwanted takeovers. If a substantial amount of stock is in the hands of founders or employees, a company may be able to provide a united front against unwanted suitors.

Know How the Tax Advantages Work

Congress has provided certain tax incentives that make ESOPs a good deal for the owners of the business as well as for the new owners created by the ESOP:

- ✔ **Deduction for ESOP contributions:** ESOP contributions (in cash or securities) are tax deductible to the sponsoring corporation based on certain limits. When employers contribute their securities directly, they may take a deduction for the full value of the stock contributed. That deduction may allow an employer to increase her profits thanks to the taxes saved.

  If the ESOP is *leveraged* — that is, financed by a loan from a bank or other source — the tax advantages can be sweeter. Because contributions to a tax-qualified employee benefit plan are tax deductible, thereafter the employer may deduct contributions to the ESOP that are used to repay not only the interest on the loan but principal as well.

- ✔ **ESOP rollover:** Keep in mind that an ESOP allows a shareholder or group of shareholders of a closely held company to sell stock in the company to the firm's ESOP and defer federal income taxes on the gain from the sale. The ESOP must own at least 30 percent of the company's stock immediately after the sale, and the seller(s) must reinvest the proceeds from the sale in the securities of domestic operating corporations within 15 months (3 months before or 12 months after the sale). This tax break isn't always available to current or retiring owners.

- ✔ **Deduction for dividends:** Employers who create an ESOP also get a tax deduction for cash dividends paid on stock purchased with a loan for those ESOP securities. A deduction is also available for dividends paid on ESOP leveraged stock to the extent that the dividends are used to reduce the principal or to pay interest on a loan incurred to buy that stock.

Examine How Valuation Comes In

We start this section by saying that the U.S. Department of Labor — which puts out most of the rules and regulations for ESOPs — demands that you get an appraiser trained in ESOP work to do a valuation of the company to determine what the ESOP will actually pay for all or part of the company. Remember that the ESOP represents the employees who have a majority or minority ownership stake in the company.

This process gets pretty complicated. For full details, you can consult plenty of books on ESOPs. But valuation experts in an ESOP situation do the same thing that valuation experts do in other situations: They value the assets of the company and apply certain discounts to their price based on certain facts about the way the company will be owned and how marketable it would be to new buyers if an ESOP were in place.

Bottom line: Setting up an ESOP for your company isn't like giving yourself a hammer to break a piggy bank with. An ESOP is a complicated strategic transaction that has consequences for the value of the company based on the way you structure it. The appraiser or valuation professional isn't the only expert you involve in this process; you also need to work with estate and tax attorneys, as well as financial advisors.

Get a Handle on Your Launch Steps

Setting up an ESOP involves not only time but also a fairly considerable paper trail. Here are just a few of the tasks involved over the time it takes to form an ESOP:

- ✔ Hire attorneys to design, draft, and implement ESOP plan documents and various trust agreements.
- ✔ Work with these attorneys to obtain favorable determination letters from the Internal Revenue Service.
- ✔ Create ESOP feasibility and business succession studies.
- ✔ Start your business succession plans.
- ✔ Consider and put into place the financing options to launch the ESOP.
- ✔ Structure and record ESOP and related transactions.
- ✔ Advise fiduciaries on the status of the transition.

✔ Inform clients and customers.

✔ Settle all legal matters that could threaten the transition.

✔ Change over all tax-reporting structures to fit the ESOP structure.

You always need a valuation professional who understands your industry and the particular objective for which you're doing the valuation. Anyone who does your valuation work on an ESOP should have verifiable experience in valuing ESOPs.

Prepare for Preparation Costs

No one-size-fits-all cost applies to doing an ESOP, but fees are the only really easy thing to quantify in this process. Attorneys and tax/valuation experts may cost anywhere from $10,000 to $20,000, but you can vary those amounts based on how much preparation and study you bring to the process.

The tougher part to quantify is your time, especially the time you need to spend educating your officers and employees about the process. An ESOP isn't something that you can do — or should do — in a couple of months. The best-laid ESOPs are planned well in advance, with firm ideas about how that ownership structure will serve the growth of the company going forward.

Get Ready to Train Next-Generation Leadership

Training next-generation leaders is the succession-planning component of the ESOP process. If the ESOP enables a primary owner or a founder to retire with a sizable cash payment, it doesn't signal the end of that person's interest in the company. Family and friends will remain, and it's in everyone's best interest that the value of the company be maintained over the long term.

Many owners plan an ESOP well before their retirement — sometimes, 10 to 15 years before. The advantage is that not only do you get to review and assemble management talent for the next generation, but you also get to oversee the cultural change that ESOPs should bring. If you're making owners out of your officers and staff members, they should start acting like owners, setting and reaching performance targets that should guide all their actions going forward.

Plan Ongoing Training for Employees

You can't stop looking for talent on the lower rungs of top management. In an ownership culture, you need to train and educate employees at all levels about what's going on with the company so they know exactly what their responsibilities are in continuing to build value at the company they will own.

This process is important because a company stops being a paternalistic organization the minute it becomes an ESOP. The organization still has leaders and employees, but tremendous advantages exist when you make employees at all levels aware of what it takes to keep the company growing.

Estimate ESOP Costs after Launch

According to the National Center for Employee Ownership, a company with 20 employees might spend $2,000 a year for plan administration costs, such as filing reports, keeping records, and sending account statements, plus an additional $30 to $60 per employee for special situations such as retirement or plan asset allocations.

Also keep in mind that if a company has to borrow to launch the ESOP and the loan comes at a high rate, it's particularly important to think carefully about how that debt will be managed and eventually extinguished — which brings us to the last and most important item, which follows.

Realize That ESOPs Can Fail

The idea that ESOPs can fail is an important one. In fact, while we were editing this book, one of the biggest ESOPs in history came dangerously close to failing. The Tribune Company, parent of the *Chicago Tribune* newspaper, was transformed into an ESOP as a way for real estate investor Sam Zell to take over the company in mid-2008. Thanks to factors including the failing economy and the rapid decline of the newspaper industry, the company filed for bankruptcy protection by the end of 2008. Reports circulated that the company's employees were particularly vulnerable because their accounts were 100 percent invested in company stock, which can be decimated by bankruptcy.

When considering bankruptcy, owners and all their experts need to be particularly vigilant about the prospects of the company's industry and all the possible disasters that may happen.

Glossary

accounting change: Any variation in the way that accounts are prepared. Various events could account for the change, such as new Internal Revenue Service regulations or the adoption of new methods in allowing for doubtful (probably noncollectible) accounts receivable. Whenever such a change occurs, accountants are expected to footnote any financial statement, offering a full explanation of the reason for the change.

accounts payable: What a company owes to outside suppliers/vendors. Accounts payable are considered to be part of a company's short-term debt and are recorded as a liability on the balance sheet.

accounts receivable: What a company is owed from customers who have purchased its goods or services. Accounts receivable are considered to be an asset on the company's balance sheet.

accretion: Growth in the value of assets.

acid-test ratio: See *quick ratio*.

addbacks: Discretionary (nonessential to operations) items in the profit-and-loss statement. These items are added back to net pretax operating profit to estimate a company's economic cash flow versus cash flow produced for tax purposes.

adjusted book value: The book value that results after asset or liability amounts are added, deleted, or changed from their respective book amounts to their fair market value.

adjusted book value method: A valuation method based mainly on the balance sheet of a business in which owners' equity — total assets minus total liabilities — sets the price. In essence, the entire balance sheet is restated to current fair market value. The resulting equity is the adjusted book value.

AICPA: American Institute of Certified Public Accountants, the leading organization of CPAs, many of whom are trained to do business valuations.

amortization: The gradual, periodic reduction of any amount, such as an intangible asset, a bond premium, or the payment of a mortgage or business loan.

angel investor: A person who provides capital to one or more startup or early-stage companies, usually someone who is affluent or has a personal stake in the success of the venture. Valuation professionals may be brought in to put a dollar value on the potential business or idea.

appraisal: A professional written opinion of the value of an asset. An appraisal usually is required when a property is bought, sold, taxed, insured, or financed.

appraisal date: Same as the valuation date.

appraiser: A trained professional who has the knowledge and expertise necessary to estimate the value of an asset. An appraiser acts independently of the buying and selling parties in a transaction to arrive at the fair market value of an asset without allegiance to either party.

appreciation: An increase in the value of an asset.

asset: An item with an economic value that can be measured. Example assets include office equipment, accounts receivable, securities, real estate, and vehicles.

asset approach: A set of business valuation methods that determines a company's value based on the value of its assets. The valuation methods commonly used in this approach are book value; adjusted book value; liquidation value; and sometimes the capitalized excess earnings method, which is a hybrid of the asset and income approaches. See also *income approach*.

audit: A review of a company's finances or procedures. The four basic kinds of company audits are

- ✔ **Financial:** A formal review of a company's financial records by a licensed certified public accountant to make sure that they conform to generally accepted auditing procedures, leading to an audit opinion

- ✔ **Compliance:** An audit that determines whether a company is operating according to national rules and regulations, as well as the regulations of the jurisdiction in which it operates

- ✔ **Management:** An audit that evaluates how well a company's executives are doing their jobs

- ✔ **Internal:** An audit that represents an investigation by the company of its own procedures.

audit documentation: The written record of the basis for an auditor's findings. This record may also be referred to as *work papers or working papers*.

auditor: A person who tests the accuracy of financial accounts and records kept by others. Auditors typically are employed by public accounting firms.

bad debt: All or a portion of an account, loan, or other form of receivable that's considered to be uncollectible.

balance sheet: The assets, liabilities, and equity of a public or private corporation at a specific point in time. This document is where you go to determine what the company is actually worth on a book-value basis. See also *book value.*

bankruptcy: A federal court proceeding in which the assets of an insolvent debtor or company are liquidated and the debtor or company is relieved of further liability.

bonds: An interest-bearing certificate, usually issued by corporations and government agencies, that promises to pay interest and principal at specified times. Typically, investors try to diversify their investment portfolios with both stocks and bonds, because the value of bonds typically moves inversely to the value of stocks.

book value: The net value (original cost less depreciation) shown for an asset on a company's balance sheet; also called *net asset value.* Book value is considered to be one of the most controversial measurements in value investing; some people maintain that book values can be outdated and therefore are not good current measurements of a company's liquidating value.

business broker: A professional who assists in the buying and selling of businesses.

business plan: A written document created by a potential business owner that lists the objectives of the business and the steps and financing necessary to achieve those objectives.

buy/sell agreement: A provision of a franchise agreement that states specifically when and how an existing franchise can be bought or sold.

capital: Cash or goods used to generate income either by investing in a business or a different income property.

capital gains: The monetary gains on an investment when an investor sells and the principal has increased in value.

capitalization: The total market value of a stock, determined by multiplying the number of shares by the market price.

capitalization of earnings method: A method that sets a company's value by dividing the expected economic benefit to the business (such as the seller's discretionary cash flow) by its capitalization rate.

capitalization of excess earnings method: A hybrid of the asset and income approaches that calculates a company's value as the total of its net tangible assets and its goodwill. See also *asset approach* and *income approach.*

capitalization rate: A calculation that converts a single year's income expectancy to an indication of value by dividing the income estimate by an appropriate rate.

cash flow: Cash receipts less cash disbursements for a particular period. If, in a given month, a company pays out $30,000 and collects $40,000, its cash flow for the month is $10,000. *Free cash flow* is the amount left after all normal capital spending, debt service, and tax payments have occurred.

certified public accountant (CPA): An accountant who has passed the Uniform SPA Examination administered by AICPA and is licensed by the state in which he or she practices to use that title. A CPA is authorized to write an audit opinion or audit report on a company's financial statements and can act as a final auditing authority. See also *AICPA.*

closely held corporation: A company that has only a few shareholders. It differs from a privately held corporation in that it trades shares (but very few shares are actually traded).

combined financial statement: A financial statement in which the income statements and balance sheets of related business entities (such as subsidiaries of the same holding company) are combined so that they may be considered to be one reporting entity.

company: A formal business enterprise set up to make a profit. Companies include corporations, partnerships, and sole proprietorships.

consolidated statement: A report issued by a holding company that consolidates all of its subsidiaries' earnings, assets, and liabilities. Sometimes, a consolidated statement makes it tough to look at the results of individual operations.

corporation: A business entity with legal status in which ownership is vested in those who purchase its stock and in so doing contribute capital to fund the business. For purposes of taxation or responsibility for liabilities, however, a corporation is regarded as being a legal entity separate from its shareholder–owners. A corporation is formed when its founders file articles of incorporation with the relevant state authority — usually, the secretary of state.

current assets: All assets that are convertible to cash within one year.

debt restructuring: A change in a company's debt structure reflecting concessions granted by its creditors. Debt restructuring usually is an indication that a company is in financial difficulties.

debt-to-equity ratio: A way to figure out which group provides most of the firm's capital: owners or lenders. This ratio also indicates whether a company can repay its obligations. If the ratio climbs, the company may be taking on too much debt.

discounted cash flow method: A valuation method that measures the value of the expected economic benefits stream in present-day dollars, given the risks associated with owning and operating a small business.

earnings: The amount of money that a company has left over after paying all its bills and other obligations. The company may distribute a portion or all of its earnings to investors in the form of stock or cash dividends, or it may reinvest those earnings in the business to help it grow.

employee stock ownership plan: A trust set up by a company to give its stock to employees over time as a tax- and estate-planning vehicle.

equity: Also called *net worth.* In accounting, equity is assets minus liabilities. In a sole proprietorship, equity belongs to the owner; in a corporation, it belongs to the stockholders.

equity financing: A way to finance a company by issuing stock to investors who give money in exchange to build the business.

extraordinary item: A one-time event that affects the company's earnings for one quarter or year. From a valuation standpoint, extraordinary items are important signals that a company is in for long-term problems that may depress or raise its value.

fair market value: The monetary amount that a buyer may reasonably offer and a seller may accept in exchange for the asset.

fairness/solvency opinion: Independent, objective analysis of a proposed deal's financial aspects from the point of view of one or more of the parties in the transaction.

franchise: A license that awards rights from a franchisor to a franchisee to use specific trademarks, business systems, and a business concept.

franchise agreement: The legal document that governs the franchisor–franchisee relationship and specifies the terms of the franchise purchase. A typical franchise agreement may include specific details on the following:

- The franchise system, such as use of trademarks and products
- Territory
- Rights and obligations of the parties: standards, procedures, training, assistance, advertising, and so on
- Term (duration) of the franchise agreement
- Payments made by the franchisee to the franchisor
- Termination and/or right to transfer the franchise

fundamental analysis: A method of stock analysis that relies on the reported numbers of a company for investment decisions, as opposed to technical analysis, which looks at the price and volume history of a stock. Fundamental analysis is an important factor in value investing.

generally accepted accounting principles (GAAP): The financial reporting standards with which all public companies must comply so that each annual or quarterly report is uniform. Whenever a company's results fail to meet these principles, this failure indicates problems or changes in the company's financial fortunes.

generally accepted auditing standards (GAAS): Guidelines that auditors follow in preparing (and certifying) financial statements for clients. Any certified public accountant who doesn't follow these guidelines is in violation of AICPA rules and can be held legally liable by clients. See also *AICPA*.

goodwill: An intangible asset of a company, usually quantified when a company is purchased, the amount being the excess over book value.

income approach: A family of valuation methods that determines the value of a business based on its ability to generate desired economic benefit for the owners.

income statement: Also called the *profit-and-loss statement* or *P&L*. This document is used in combination with the company's balance sheet to provide an overall look at the company's finances.

incorporation: It is the process of turning a business into one that is separate from its owners. A corporation accomplishes several goals. It protects the owner's assets against the company's liabilities, can achieve a lower tax rate than on an owner's personal income and allows owners to raise capital through the sale of stock.

intangible assets: Assets without a strict dollar value in the form of goodwill, patents, trademarks, copyrights, and trade names.

inventory: Goods made and held by a company for sale. Inventory is important as long as a company keeps up with demand, but if demand falls, inventory is a burden.

liabilities: What a company owes in the form of accounts payable, bank borrowings, or bond indebtedness.

liquid asset: An asset that can be converted to cash within 30 days.

liquidation value: The value of a company based on a plan to close it as a going concern and simply sell off the assets.

liquidity: The degree of ease and certainty of value with which a security can be converted to cash.

market-based business valuation: A general way of setting value by comparing the business with similar businesses.

multiple of discretionary earnings business valuation method: A method that establishes value by multiplying the seller's discretionary cash flow by a factor derived from the business, industry, and market, as well as owner preferences.

net income: The amount of income, or profit, after all the bills and obligations have been paid at a company.

partnership: A kind of business organization in which two or more people contribute capital and their services to the organization.

portfolio: A group of investments.

preferred stock: A security representing prior claim to common stock on the firm's earnings and assets. Preferred stockholders normally forgo voting rights and receive a fixed dividend that takes precedence over payment of dividends to common stockholders.

price-to-book ratio: Market price per share divided by book value (tangible assets less all liabilities) per share; a measure of stock valuation relative to net assets.

pro forma statement: A calculated guess about the future earnings or balance sheet of a company, usually part of initial public offering documents or merger and acquisition proposals.

quick ratio: A method of analyzing a balance sheet, in which inventory is subtracted from current assets and the result is divided by current liabilities. The quick ratio is also known as the *acid-test ratio* because it indicates how much money is truly available for current needs.

receivables: Money owed to a company that is payable within a specified period.

retained earnings: The earnings that a company keeps after paying interest, dividends, salaries, and all bills.

return on assets (ROA): A way to assess how much a company earns on each dollar of assets.

return on investment (ROI): The most common profitability ratio, reached by dividing net profit by net worth.

revenue: Total sales of a company.

S corporation: A profitmaking corporation whose shareholders have received subchapter S corporation status from the Internal Revenue Service.

seller's discretionary cash flow: The pretax earnings of a business before noncash expenses, a single owner's compensation, interest expense, or income, as well as one-time and nonbusiness-related income and expense items.

Small Business Administration: A federal agency that helps small business with operational, financial, and regulatory issues: www.sba.gov.

sole proprietorship: An unincorporated business (usually, a small business) with just one owner. The disadvantage of such a business entity is that the sole proprietor is directly responsible for all the debts of the business.

undercapitalization: A company's lack of enough cash on hand to continue business operations or pay its creditors.

value: A quality, feature, or function of a business that makes customers and investors want to put money into it.

valuation date: The official date of a company's valuation – a frozen point in time where all parties can look at it's valuation as a means of making a business decision.

venture capital: A fund-raising technique for companies that are willing to exchange equity for money to grow or expand the business. See also *angel investor.*

working capital: The excess of a company's current assets over its current liabilities — that is, cash plus accounts receivable plus inventory minus the sum of accounts payable plus accrued liabilities and short-term loans.

Index

• E •

• G •

• H •

• U •

• V •

• W •

USINESS, CAREERS & PERSONAL FINANCE

ounting For Dummies, 4th Edition*
-0-470-24600-9

okkeeping Workbook For Dummies†
-0-470-16983-4

mmodities For Dummies
-0-470-04928-0

ing Business in China For Dummies
-0-470-04929-7

E-Mail Marketing For Dummies
978-0-470-19087-6

Job Interviews For Dummies, 3rd Edition*†
978-0-470-17748-8

Personal Finance Workbook For Dummies*†
978-0-470-09933-9

Real Estate License Exams For Dummies
978-0-7645-7623-2

Six Sigma For Dummies
978-0-7645-6798-8

Small Business Kit For Dummies,
2nd Edition*†
978-0-7645-5984-6

Telephone Sales For Dummies
978-0-470-16836-3

USINESS PRODUCTIVITY & MICROSOFT OFFICE

ess 2007 For Dummies
-0-470-03649-5

el 2007 For Dummies
-0-470-03737-9

ice 2007 For Dummies
-0-470-00923-9

tlook 2007 For Dummies
-0-470-03830-7

PowerPoint 2007 For Dummies
978-0-470-04059-1

Project 2007 For Dummies
978-0-470-03651-8

QuickBooks 2008 For Dummies
978-0-470-18470-7

Quicken 2008 For Dummies
978-0-470-17473-9

Salesforce.com For Dummies,
2nd Edition
978-0-470-04893-1

Word 2007 For Dummies
978-0-470-03658-7

UCATION, HISTORY, REFERENCE & TEST PREPARATION

ican American History For Dummies
-0-7645-5469-8

ebra For Dummies
-0-7645-5325-7

ebra Workbook For Dummies
-0-7645-8467-1

History For Dummies
-0-470-09910-0

ASVAB For Dummies, 2nd Edition
978-0-470-10671-6

British Military History For Dummies
978-0-470-03213-8

Calculus For Dummies
978-0-7645-2498-1

Canadian History For Dummies, 2nd Edition
978-0-470-83656-9

Geometry Workbook For Dummies
978-0-471-79940-5

The SAT I For Dummies, 6th Edition
978-0-7645-7193-0

Series 7 Exam For Dummies
978-0-470-09932-2

World History For Dummies
978-0-7645-5242-7

OOD, GARDEN, HOBBIES & HOME

dge For Dummies, 2nd Edition
-0-471-92426-5

n Collecting For Dummies, 2nd Edition
-0-470-22275-1

oking Basics For Dummies, 3rd Edition
-0-7645-7206-7

Drawing For Dummies
978-0-7645-5476-6

Etiquette For Dummies, 2nd Edition
978-0-470-10672-3

Gardening Basics For Dummies*†
978-0-470-03749-2

Knitting Patterns For Dummies
978-0-470-04556-5

Living Gluten-Free For Dummies†
978-0-471-77383-2

Painting Do-It-Yourself For Dummies
978-0-470-17533-0

EALTH, SELF HELP, PARENTING & PETS

ger Management For Dummies
-0-470-03715-7

xiety & Depression Workbook
Dummies
-0-7645-9793-0

ting For Dummies, 2nd Edition
-0-7645-4149-0

g Training For Dummies, 2nd Edition
-0-7645-8418-3

Horseback Riding For Dummies
978-0-470-09719-9

Infertility For Dummies†
978-0-470-11518-3

Meditation For Dummies with CD-ROM,
2nd Edition
978-0-471-77774-8

Post-Traumatic Stress Disorder For Dummies
978-0-470-04922-8

Puppies For Dummies, 2nd Edition
978-0-470-03717-1

Thyroid For Dummies, 2nd Edition†
978-0-471-78755-6

Type 1 Diabetes For Dummies*†
978-0-470-17811-9

parate Canadian edition also available
parate U.K. edition also available

lable wherever books are sold. For more information or to order direct: U.S. customers visit www.dummies.com or call 1-877-762-2974.
customers visit www.wileyeurope.com or call (0)1243 843291. Canadian customers visit www.wiley.ca or call 1-800-567-4797.

INTERNET & DIGITAL MEDIA

AdWords For Dummies
978-0-470-15252-2

Blogging For Dummies, 2nd Edition
978-0-470-23017-6

**Digital Photography All-in-One
Desk Reference For Dummies, 3rd Edition**
978-0-470-03743-0

Digital Photography For Dummies, 5th Edition
978-0-7645-9802-9

**Digital SLR Cameras & Photography
For Dummies, 2nd Edition**
978-0-470-14927-0

**eBay Business All-in-One Desk Reference
For Dummies**
978-0-7645-8438-1

eBay For Dummies, 5th Edition*
978-0-470-04529-9

eBay Listings That Sell For Dummies
978-0-471-78912-3

Facebook For Dummies
978-0-470-26273-3

The Internet For Dummies, 11th Edition
978-0-470-12174-0

Investing Online For Dummies, 5th Edition
978-0-7645-8456-5

iPod & iTunes For Dummies, 5th Edit
978-0-470-17474-6

MySpace For Dummies
978-0-470-09529-4

Podcasting For Dummies
978-0-471-74898-4

**Search Engine Optimization
For Dummies, 2nd Edition**
978-0-471-97998-2

Second Life For Dummies
978-0-470-18025-9

**Starting an eBay Business For Dumm
3rd Edition†**
978-0-470-14924-9

GRAPHICS, DESIGN & WEB DEVELOPMENT

**Adobe Creative Suite 3 Design Premium
All-in-One Desk Reference For Dummies**
978-0-470-11724-8

**Adobe Web Suite CS3 All-in-One Desk
Reference For Dummies**
978-0-470-12099-6

AutoCAD 2008 For Dummies
978-0-470-11650-0

**Building a Web Site For Dummies,
3rd Edition**
978-0-470-14928-7

**Creating Web Pages All-in-One Desk
Reference For Dummies, 3rd Edition**
978-0-470-09629-1

**Creating Web Pages For Dummies,
8th Edition**
978-0-470-08030-6

Dreamweaver CS3 For Dummies
978-0-470-11490-2

Flash CS3 For Dummies
978-0-470-12100-9

Google SketchUp For Dummies
978-0-470-13744-4

InDesign CS3 For Dummies
978-0-470-11865-8

**Photoshop CS3 All-in-One
Desk Reference For Dummies**
978-0-470-11195-6

Photoshop CS3 For Dummies
978-0-470-11193-2

Photoshop Elements 5 For Dummi
978-0-470-09810-3

SolidWorks For Dummies
978-0-7645-9555-4

Visio 2007 For Dummies
978-0-470-08983-5

Web Design For Dummies, 2nd Edi
978-0-471-78117-2

Web Sites Do-It-Yourself For Dumm
978-0-470-16903-2

Web Stores Do-It-Yourself For Dumm
978-0-470-17443-2

LANGUAGES, RELIGION & SPIRITUALITY

Arabic For Dummies
978-0-471-77270-5

Chinese For Dummies, Audio Set
978-0-470-12766-7

French For Dummies
978-0-7645-5193-2

German For Dummies
978-0-7645-5195-6

Hebrew For Dummies
978-0-7645-5489-6

Ingles Para Dummies
978-0-7645-5427-8

Italian For Dummies, Audio Set
978-0-470-09586-7

Italian Verbs For Dummies
978-0-471-77389-4

Japanese For Dummies
978-0-7645-5429-2

Latin For Dummies
978-0-7645-5431-5

Portuguese For Dummies
978-0-471-78738-9

Russian For Dummies
978-0-471-78001-4

Spanish Phrases For Dummies
978-0-7645-7204-3

Spanish For Dummies
978-0-7645-5194-9

Spanish For Dummies, Audio Set
978-0-470-09585-0

The Bible For Dummies
978-0-7645-5296-0

Catholicism For Dummies
978-0-7645-5391-2

The Historical Jesus For Dummies
978-0-470-16785-4

Islam For Dummies
978-0-7645-5503-9

**Spirituality For Dummies,
2nd Edition**
978-0-470-19142-2

NETWORKING AND PROGRAMMING

ASP.NET 3.5 For Dummies
978-0-470-19592-5

C# 2008 For Dummies
978-0-470-19109-5

Hacking For Dummies, 2nd Edition
978-0-470-05235-8

Home Networking For Dummies, 4th Edition
978-0-470-11806-1

Java For Dummies, 4th Edition
978-0-470-08716-9

**Microsoft® SQL Server™ 2008 All-in-One
Desk Reference For Dummies**
978-0-470-17954-3

**Networking All-in-One Desk Reference
For Dummies, 2nd Edition**
978-0-7645-9939-2

**Networking For Dummies,
8th Edition**
978-0-470-05620-2

SharePoint 2007 For Dummies
978-0-470-09941-4

**Wireless Home Networking
For Dummies, 2nd Edition**
978-0-471-74940-0

OPERATING SYSTEMS & COMPUTER BASICS

Mac For Dummies, 5th Edition
978-0-7645-8458-9

Laptops For Dummies, 2nd Edition
978-0-470-05432-1

Linux For Dummies, 8th Edition
978-0-470-11649-4

MacBook For Dummies
978-0-470-04859-7

Mac OS X Leopard All-in-One Desk Reference For Dummies
978-0-470-05434-5

Mac OS X Leopard For Dummies
978-0-470-05433-8

Macs For Dummies, 9th Edition
978-0-470-04849-8

PCs For Dummies, 11th Edition
978-0-470-13728-4

Windows® Home Server For Dummies
978-0-470-18592-6

Windows Server 2008 For Dummies
978-0-470-18043-3

Windows Vista All-in-One Desk Reference For Dummies
978-0-471-74941-7

Windows Vista For Dummies
978-0-471-75421-3

Windows Vista Security For Dummies
978-0-470-11805-4

SPORTS, FITNESS & MUSIC

Coaching Hockey For Dummies
978-0-470-83685-9

Coaching Soccer For Dummies
978-0-471-77381-8

Fitness For Dummies, 3rd Edition
978-0-7645-7851-9

Football For Dummies, 3rd Edition
978-0-470-12536-6

GarageBand For Dummies
978-0-7645-7323-1

Golf For Dummies, 3rd Edition
978-0-471-76871-5

Guitar For Dummies, 2nd Edition
978-0-7645-9904-0

Home Recording For Musicians For Dummies, 2nd Edition
978-0-7645-8884-6

iPod & iTunes For Dummies, 5th Edition
978-0-470-17474-6

Music Theory For Dummies
978-0-7645-7838-0

Stretching For Dummies
978-0-470-06741-3

Get smart @ dummies.com®

- **Find a full list of Dummies titles**
- **Look into loads of FREE on-site articles**
- **Sign up for FREE eTips e-mailed to you weekly**
- **See what other products carry the Dummies name**
- **Shop directly from the Dummies bookstore**
- **Enter to win new prizes every month!**

Separate Canadian edition also available
Separate U.K. edition also available

CPSIA information can be obtained at www.ICGtesting.com
Printed in the USA
BVOW03n1350051215

429034BV00002B/5/P